CHICAGO DAYS

CHICAGO DAYS

150 Defining Moments in the Life of a Great City

By the staff of the Chicago Tribune

Edited by Stevenson Swanson

Foreword by Howard A. Tyner, Editor of the Chicago Tribune

 CANTIGNY FIRST DIVISION FOUNDATION

Produced and distributed by Contemporary Books

Library of Congress Cataloging-in-Publication Data

Chicago days : 150 defining moments in the life of a great city / by
    the staff of the *Chicago Tribune* ; edited by Stevenson Swanson ;
    foreword by Howard A. Tyner.
        p.   cm.
    ISBN 1-890093-03-3 (cloth)
    ISBN 1-890093-04-1 (paper)
    ISBN 1-890093-05-X (leather)
        1. Chicago (Ill.)—History—Anecdotes.   I. Swanson, Stevenson.
II. Chicago Tribune (Firm)
F548.36.C46   1997
977.3'11—dc21   96-51735
                                                                 CIP

The contributors to this volume conducted independent research and
writing without editorial participation from the officers and directors
of the Cantigny First Division Foundation. The resulting stories are
exclusively the work of the contributors and their editors.

Cover design and interior design by Kim Bartko.

Cover photo: Crowd at the corner of Randolph and Dearborn
Streets cheers the news of Japan's surrender, August 14, 1945.
Tribune file photo (*Chicago Herald-American* photo by Joe Mastruzzo).

Acknowledgment of permissions for interior illustrations begins on page 269.

Copyright © 1997 by Cantigny First Division Foundation
All rights reserved
Published by Cantigny First Division Foundation
1 South 151 Winfield Road, Wheaton, Illinois 60187-6097
Produced and distributed by Contemporary Books,
an imprint of NTC/Contemporary Publishing Company
4255 West Touhy Avenue, Lincolnwood, Illinois 60646-1975
Manufactured in the United States of America
International Standard Book Number: 1-890093-03-3 (cloth)
                                    1-890093-04-1 (paper)
                                    1-890093-05-X (leather)
10   9   8   7   6   5   4   3   2   1

Contents

Foreword

By Howard A. Tyner,
Editor of the
Chicago Tribune

H istory and newspapers are an odd couple in the world of letters. History recounts people's lives and times; so do newspapers. News, after all, is history that just happened. Yet newspaper journalists rarely can afford to operate as true historians. The writing of history involves a luxury their profession must deny them: time. The reflection and perspective that time permits are at the heart of a historian's craft, but they are lost to the men and women whose world is defined by the deadline for tomorrow's edition.

Chicago Days, published during the *Tribune*'s 150th year, looks at the history of the Chicago community, including that of the newspaper itself. Events big and small contributed to making Chicago what it is today—a boisterously grand metropolis known around the world for its commerce, its culture, its institutions, and its beauty. The authors of the book's 150 historical vignettes are *Tribune* journalists, who were able go back through time—and through the back issues of the newspaper— to provide the context their predecessors could not under the pressure of daily deadlines. Each "moment" is thus history and news combined.

The publisher of this panoramic view of the Chicago area's past is the Cantigny First Division Foundation. The foundation, which receives its support from the Robert R. McCormick Tribune Foundation, pursues the dual mission of preserving the institutional history of the U.S. Army's First Division and the personal history of Colonel Robert R. McCormick, a veteran of the unit and the longtime publisher of the *Tribune*.

The foundation operates the First Division Museum and the Robert R. McCormick Research Center, which includes a Tribune Company archive, on the grounds of Cantigny, McCormick's estate in Wheaton, Illinois. In addition, it is an active sponsor of research, conferences, publications, and educational programs. The foundation is publishing *Chicago Days* in the spirit of the Colonel's lifelong devotion to the Chicago area and its people.

▼ *The* Chicago Tribune
newsroom, circa 1920

Acknowledgments

To produce a book that covers so many topics, spread over a century and a half, with photographs and illustrations, required an almost epic cast of editors, writers, researchers, and many others. In addition to the writers of the 150 moments, whose contributions of both text and ideas made the editing of this book a fascinating and educational experience, I gratefully acknowledge the help and support of the following individuals:

This book could not have been produced without the commitment and encouragement of Jack Fuller, publisher of the *Chicago Tribune*, and editor Howard Tyner. In an especially busy news year, managing editor Ann Marie Lipinski not only gave me the opportunity to edit this book but also made available the necessary staff. Senior editor John Twohey, who managed the *Tribune*'s sesquicentennial observances, was always available to provide guidance and to marshal any additional assistance when that was necessary. Associate editor Joe Leonard facilitated the production of *Chicago Days* by providing access to *Tribune* photographs and historic front pages so they could be reproduced for use in the book.

Neal Creighton, president of the Robert R. McCormick Tribune Foundation, and John Votaw, executive director of the Cantigny First Division Foundation, generously supported the publication of *Chicago Days*. Researcher Eric Gillespie at the Robert R. McCormick Research Center provided a wealth of archival material concerning the *Tribune*.

Mary Wilson, manager of the *Tribune*'s photo library, has an encyclopedic knowledge of the newspaper's seven-million-plus collection of photographs, which made the photoediting of this project immeasurably easier and the result immeasurably better. Her willingness to take on the onerous clerical work and photocopying involved in a complicated project of this nature is deeply appreciated. (And she has a wonderful sense of humor.)

Photographs from sources outside the *Tribune* library were the responsibility of freelance photo researcher Cecily Rosenwald, whose diligence, thorough organization, and imagination in tracking down photographs yielded one wonderful image after another. Her advice and counsel helped greatly in making final photo selections, and she, too, spent much time at the copying machine as the project entered its final stages.

A special word of thanks goes to senior news editor Bill Parker, who gave freely of his time and whose advice on photographs and photoediting was invaluable.

The following *Tribune* editors and managers made writers, copy editors, and researchers available for this project: Jim O'Shea, Gerould Kern, Geoff Brown, Karen Callaway, George de Lama, Tim Franklin, Janet Franz, Denis Gosselin, Mark Hinojosa, John Jansson, Denise Joyce, Paul Weingarten, Pat Widder, and N. Don Wycliff.

Copyediting assistance was provided by Doug Balz, Tim Bannon, Margaret Carroll, John Cooper, Randy Curwen, Charles Dickinson, David Elsner, Eric Gwinn, Jim Haglund, Susan Hilkevitch, Larry Kart, Karen Klages, Ken Knox, Rick Kogan, Rich Lorenz, Wendy Navratil, Yolette Nicholson, Clarence Petersen, Richard Phillips, Ron Silverman, Nancy Watkins, and Pat Worklan.

Tribune staff members who contributed in various valuable ways to the completion of the book include Judie Anderson, Lisa Anderson, Linda

Balek, Don Bierman, Victoria Boylan, Torry Bruno, Abby de Shane, Mary Ellen Hendricks, Linda Hubbs, Kemper Kirkpatrick, Michael Mahaley, Judi Marriott, Steve Marino, Joe Pete, Alan Peters, Mary Schmich, Larry Underwood, Arthur Walker, and Melanie Walker.

For guiding newspaper journalists through the world of book publishing, appreciative thanks go to the following at NTC/Contemporary Publishing Company: chief executive officer Mark Pattis, publisher Christine Albritton, editor Nancy Crossman, managing editor Kathy Willhoite, art director Kim Bartko, prepress manager Terry Stone, layout artist Mary Lockwood, and project editors Craig Bolt, David Bramer, and Julia Anderson.

Apart from *Tribune* files, the major source of photographs was the Chicago Historical Society. The *Tribune* is deeply grateful to president Douglas Greenberg, assistant director Russell Lewis, and photo researchers Cynthia Mathews and Linda Ziemer for making this treasure trove of all things Chicago available to the *Tribune*.

For their wise counsel, good humor, moral support, and constant friendship, I extend my heartfelt thanks to Kathleen Byrne, Steve Buckman, Ted Cox, Kevin Grandfield, Eric Greenberg, Janet Hieshetter, Wendi Williams, and Mark Wukas. For my early interest in Chicago history, I owe a son's unredeemable debt of gratitude to my mother, Elaine Swanson, whose stories about the Chicago of her youth first filled me with curiosity about that faraway metropolis when I was growing up in Omaha, Nebraska. Finally, I could not have completed the editing of *Chicago Days* without the unwavering support of my wife, Ann Dumas-Swanson. Her patience during my long absences while I was working on the book knew no bounds, and her understanding and encouragement kept me moving forward when the end seemed far off.

—*Stevenson Swanson*

Introduction

By Stevenson Swanson

Among the great cities of the world, Chicago is a youngster. When French explorers first passed through the swampy region where the city would one day rise, Paris was already some sixteen hundred years old. Chicago's most historic structure—the Water Tower, survivor and reminder of the Great Fire of 1871—was completed as recently as 1869, about eight hundred years after William the Conqueror started construction of the Tower of London. From the time Chicago was incorporated as a town until it became the second-largest city in the nation, a mere fifty-seven years passed.

But in its short life, Chicago has packed in more than its share of historic days and great moments. *Chicago Days* tells the story of 150 such moments that have become part of the history of the metropolitan area.

These are not necessarily the "greatest" moments in Chicago's history. Rather, they are the events—big and small, tragic and comic—that have shaped the metropolitan area, stamped themselves on the memories of its people, or contributed to Chicago's reputation across the country and around the world. The city, for instance, is inevitably and probably forever associated with the Prohibition era and Al Capone, but it is also known for its architecture and its music—jazz and blues—as well as its contribution to the waistlines of the world, thanks to deep-dish pizza.

The moments are not limited to things that happened only in Chicago or its suburbs; wars, assassinations, the resignation of a president—these are so momentous that to exclude them would be to distort history. For example, the Civil War was fought far from Chicago, but it touched the city in myriad ways. This book looks at what these national events meant to Chicago and the role that Chicagoans played in them. A list of such moments is almost made to be argued with, but, in general, the selections were intended to pin down the points in time when something changed, when something started or ended—when, figuratively speaking, a light switched on, glowed most brightly, or switched off.

▼ *This engraving, based on a drawing by H. R. Schoolcraft, shows Fort Dearborn (center) and virtually every house in the village of Chicago in 1820.*

▶

Chicago's first non–Native American resident was black fur trader Jean Baptiste Point du Sable (inset), who built a cabin on the north bank of the Chicago River in 1779.

Since the impetus for this book is the *Chicago Tribune's* 150th anniversary, the number of moments to include in *Chicago Days* was clear, as was the starting point: June 10, 1847, the day the first *Tribune* was published. But this book is primarily a history of the Chicago area and not of the *Tribune*. The newspaper and its legendary figures enter the story at points, however, because a major newspaper not only reports the news. At times, it makes news—and not always the kind that it would like to make. See, for instance, the entry for November 3, 1948.

The text was written by *Tribune* staff members, some of whom wrote about events that they originally covered for the newspaper. As much as possible, the photographs and other illustrations come from the *Tribune's* voluminous files, which include the photographs and irreplaceable glass negatives from *Chicago Today*, the afternoon newspaper that Tribune Company published until 1974. That paper's ancestry reached back to 1900 under different owners and a variety of names, including *Chicago's American*, the *Chicago Herald-American*, and the *Chicago Herald and Examiner*.

Selecting 150 moments meant, ultimately, selecting 150 dates. Many events are easy to pin down: the *Eastland* disaster happened on July 24, 1915. But when exactly did the Chicago expressway system open? It was built in stages; picking just one date is difficult. And yet to ignore the expressway system would be to ignore something that has had a major impact on the metropolitan area's land use and housing patterns (see December 15, 1955). Tracking down some dates—even fairly recent ones—proved daunting, but ultimately only one remained elusive: the date on which Hugh Hefner sold his first copy of *Playboy*. Because he was not sure how the magazine would be received, he did not even put the month—December—on the cover. Hefner's best guess is that on or about December 1, 1953, the magazine made its first appearance on newsstands.

The year 1847 turns out, by a happy coincidence, to be a good starting point for a history of Chicago's development into a major metropolitan area. By then, the city had reached the end of its childhood and was about to enter a precocious period of adolescent growth. That a permanent settlement ever grew up along the marshy banks of a sluggish prairie river was something of a surprise, but events during the last Ice Age, which ended more than ten thousand years ago, gave the area an importance that outweighed its drawbacks. Glaciers scoured out river valleys to form the Great Lakes, and they also planed flat the territory west of the lakes. A low ridge ran roughly north and south a few miles from the shore of the inland sea that would be named Lake Michigan. Streams east of the ridge flowed into the lake, which was part of a watershed that emptied into the Atlantic Ocean via the St. Lawrence River. Streams to the west ran south and west to what some Indian tribes called the Big Water—the Mississippi River, which flowed into the Gulf of Mexico.

In September 1673, the first Europeans known to have visited the area discovered it was easy to cross from one watershed to the other. Jacques Marquette, a Jesuit priest, and Louis Joliet, a fur trader and explorer, had explored the Mississippi River during the summer. On their way back to Marquette's mission at St. Ignace (on the upper peninsula of present-day Michigan), they paddled up the Illinois and Des Plaines Rivers. They then reached a low point where they could carry their canoes to a river that flowed in the opposite direction—the south branch of the Chicago River, which took them to Lake Michigan. Joliet saw the potential of the dismal region. "It would only be necessary," he reported to French authorities, "to make a canal by cutting through [a short distance] of prairie, to pass from the foot of the Lake of the Illinois [Lake Michigan] to the river Saint Louis [the Illinois River]."

His idea would not become reality for 175 years, when the Illinois and Michigan Canal opened in 1848 (see April 10, 1848). In the meantime, the area that came to be called Chicago—after an Indian word for the wild onion plants that thrived on the banks of the river near the lake—passed from French to British to American ownership. A black fur trader named Jean Baptiste Point du Sable built a cabin on the north bank of the Chicago River in about 1779, roughly where the Equitable Building stands. The French-speaking du Sable, who stayed until 1800, is considered Chicago's first permanent non–Native American resident.

To guard the mouth of the river, the federal government built Fort Dearborn on the south bank near the lake in 1803. This fort, whose location is marked in the sidewalks at the south end of the Michigan Avenue bridge, was destroyed in 1812 as fighting broke out on the frontier during the War of 1812. While a raiding party of Potawatomi Indians burned the stockade, another band killed most of the fort's garrison and their families as they fled along the lakeshore, about three miles south of the fort. Fort Dearborn and the massacre would be memorialized on Chicago's flag with a red, six-pointed star, one of four on the white-and-blue flag. (The other stars commemorate the 1871 fire and the world's fairs of 1893 and 1933–34.)

▼ *The government built Fort Dearborn on the south bank of the Chicago River in 1803. Its location is marked at the south end of the Michigan Avenue bridge.*

▶

John H. Kinzie, son of pioneer trader John Kinzie, came to Chicago in 1834 and quickly established himself as one of the town's leading citizens.

The fort was rebuilt in 1816 as surveying began for a canal that would fulfill Joliet's dream and link the two great watersheds of mid-America. The canal was to alter everything about the infant town; but for at least another decade Chicago remained a fur-trading outpost with two centers of activity. Near the mouth of the river was the fort and du Sable's house, which by this time was owned by trader John Kinzie. And at Wolf Point, where the north and south branches of the river merged into the main branch, was a rowdy precinct of inns, the most popular of which was Mark Beaubien's Sauganash. "I plays de fiddle like de debble," he once said, "an' I keeps hotel like hell."

The raw town was full of such colorful characters. Two of the most noteworthy were Gurdon Saltonstall Hubbard and "Long John" Wentworth. Hubbard, a flinty Yankee from Vermont, first came to Chicago in 1818 with a group of fur traders, but he lived in the bigger town of Danville, Illinois, until 1834. He made frequent trips to the village on the lake, though, and the trail he blazed between Danville and Chicago eventually became a state road, which in Chicago was called State Street. He was instrumental in making sure that the northern terminus of the proposed canal would be Chicago. During a long life, Hubbard made a successful transition from fur trader to industrial capitalist, building or buying warehouses, a lake shipping service, the city's first bank, and even a primitive water system that supplied drinking water through log pipes.

Wentworth arrived in Chicago on foot in October 1836. Journeying from his native New Hampshire, he walked the final stretch from Michigan City, Indiana, behind a wagon that carried his luggage. Within a month of his arrival, he was the editor of the *Chicago Democrat*, the town's first newspaper, and in short order he owned the publication. Real-estate investments and railroad developments made him a millionaire, but he is probably best remembered for his flamboyant political career, which spanned several terms in Congress and, as a member of the antislavery Republican Party, two stints as mayor. "Long John," who stood six feet six inches tall, was a tireless Chicago booster who in 1860 lured England's Prince Edward to the city. "Boys," he bellowed to a crowd from a hotel balcony, the future King Edward VII by his side, "this is the Prince of Wales. Prince, these are the boys."

▲ *Flamboyant politician "Long John" Wentworth was instrumental in promoting the city's growth.*

By the time Long John moved to Chicago, the last of the native inhabitants of the area had left. Following the Fort Dearborn massacre, the Potawatomi more or less coexisted with the fur-trading community, but in the spring of 1832 a chief named Black Hawk led at least one thousand Fox and Sauk Indians in Iowa across the Mississippi River into Illinois. They sought to reclaim lands ceded to the United States under a treaty of shaky legality. Fearing the Indians, settlers in northwestern Illinois raised the alarm, and volunteers such as Hubbard and a young self-taught lawyer named Abraham Lincoln answered the call. The so-called Black Hawk War was over by early August, after Army troops shot down dozens of Indian men, women, and children at the Battle of Bad Axe as they attempted to flee back across the Mississippi River.

The conflict, fought far from Chicago, brought about an end to the Potawatomi presence in the area. Anxious to remove any potential threats to the settlers who were rushing to Illinois, the government concluded treaties with the Potawatomis in 1833, under which they ceded the last five million acres they held in northeastern Illinois and southeastern Wisconsin. In the summer of 1835, the last several hundred Potawatomis held an impressive war dance that snaked through the streets of Chicago and shortly afterward departed for the West. They left behind a wealth of place names and many centuries-old trails that later became major roads in the metropolitan area.

▲ *Chat-O-Nis-Sec, a Potawatomi chief*

▼ *The north and south branches of the Chicago River merged at Wolf Point, where a rowdy precinct of inns sprang up.*

▲ *James Thompson's plat of the original town—a rigid grid system that could be extended easily*

The departure of the Indians was only one sign of the accelerating pace of change in the 1830s. As part of the canal project, surveyor James Thompson platted Chicago for the first time in 1830, laying out the streets in a rigid grid system that could be extended easily from horizon to horizon on the flat terrain. In 1833, Chicago became an official place when it was incorporated as a town. The federal government cut a channel through the sandbar at the mouth of the Chicago River that until then had forced the sluggish stream to turn sharply to the south before emptying into Lake Michigan. The new channel, opened in 1834, allowed lake ships to enter the river and dock along its banks rather than having to transfer cargo or passengers to smaller craft.

Although Chicago numbered only a few hundred residents at the time of incorporation, the population began to increase quickly as land speculators arrived. Gambling on real estate was a national craze in the 1830s, but Chicago had the added attraction of the canal project. Construction did not begin until 1836, but simply the anticipation of the boom that the canal would cause was enough to stoke feverish buying and selling. Passing through New York in 1835, Hubbard auctioned off part of a barren eighty-acre tract that he and two partners had purchased along the north branch of the river. He left with $75,000; the entire tract had cost the three men $5,000.

At about the same time, a young lawyer from western New York named William Butler Ogden came to Chicago to look after his brother-in-law's property, which had cost $100,000. He overcame his grave doubts about the town's future after he was able to sell a third of his brother-in-law's property—for $100,000. With the settlement's population at more than four thousand, Chicago leaders lobbied the state for a city charter, which was granted March 4, 1837, Chicago's official birthday.

The newcomer Ogden beat John Harris Kinzie, son of the old trader, in the young city's first mayoral election. As the settlement grew, the demand for housing and commercial structures led to the first of Chicago's architectural innovations, the balloon-frame method of constructing wooden buildings. Until 1833, when the first balloon frames seem to have been constructed, carpenters joined timber beams and posts one at a time with hand-cut joints and wooden pegs. But by using standard-length boards and mass-produced nails, unskilled workers could easily bang together frames and throw up buildings seemingly overnight. If the result looked as if it might blow away like a balloon, it was nonetheless cheap and served its purpose. This method of building has become so universal as to seem unremarkable, but at the time it revolutionized construction.

In 1837, the city became home to the first of the many architects who have made Chicago synonymous with great architecture. John Van Osdel, a carpenter and self-trained architect, moved to Chicago to design a house for Ogden, the new mayor. During a long career that lasted until his death in 1891, Van Osdel built scores of houses and large buildings, including the Cook County courthouse, where Abraham Lincoln's body lay in state (see April 14, 1865). The courthouse shared the fate of many of Van Osdel's buildings when it burned to the ground during the 1871 fire (see October 8, 1871).

The speculative fever that gripped the country finally burst in the Panic of 1837. In the ensuing depression, the state of Illinois defaulted on its loans and business came to a near standstill. The country did not recover from the panic until the early 1840s, by which time Chicago was poised for a new era. Fort Dearborn sat abandoned (it was finally demolished in 1857), and the fur trade had ended. The new channel to Lake Michigan was turning the Chicago River into a busy confusion of lake schooners and tugboats, and a lively retail district had taken shape on Lake Street. As the 1840s progressed and more settlers broke the prairie sod of the Midwest, trade grew quickly in new commodities, such as grain and lumber. Great days awaited Chicago, and the city hurried toward them.

▲ *The balloon-frame method of constructing wooden buildings was an architectural innovation that contributed greatly to the city's rapid growth.*

First Edition of the *Chicago Tribune*

Four pages and four hundred copies: a new publication enters the "stormy sea" of Chicago journalism.

JUNE 10, 1847

By the middle of 1847, Chicago had shaken off much of the transient appearance of a frontier settlement and was attracting the country's attention as an up-and-coming city. In July, twenty thousand visitors from across the nation would stream into Chicago—population sixteen thousand—for the Rivers and Harbors Convention, foreshadowing the city's future as a convention center. The visitors would leave impressed with Chicago's potential.

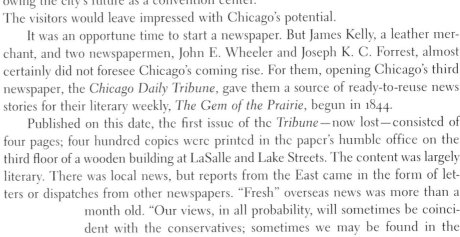

▲ *The first office of the* Chicago Tribune *was at Lake and LaSalle Streets. The first issue of the paper was printed on a hand press in a barren loft on the third floor.*

It was an opportune time to start a newspaper. But James Kelly, a leather merchant, and two newspapermen, John E. Wheeler and Joseph K. C. Forrest, almost certainly did not foresee Chicago's coming rise. For them, opening Chicago's third newspaper, the *Chicago Daily Tribune*, gave them a source of ready-to-reuse news stories for their literary weekly, *The Gem of the Prairie*, begun in 1844.

Published on this date, the first issue of the *Tribune*—now lost—consisted of four pages; four hundred copies were printed in the paper's humble office on the third floor of a wooden building at LaSalle and Lake Streets. The content was largely literary. There was local news, but reports from the East came in the form of letters or dispatches from other newspapers. "Fresh" overseas news was more than a month old. "Our views, in all probability, will sometimes be coincident with the conservatives; sometimes we may be found in the ranks of the radicals; but we shall at all times be faithful to humanity—to the whole of humanity—without regard to race, sectional divisions, party lines, or parallels of latitude or longitude," the paper said.

The city's first newspaper, the *Chicago Democrat*, founded in 1833, took no notice of the newcomer. However, the *Chicago Journal* welcomed the *Tribune* to "the stormy sea" of Chicago journalism. Within six weeks, the founding partnership hit rough water: Kelly quit because of failing eyesight. Forrest pulled out in September, questioning the wisdom of his $600 investment. Wheeler, the editor, bowed out in 1851. But as the city grew, so did *Tribune* circulation, reaching eighteen hundred by 1851. Ownership would change hands several times, but the paper's politics remained constant. The *Tribune* supported anybody who was not a Democrat—Whigs, Free Soilers, and even members of the short-lived Know-Nothing party.

That stance differed dramatically from the first *Chicago Tribune*, a Democratic weekly launched in 1840 to support a second term for President Martin Van Buren. It followed Van Buren's lead and folded after a year. But, like the first adhesive United States postage stamp, also introduced in 1847, the second *Chicago Tribune* would stick.

— *Tim Jones*

◀ *The front page of the earliest* Chicago Tribune *known to exist, dated April 23, 1849. Between fires in the newspaper's offices and the Chicago Fire, in 1871, many early issues of the paper were lost.*

Cyrus McCormick Moves to Chicago

The Virginia inventor's reaper factory becomes Chicago's first great industrial venture.

▼ *A McCormick reaper at work, probably about 1875. McCormick constantly improved his original 1831 reaper by adding such things as a seat for the driver and a device that would bind sheaves of grain with twine.*

AUGUST 30, 1847

Cyrus Hall McCormick had moved from Virginia to Cincinnati just two years earlier, but he was ready to move again by the summer of 1847. The country was pushing west across the sprawling prairies, and as those prairies came under the plow, McCormick wanted to be closer to the farmers who would be the customers for his invention, the mechanical reaper. And so on this date, McCormick and his two brothers bought land on the north bank of the Chicago River, about 300 feet east of the present Michigan Avenue bridge.

When a three-story brick plant opened that fall, some thirty-three workers operated six forges, lathes for turning iron, and a steam engine that drove other machines, saws, and grindstones. Within a year, riverside docks had been built to receive supplies from lake schooners and to ship finished reapers. McCormick's reaper works quickly became the city's leading manufacturing plant and presaged the Chicago region's rise as an industrial powerhouse, a place where, above all else, people made things.

McCormick knew that the most crucial labor problem on a farm came at harvest time. Ripe grain had to be harvested almost all at once or precious kernels would drop and be lost. His creation, built on models developed by his father in the fields of Virginia, gave farmers a tireless device that could do the work of half a dozen field hands.

Dark, strong, and vigorous, McCormick was the son of a well-to-do tinkerer who spent most of his life trying to develop a mechanical device to replace back-breaking hand sickles. None worked—at least not under conditions that farmers faced each autumn when rains often flattened grain stocks.

Young Cyrus worked out a deft combination of back-and-forth blade motions, with projecting fingers to catch and hold the stocks, plus a rotating wheel that pulled up grain that had fallen to the ground. "It was as clumsy as a Red River ox-cart," said one writer of the day, "but it reaped."

In 1848, the factory's first full year of operation, McCormick sold eight hundred machines; the next year, fifteen hundred. By the time McCormick died, in 1884 in his Rush Street mansion, five hundred thousand copies of Chicago's first great machine were in use.

—*Jon Anderson*

▲ *Cyrus McCormick not only invented the reaper but also was among the first businessmen to offer deferred payments and written guarantees.*

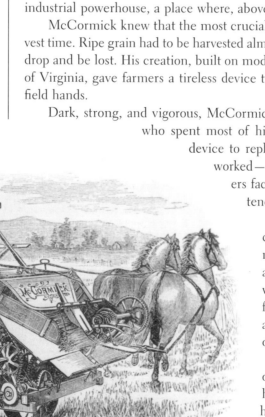

The Chicago Board of Trade

At first, even a free lunch was not enough to entice traders.

▲ *Frenzied shouting and specialized hand signals have long since taken the place of grain merchants and their samples. In this 1987 photo, the first session of night trading has just begun.*

▶

In the Board of Trade's early years, grain merchants and farmers brought samples of wheat and other grains to the trading floor for buyers to inspect.

MARCH 13, 1848

Founded on this date to promote and monitor Chicago commerce, the Chicago Board of Trade started with eighty-two members and no special interest in the grain business. The city's grain traders and merchants had no special interest in the Board of Trade, either. In the early days, the board lured members with free lunches. Even that was not sufficient inducement: on four days in July 1851, only one member showed up, and no one showed up on four other days. Traders preferred to do business on the city's streets, amid mounds of wheat and oats.

The Crimean War, in the mid-1850s, changed all that. The war boosted demand for American grain, which meant wheat shipments through Chicago rose in volume until it became easier for grain brokers to do their buying and selling in one central place. That place was the Board of Trade, which was firmly launched as a financial institution with worldwide influence.

As its power over the grain trade grew, the board adopted standards for the quality of commodities, with a bottom grade of "rejected." The grading system, first established in 1856, made it possible for traders to buy and sell not specific sacks of wheat—which was cumbersome at best—but quantities of a certain grade of wheat. From there, it was a short step to buying and selling contracts for delivery of grain in the future. The trading of futures, which took off after the Civil War, quickly outstripped trading of the real thing. By 1875, the *Tribune* reported the city's grain trade as $200 million; the sale of grain futures was ten times that—$2 billion.

A new marketplace, the Chicago Produce Exchange, had been established the year before for organized trading in butter, eggs, poultry, and other farm products. Its members developed the now worldwide "open outcry" system of floor trading, which can make commodities trading seem like little more than a shouting match. In 1919, part of the Produce Exchange changed its name to the Chicago Mercantile Exchange, or the Merc for short. The Merc, the Board of Trade's great rival, trades principally in futures and options on the world's currencies but continues to have markets in live animals, milk, and frozen meats. The Board of Trade, however, has remained the world's largest futures exchange, with markets not only in agricultural products but also treasury notes, municipal bonds, and metals. And, far from the days of the free lunch, traders pay dearly for memberships. In 1995, a seat cost as much as $710,000.

—*Kenan Heise*

The Illinois and Michigan Canal

After many delays, the link between the Great Lakes and the Mississippi River finally opens.

▼ *A view of a canal lock in Summit, Illinois, southwest of Chicago*

APRIL 10, 1848

Since it was the Illinois and Michigan Canal that turned a fur trading post into a thriving town, its opening on this date should be considered the seminal event in Chicago's early development. But history is never that simple: it was the *anticipation* of the canal that had led to Chicago's first boom in the early 1830s. By the time the steam tug *A. Rossitor* towed the first canal boat through Chicago, the age of canals was almost over.

As early as the 1670s, French explorers had proposed a canal to connect the Great Lakes and Mississippi River waterways, but it was not until 1810 that the United States took up the idea as a way to develop the vast interior of the new country. With no railways and few roads, the only way to move large quantities of goods inland was on rivers, lakes, and canals. Congress granted Illinois a strip of land for a canal in 1822, but raising the capital to pay for construction proved so difficult that work did not begin until 1836. The Panic of 1837, a severe national economic depression, then interrupted construction from 1841 to 1845.

Some of the first immigrants to the Chicago area were Irish and German workers who came to take jobs digging the ninety-six-mile waterway, which ran from the Chicago River to La Salle, the head of navigation on the Illinois River at the time. Many of the Irish settled along the Chicago River south of the city in a community that was called Hardscrabble at first but came to be known as Bridgeport. In addition to locks and stone-lined sides, the canal was designed with towpaths for mules, but, like the canal itself, the paths were practically past their time when the canal opened. Some boats were towed by mules in the early days, but steam-powered canal boats were common by 1848.

The canal never achieved the success that its proponents had projected because the railroads came along soon after it opened and took away some of its most profitable business. After 1853, for example, the new Chicago & Rock Island Railroad lured away passengers and shipments of package freight. And yet the Illinois and Michigan is considered one of the more successful American canals. It funneled to Chicago and New York the agricultural harvest of the Illinois River valley that formerly flowed downstream to rivals St. Louis and New Orleans. Trade in St. Louis declined by 316,625 bushels of corn and 237,000 bushels of wheat in the first year the canal was open.

Despite the railroads, lumber and many manufactured goods continued to move west on the canal, and large quantities of grain moved east. Traffic on the Illinois and Michigan Canal peaked in 1882 at more than a million tons but dropped sharply after that, although western portions remained open for decades. Sections of the canal have been preserved for their historic value and for recreational uses. Bicyclists, for instance, have turned the canal's little-used towpaths into well-traveled trails.

—David Young

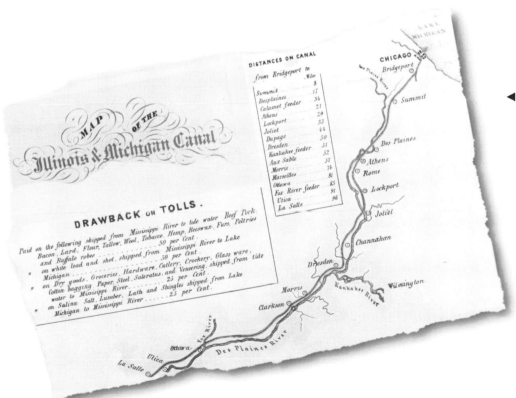

▲ The canal boat Elizabeth at the Norton & Company flour mill in Lockport, about 1880. The size of canal boats was limited by the long, narrow locks on the canal.

◀ The Illinois and Michigan Canal ran parallel to the Des Plaines and Illinois Rivers for ninety-six miles, from Bridgeport, on the banks of the Chicago River, to La Salle.

The Galena & Chicago Union

Chicago's rise as a rail center begins with an obsolete, wood-burning locomotive.

▼ *From humble beginnings with the* Pioneer, *Chicago quickly grew into the greatest railroad center on earth. Here streamliner diesel engines await servicing at the 40th Street yards of the Chicago & North Western Railway, which in 1864 absorbed the Galena & Chicago Union.*

NOVEMBER 20, 1848

The Galena & Chicago Union Railroad outfitted a couple of baggage cars with temporary seats and invited dignitaries, politicians, and the press on this date to take a free inaugural run west from Chicago. The only locomotive that was available and affordable was a twelve-year-old wood burner called the *Pioneer* that was obsolete even by the standards of 1848. Returning from the area that became the suburb of Oak Park, the train hauled a farmer's load of wheat and hides as a demonstration.

Thus began Chicago's transformation into the largest railroad center on earth. However, the city that would be so closely identified with railroads had shown little interest and less faith in the new mode of transportation. Former Mayor William B. Ogden and several other entrepreneurs had been able to raise only $20,000 from Chicagoans toward the $365,000 needed to get the project started. That forced Ogden and his partners to travel the prairies of northern Illinois and ask farmers, store proprietors, and mill operators to chip in. Warren L. Wheaton, a farmer who lived about twenty-five miles west of Chicago, provided some land for the right of way on the site of the town that was later named for him, and many farmers pledged to buy stock later when they got money for their crops.

▲ *William B. Ogden, who had already made a mark on Chicago history by serving as the city's first mayor, led the entrepreneurs who founded the Galena & Chicago Union.*

▲ *The first of thousands of locomotives to operate in Chicago was the* Pioneer, *an old wood burner that was bought used and brought to the city by ship. In the 1870s, when this photo was taken, the locomotive was still in service. It is on display at the Chicago Historical Society.*

The new railroad proved an instant success. Organizers were able to report that during the first full year of operation the company posted a profit of almost $30,000 on revenues of only $48,331. Investors who had been reluctant to put their money into frontier railroads in 1847 stampeded to them in 1850, and money poured in from as far away as Europe. By the eve of the Civil War, just twelve years after the *Pioneer*'s first trip, Chicago was a terminal to ten railroads and a network of track that stretched for four thousand miles.

As it continued to develop, that network boosted Chicago's meat-packing, lumber, and commodities industries as well as a host of other manufacturing and wholesale businesses. It created suburbia as well-to-do residents fled the bustling city to the relative quiet of outlying towns from which they could commute to work on the train. It turned the city into the nation's transfer point, with twenty-five million passengers funneling through the city's railroad stations in 1913.

To imagine Chicago without railroads is to imagine Chicago without Lake Michigan. In the 1990s, New York City's system carried more commuters, and more rail passengers traveled in the northeastern corridor between New York and Washington than passed through Chicago's Union Station. Still, the city was by far the largest rail center in the nation in volume of freight traffic and total amount of trackage. As for the Galena & Chicago Union, it was absorbed in 1864 by the Chicago & North Western Railway, which in turn disappeared in a merger with the Union Pacific in 1995.

— *David Young*

▲ Ginger Rogers, *traveling to the East Coast, steps off the Santa Fe Super Chief from Los Angeles at the Dearborn Street Station in 1942. Because no single railroad spanned the country, a cross-country trip inevitably involved a change of trains in Chicago.*

Northwestern University

The Chicago area's first institution of higher education begins as a haven for "sanctified" learning.

MAY 31, 1850

On this date, an energetic band of young Methodist brethren gathered in a law office over a hardware store at Lake and Dearborn Streets in Chicago. Led by John Evans, a physician; Grant Goodrich, a lawyer and temperance crusader; and Orrington Lunt, a cautious businessman, the group sought guidance in prayer and then resolved that "the interests of *sanctified* learning" required the immediate establishment of a university for the Methodist youth of the original Northwest Territory.

A mixture of cost consciousness, investment savvy, and religious zeal infused the founders of Northwestern University, the first institution of higher education in the Chicago area. The university, which was incorporated the following January, was at first under church patronage. But no particular faith would be required of students and faculty, and it would have a private endowment with many real-estate investments.

Finding a suitable location fell to Lunt; his quest took him south to the Indiana border and north to present-day Winnetka. On a final trip north of Chicago, he happened on a spectacular property—a lakeshore farm so lovely that Lunt saw it in his sleep that night, "the fairy visions constantly presenting themselves in fanciful beauties—of the gentle waving lake—its pebbly shore, the beautiful oak openings and bluffs beyond." The site delighted the trustees. "Some of the brethren threw up their hats," Lunt reported. They acquired 379 acres of farmland for $25,000; Evans assumed the mortgage. In 1855, the three-story frame structure known to succeeding generations as Old College was finished, and the first students enrolled.

▲ *John Evans, one of Northwestern's founders, after whom Evanston was named*

◄ *Town and gown: In this 1936 aerial view looking north, Northwestern University's campus hugs the lakeshore, while the tree-lined streets of Evanston enclose it to the west and south. The university expanded its campus in 1962 with construction of an eighty-five-acre landfill in Lake Michigan.*

◀ *Old College, shown here circa 1874, was the campus's first building. It was razed in 1973.*

▼ *Northwestern is known for its theater program, among other things. Three students, including future Hollywood star Warren Beatty (right), perform in the 1956 Waa-Mu show, the university's annual talent showcase.*

Also that year, the state legislature bowed to Goodrich and prohibited sales of intoxicating liquor within four miles of the university (a policy that would endure for more than a century) and declared that all Northwestern property "shall be forever free from taxation." That paved the way for a perennial argument with Evans's namesake, the city of Evanston. The town owed its existence to the university, but it had two advantages that ensured its independent development: an attractive location on the lakeshore and a rail link to Chicago's business district, a dozen miles to the south. Evanston was soon dotted with the imposing mansions of Chicago merchants. For decades, it was the city's largest suburb.

Northwestern's links to Chicago were strengthened in 1933 with the completion of its downtown campus on Lake Shore Drive, between Chicago Avenue and Superior Street. The university flowered in the years after World War II, with highly regarded programs in journalism, theater, music, law, and medicine. Its business school consistently has ranked at or near the top in the nation. The vision of the original brethren has held true; a university and a residential community have grown up together to create mutual desirability and excellence.

— *Peter Gorner*

Joseph Medill Buys the *Tribune*

A young editor from Ohio moves west to run a small, struggling paper.

▶

Joseph Medill in 1855, when he left Cleveland and formed a partnership to buy the struggling Tribune. Medill, who was born in St. John, New Brunswick, and grew up in rural Ohio, would spend the rest of his life building the foundations of one of America's major newspapers.

June 18, 1855

The little newspaper on Clark Street was certainly no great prize. Neither, in the eyes of Joseph Meharry Medill, was Chicago, which he viewed as a "quagmire on the lake." The thirty-two-year-old crusading editor of the *Cleveland Morning Leader* could not be blamed for being reluctant to leave the security of Cleveland; he had already made a mark as an organizer of the Republican Party. But his heart said to go. So, predictably, did Horace Greeley, the editor of the *New York Tribune*, who was prone to urge young men to go west. "Go to Chicago," Greeley advised Medill. "Buy the *Tribune*."

And so with Dr. Charles Ray, a political firebrand and medical doctor who had newspaper experience in Galena and Springfield, Medill pieced together a partnership to buy the *Tribune*; the new ownership was announced on this date in the pages of the paper. The new owners not only put the struggling eight-year-old daily on solid financial footing but also created a forceful antislavery voice. In March 1857, the Supreme Court ruled in the Dred Scott decision that slaves had to be returned to their masters from non-slave territory. "Slavery is now national," the *Tribune* editorialized. "Freedom has no local habitation nor abiding place save in the hearts of Freemen. Illinois in law *has ceased to be a free State!*"

The paper's remedy was published a few days later: "Let the next President be a Republican and 1860 will mark an era kindred

[handwritten letter in Medill's hand]

▲ *In 1882, Medill wrote out his instructions for how he wanted the paper to be run after his death. "I want the Tribune to continue to be after I am gone as it has been under my direction: an advocate of political and moral progress and in all things to follow the line of common sense. I desire the Tribune as a party organ never to be the supporter of that party which sought to destroy the American Union or that exalts the State above the Nation."*

with that of 1776." Medill worked tirelessly for the election of Abraham Lincoln as president and grimly set himself and his newspaper to support the savage war that followed Lincoln's election. His fervor for the Union cause was put to the test: two of his brothers were killed in the Civil War.

Ray left the paper in 1863; in 1874, Medill purchased a controlling interest. In the decades following the Civil War, Medill's *Tribune* sided with the working man in battles against such high-handed industrialists and monopolists as the Rocke-fellers and the Vanderbilts. His favorite editorial writer in those years was pioneering muckraker Henry Demarest Lloyd, who dubbed the robber barons "American Pashas." And yet Medill had little use for unions and other labor causes. The eight-hour day might be practical in some industries, he felt, but not all.

Medill not only laid the foundations of one of the country's major newspapers; he also established a publishing dynasty. Three of his grandchildren went on to run papers: Robert R. McCormick (*Chicago Tribune*), Joseph M. Patterson (*New York Daily News*), and Eleanor M. Patterson (*Washington Times-Herald*). Medill died in 1899, shortly before his seventy-sixth birthday. But in forty-four years at the *Tribune*, he charted the newspaper's partisan course for decades to come.

—Tim Jones

◄ *Dr. Charles Ray, a partner of Medill's, was a political firebrand and newspaperman who had worked in Galena and Springfield.*

◄ *Medill was photographed shortly before his death in 1899 with his grandchildren, three of whom became newspaper publishers: (left to right) Robert R. McCormick (later publisher of the* Chicago Tribune*), Eleanor M. Patterson (*Washington Times-Herald*), Medill, Medill McCormick (who later was elected to the United States Senate from Illinois), and Joseph M. Patterson (*New York Daily News*).*

Raising the Streets

The city decides on an ambitious plan to pull itself out of the mud.

▼ *Walking along a Chicago sidewalk in the 1850s had its ups and downs, as many store owners put off the inevitable but expensive job of raising their buildings. The view shows Clark Street in 1857.*

DECEMBER 31, 1855

As Chicago boomed in the 1850s, growing into a major lake port and industrial center, mud became a major problem. The lakeshore marsh on which the city was being built seemed bottomless. According to a popular story of the time, a passerby came upon a man whose head and shoulders protruded from the muck in the middle of the street. "Can I help?" asked the passerby. "No, thank you," replied the man. "I have a fine horse under me."

The humor belied the serious nature of the problem. The quagmire made Chicago a breeding ground for deadly cholera, which swept the city periodically and in 1854 killed more than 5 percent of the population. The city first had tried grading its streets so that water ran into the Chicago River. When that failed, it tried planking them over; but the planks warped and rotted from all the moisture beneath. On the last day of 1855, the newly created Chicago Board of Sewerage Commissioners finally came up with a plan to lift Chicago out of the ooze.

Engineer E. S. Chesbrough of Boston, whom the board had hired to study the problem, recommended installing a storm-sewer system, the first comprehensive sewage system in the country. But since the city was only three or four feet above the level of Lake Michigan, underground sewers would not drain properly into the river and the lake unless the entire elevation of Chicago was raised. And so the Common Council, as the city council was then called, passed ordinances that called for raising the grade level of streets across the city. The increases varied, but for streets next to the river, the boost amounted to about ten feet.

Over a period of almost two decades, Chicago's buildings were jacked up four to fourteen feet, higher foundations were built beneath them, the storm sewers were placed on top of the streets, and the streets were then filled up to the level of the front doors of the raised buildings. To raise larger buildings, an enterprising newcomer to the city named George Pullman perfected a method involving hundreds of men turning thousands of large jackscrews at the same time. Many smaller structures, especially houses, were simply moved to new locations. "Never a day passed,"

noted a visitor at the time, "that I did not meet one or more houses shifting their quarters. One day I met nine."

The raising of Chicago became the talk of the nation, but for the people of Chicago, the enormous undertaking not only solved a problem; it also testified to the young city's character. "Nothing," noted an early Chicago historian, "better illustrates the energy and determination with which the makers of Chicago set about a task when once they had made up their minds, than the speed and thoroughness with which they solved the problem of the city's drainage and sewage."

— *David Young*

▲ *Raising the Briggs House, a hotel at Randolph and Wells Streets, in 1857 involved the coordinated efforts of hundreds of men, but meanwhile the hotel was open for business. "The people were in it all the time, coming and going, eating and sleeping," an observer noted.*

◄ *George Pullman, shown in 1857 when he was twenty-six, perfected the raising of large buildings. The fortune he made allowed him to go into the railroad sleeping car building business.*

The Lincoln-Douglas Debates

A lanky lawyer from Springfield takes on "the little giant."

JULY 24, 1858

A note to Stephen A. Douglas, which was handed to him in Chicago on this date, seemed to offer a bad deal for the politician. His rival for a seat in the United States Senate—a former postmaster, deputy county surveyor, state legislator, circuit-riding lawyer, and one-term congressman named Abraham Lincoln—wanted to debate him on slavery. For the nationally prominent Douglas, the debates would simply give his relatively little-known opponent prestigious exposure. And yet slavery was the great issue of the day. Douglas agreed to seven debates at various sites throughout Illinois.

Through the late summer and early fall, the two candidates followed a format that a later, less-patient age doubtless would find tedious. The first speaker had an hour to frame his position, after which the other speaker responded for an hour and a half. The first speaker then returned for a half hour. Douglas was an imposing if compact figure with a broad brow; dark, fiery eyes; and bass voice. His lanky opponent spoke in a high-pitched tone, and his ankles and wrists showed beyond the confines of a too-small suit. "Senator Douglas wants to keep me down," Lincoln said. "Put me down I should not say, for I have never been up."

But Lincoln's folksy oratory complemented the precise logic of his arguments against slavery, "a moral, social, and political wrong." Douglas argued for each state's right to decide the issue for itself. By the fifth debate, in Galesburg, Horace White was writing in the *Daily Press and Tribune* (as the *Tribune* was known briefly following a merger): "Like a whale in his 'flurry,' Mr. Douglas, pierced to the very vitals by the barbed harpoons which Lincoln hurls at him, goes around and around, making the water foam, filling the air with roars of rage and pain, spouting torrents of blood, and striking out fiercely but vainly at his assailant, who seems to enjoy the noble sport in which he is engaged."

Papers outside Illinois first published only Douglas's speeches. Later, as Lincoln's fame spread, his side of the debates began to appear in print also. Although Lincoln won the popular vote, he lost in the Illinois legislature at a time when state legislators, not voters, chose senators. But the debates established Lincoln as a national figure who would be heard from in the future.

—*Charles Leroux*

◀ *Abraham Lincoln holds the floor during the fifth debate, at Knox College, in Galesburg. Because the artist, Fletcher Seymour, was not sure where Stephen A. Douglas sat, Lincoln's rival appears twice in this depiction—seated second from the right and second from the left.*

The 1860 Republican Convention

Politics Chicago-style puts Lincoln over the top.

▼ *Chicago photographer Alexander Hesler took this photograph of the Wigwam, a barnlike building at Lake and Market Streets, in May 1860, during the Republican convention. The pine-board building was razed shortly after the convention.*

MAY 18, 1860

A large and noisy crowd had already filled the meeting hall to capacity by the time the supporters of William H. Seward showed up for the third day of the Republican convention. It was no accident that the crowd—which bellowed its backing for Illinois' favorite son, Abraham Lincoln—had arrived early. In retrospect, the hand of destiny is easy to see in Lincoln's nomination on this date, but fate received considerable help from local admirers of "Honest Abe."

The eloquent, self-assured Seward, a U.S. senator from New York, was widely thought to have the nomination wrapped up; many deals had been cut, one of which put Chicago mayor "Long John" Wentworth in the Seward camp. Lincoln had grown in national standing in the two years since his debates with Stephen A. Douglas, but he was still seen as something of a provincial.

Fortunately for him, Chicago, which was hosting its first national political convention, was the heart of Lincoln country. To be sure that a friendly crowd would be on hand to outshout the competition, batches of admission tickets were printed at the last moment and handed out to Lincoln supporters, who were told to show up early at the Wigwam, a rickety hall that held ten thousand people. And, for good measure, Illinois delegation chairman Norman Judd and Joseph Medill, of the *Chicago Daily Press and Tribune*, placed the New York delegates off to one side, far from key swing states such as Pennsylvania.

No candidate had a majority after two ballots. During the third ballot, with Lincoln tantalizingly close to winning the nomination, Medill sat close to the chairman of the Ohio delegation, which had backed its favorite son, Salmon P. Chase. Swing your votes to Lincoln, Medill whispered, and your boy can have anything he wants. The Ohio chairman shot out of his chair and changed the state's votes.

After a moment of stunned silence, the flimsy Wigwam began to shake with the stomping of feet and the shouting of the Lincoln backers who packed the hall and blocked the streets outside. A cannon on the roof fired off a round, and boats on the Chicago River tooted in reply. The courthouse bell rang out, and soon church bells around the city took up the peal. The Republicans had a candidate.

—*Kenan Heise*

▲ *Abraham Lincoln in 1860, at about the time of the Republican nomination*

The Civil War

The bombardment of Fort Sumter begins a bloody conflict in which Chicago will play a vital role.

APRIL 12, 1861

The election of Abraham Lincoln as president on November 6, 1860, was a watershed in American history, all but guaranteeing that the South would break from the Union. Indeed, on this date, just five months after the election, the Confederate attack on Fort Sumter, in Charleston, South Carolina, triggered a terrible, bloody struggle that would rage for four years. "Lenity and forbearance have only nursed the viper into life," the *Tribune* thundered. "Let the cry be, 'THE SWORD OF THE LORD AND OF GIDEON!'"

The young men of Chicago appeared in droves at recruitment centers, bankers wired Washington offering loans to the government, and the state militia began organizing itself. A contingent of five hundred Cook County volunteers, armed with squirrel guns, antique revolvers, and fifty muskets from the Milwaukee militia, was dispatched hastily to Cairo, at the southern tip of the state, to secure the confluence of the Ohio and Mississippi Rivers, the strategic key to controlling river traffic. Businessmen donated cash for guns and uniforms.

At the outbreak of the war, Chicago was a hotbed—politically, economically, and socially. Its population had soared from 16,000 to 109,000 in only thirteen years. It was home to more than five hundred factories, led by the McCormick reaper works, and dozens of mills, slaughterhouses, and lumberyards. It had become the railroad capital of America, the greatest primary grain port, and largest lumber market in the world. Though it was still a vast sprawl of wooden buildings and plank sidewalks built above a sea of mud, the city boasted seven first-class hotels, a fine new courthouse, and a horse-drawn trolley. As a stronghold of abolitionist sentiment and the springboard of Lincoln's presidency, Chicago was blamed in many circles for bringing on the war. The *Tribune* came in for a major share of the accusations, having long championed the abolitionist cause.

◄ *Colonel Elmer Ellsworth of Chicago, shown in this photograph by Mathew Brady, was one of the first officers to die for the Union cause. When he hauled down a Confederate flag at a hotel in Alexandria, Virginia, he was shot by the hotel manager, who in turn was killed by Ellsworth's troops.*

Chicago Tribune.

VOLUME XIV.   CHICAGO, MONDAY, APRIL 15, 1861.   NUMBER 246.

BY TELEGRAPH.

THE ATTACK ON SUMTER

THE SURRENDER!

THE BOMBARDMENT AND DEFENCE.

EFFECT OF THE NEWS IN WASHINGTON.

Absurd and Contradictory Rumors.

PRESIDENT LINCOLN'S PRO-CLAMATION.

The city was to pay dearly for its role. Some twenty-six thousand Chicagoans would be called to arms, and thousands would lose their lives. Among the first Union officers to die was Chicagoan Elmer Ephraim Ellsworth, an ex–law student of Lincoln. The city also lived uneasily with the presence of Camp Douglas, a prisoner-of-war facility at 33rd Street and the lakefront. The prison stood on the estate of Lincoln's opponent in the 1858 debates, Senator Stephen A. Douglas, who died shortly after the outbreak of war. Within the prison's squalid walls, twelve thousand rebel prisoners subsisted on meager rations.

▲ *The Tribune of April 15, 1861, brought the news of the surrender of Fort Sumter and the beginning of the Civil War.*

▲ *To raise troops without a draft, bounties were offered to enlistees. Veterans, who knew what awaited them, were paid more to reenlist. Not until late in the war was a draft needed in Chicago.*

▲ *A grim reminder of the Civil War in Chicago was Camp Douglas, where as many as twelve thousand Confederate soldiers such as these were held prisoner.*

▲ In this 1858 photograph of the Chicago lakefront by Alexander Hesler, many of the features that made the city an important part of the Northern war effort can be seen. At the right are the two grain elevators of Sturges, Buckingham and Company. Between the elevators and behind the buildings in the distance are the masts of the schooners that brought, among other things, lumber to the city. At that time, Chicago was the world's largest grain port and lumber market as well as the nation's railroad capital. In the center are the Illinois Central Railroad tracks and depot. The street that fronts the water is Michigan Avenue.

But Chicago also prospered during the Civil War. Its population almost doubled as thousands of immigrants found work in the city, the second leading war supplier after New York. Arms flowed from Chicago's factories. Its reapers freed thousands of farmers to fight. Its stockyards fed the Union armies, and its trains kept the troops supplied with bullets and cannonballs. The boom sent land values skyrocketing and spawned scores of millionaires, who spent their newfound money at such places of entertainment as the McVicker's Theatre, where a young actor named John Wilkes Booth won glittering reviews.

Despite this economic upsurge, Chicagoans celebrated with abandon in April 1865 at the news that the South had surrendered. Artillery bursts filled the air, impromptu parades broke out, and twenty thousand revelers took to the streets "to shout, sing, laugh, dance and cry for very gladness," reported the *Tribune*. But the city's joy was to be short-lived.

—*Jeff Lyon*

◄ *One of the centers of city life in Civil War–era Chicago was the courthouse, designed by John Van Osdel. It stood in the middle of the block bounded by Clark, Randolph, LaSalle, and Washington Streets.*

Lincoln's Assassination

Chicago mourns as a funeral train brings the president's body home to Illinois.

▼ *The procession to take Lincoln's casket to the courthouse leaves the memorial arch that was erected for the occasion at 12th Street and Michigan Avenue. The legends in the arch read, from left to right, "We honor him dead who honored us while living," "Rest in peace noble soul, patriot heart," and "Faithful to right, a martyr to justice."*

April 14, 1865

After holding the nation together through its darkest hours, Abraham Lincoln celebrated the end of the Civil War on this date, Good Friday, by taking in *Our American Cousin* at Ford's Theater, in Washington. As Lincoln and his wife, Mary Todd, watched the comedy, young actor and Confederate sympathizer John Wilkes Booth slipped into their box and shot the president in the head at point-blank range. Booth vaulted to the stage, breaking his left ankle, and fled.

Mortally wounded, Lincoln was carried across Tenth Street to a boarding house, where at 7:22 the next morning he died. "Now he belongs to the ages," said Secretary of War Edward M. Stanton, one of many at Lincoln's bedside. Booth was later surrounded and killed by a federal posse in Virginia.

A bulletin in the April 15 *Tribune* announced: Terrible News. President Lincoln Assassinated at Ford's Theater. A Rebel Desperado Shoots Him Through the Head and Escapes. An editorial two days later said: "President Lincoln, whose life was covered with glory by his faithfuness to his country, has ascended to his God. Pale in death, murdered by the hellish spirit of slavery, his body lies at the nation's capital—a new sacrifice upon our country's altar. All the land weeps, for we loved none as we loved him." The nation, or at least the North, grieved openly as Lincoln's black-draped funeral train retraced in reverse the zigzag, seventeen-hundred-mile route he had traveled in 1861 on his journey from Springfield to Washington for his inauguration.

On May 1, the train arrived in Chicago, which Lincoln had known well as a lawyer and rising politician. A crowd of a hundred thousand people gathered at the trestle along the lakeshore where the train stopped. Lincoln's casket was transferred to a hearse beneath a Gothic memorial arch, and then thirty-six maidens in white circled the scene, each dropping a flower near the coffin. Mourners by the tens of thousands followed the hearse to the Cook County courthouse, where Lincoln's body lay in an open casket as 125,000 people filed by. On May 3, he was laid to rest at Oak Ridge Cemetery, in Springfield.

—Bob Secter

The Stockyards Open

Chicago becomes "The Great Bovine City of the World."

DECEMBER 25, 1865

For almost a century, Chicago's stockyards were one of the city's world-famous wonders, visited by princes and maharajas and almost every tourist. "Not to see the Yards is to miss seeing Chicago," one guidebook noted. Most visitors marveled at the sight of the stock pens stretching as far as the eye could see. Others, from Upton Sinclair to Rudyard Kipling, took darker views. "One cannot stand and watch long," Sinclair wrote in *The Jungle*, his 1906 exposé of the meatpacking industry, "without beginning to deal in symbols and similes, and hear the hog-squeal of the universe."

The Union Stock Yard and Transit Company of Chicago received its first bellowing arrivals on Christmas Day 1865, in fifteen rickety cattle cars pulled by a puffing, wood-burning locomotive. Driven by the Union Army's ravenous demands for meat, Chicago's already-prosperous meatpacking industry had boomed during the Civil War to become the largest in the world; consolidating the city's scattered stockyards at one large site seemed the only way to handle the growth. To make the tract of swampland usable, some one thousand men dug thirty miles of ditches and

▲ *Trimming meat in a packing plant. In 1893, a year after this photograph was taken, almost one-fifth of Chicago's workers were employed in the meatpacking industry. But the work often involved long hours for low pay in grim conditions.*

drains that emptied into a fork of the Chicago River, later to become notorious as Bubbly Creek when its waters thickened with pungent slaughterhouse offal.

The yards, which covered a half square mile west of Halsted Street between 39th and 47th Streets, were soon filled "with so many cattle as no one had ever dreamed existed in the world," noted one writer of the day. "Red, black, white, and yellow cattle. Great bellowing bulls and little calves not an hour born. Meek-eyed milch cows and fierce, long-horned Texas steers."

Men on horseback, booted and carrying long whips, galloped up and down the alleys between pens. Drovers and stock-raisers, brokers and buyers, they would stop to inspect a herd of cattle. A buyer would nod or lower his whip, meaning that a bargain had been struck. Meanwhile, the parade of animals—cattle, hogs, and sheep—never stopped. By the following night, every creature in sight would be killed, cut up, loaded into freight cars, and taken away.

During the peak times of World War I, fifteen million animals a year moved through Chicago, almost nine million pounds of meat a day. Nor was there money only in meat. Profits for such meatpacking tycoons as Gustavus F. Swift and Philip Armour also came from hides, hair, wool, bones, horns, fertilizer, glue, fats, materials for toothbrush handles, chess pieces, and strings for musical instruments. It became a commonplace that Chicago packers used every part of a hog but its squeal.

Times changed when refrigerated trucks and the interstate highway system made the old railroad-based stockyards obsolete. Packers decentralized and moved plants west. The Union Stock Yard and Transit Company held on until 1971, when it closed forever, leaving behind only an entranceway arch.

— *Jon Anderson*

▲ *The stockyards, shown here in 1902, became a popular tourist stop. To the left are some of the rail lines that brought animals to the yards and to the right in the distance are the meatpacking plants of the two industry giants, Armour and Swift.*

▶

The limestone entrance to the stockyards, dating from 1879, became a neighborhood landmark that outlived the yards. The gate stands on Exchange Avenue at Peoria Street.

The Water Tower

Tested by fire, it becomes Chicago's most beloved structure.

MARCH 25, 1867

For a city that sits beside one of the world's largest sources of fresh water, Chicago in its early years had drinking water that was scandalously bad. Drawn mainly from the Chicago River, which was also the city's sewer, the water at best tasted foul and at worst carried such deadly diseases as cholera and typhoid fever. The groundbreaking on this date for something as prosaic as a new water tower was understandably the occasion for civic jubilation.

"To a people so long habituated to quenching their thirst by unnatural beverages, to quaffing bumpers of diluted animal matter, the outflowings of sewers and the distillations of graveyards, the [groundbreaking] event must be a happy one," noted the *Tribune*. The paper went on to mention the tiny silver minnows that wriggled through hydrants and said, "Everyone will hail the announcement as being indeed tidings of great joy . . . their tea, coffee and other beverages will be no longer fishy."

The pumping station and water tower, built on Chicago Avenue on either side of what became Michigan Avenue, were connected to a tunnel that reached two

miles out into Lake Michigan, where an octagonal crib collected water from the lake's "pure and limpid portions," the paper reported. The tower, designed by architect W. W. Boyington, disguised a three-foot diameter, 140-foot-tall iron standpipe that was needed to provide water pressure for the city's North Side. Surely no pipe was ever so ornately wrapped as this one, clad in a pale golden limestone carved from quarries around Lemont, Illinois. Boyington's tower, completed in 1869, became a near-instant object of great affection for Chicagoans and visitors alike.

Lady Duffus Hardy, a British novelist and travel writer, touring the city in 1880, wrote: "The new water works are the most beautiful illustrations of the vagaries of the architectural brain. . . . Never were so many cupolas and buttresses, pinnacles and towers grouped together on one spot; none but a true artist could have arranged them into so harmonious a whole." Two years later, Oscar Wilde, the Irish aesthete but not yet the famed playwright, arrived at a quite different conclusion. The *Tribune* reported that during a lecture at the Central Music Hall, he called the structure a "castellated monstrosity with pepper boxes stuck all over it" and won-

◀ *Architect W. W. Boyington with his drawing of the Water Tower*

dered why anyone would make a water tower masquer-
ade as a miniature medieval castle.

The pumping station has remained in use, but the
Water Tower outgrew its original function. Instead, as
one of the few buildings to survive the Chicago Fire, in
1871 this flamboyant piece of plumbing became a civic
symbol of the city's will to survive.

—*Charles Leroux*

▲ *The Water Tower and pumping
station, shown here sometime
before the Chicago Fire, were
part of the city's effort to
improve its foul drinking water.*

◄ *Oscar Wilde in 1882, the year
he visited Chicago and
dismissed the Water Tower as
a "castellated monstrosity"*

The Village of Riverside

Frederick Law Olmsted designs one of the first planned suburbs in the United States.

AUGUST 19, 1868

On this date, landscape architect Frederick Law Olmsted headed west from Chicago, where he had arrived by train from New York, to a spot about ten miles from the city. His mission was to inspect sixteen hundred acres of land that a group of eastern businessmen had recently purchased. Olmsted took a carriage out to the site, which lay along the Des Plaines River and was graced with thick groves of oak and hickory trees.

"I was ill when I reached Chicago but to keep my engagement, drove twenty miles over open prairie, [in] bleak & raw wind, & walked a good deal," Olmsted wrote his wife, Mary. "Next day [I] could not speak easily & had to keep [to] my bed." Olmsted, who was already well known for his design of New York's Central Park, had been hired to draw up plans to develop the property. The result was the village of Riverside, one of the first planned communities in the country.

In designing Riverside, Olmsted laid out a model suburb at a time when the notion of a suburb as a new kind of community—neither urban nor rural—was taking shape. Referring to Chicago, he wrote: "The city, as yet, has no true suburb . . . in which urban and rural advantages are agreeably combined." Olmsted envisioned Riverside as a sylvan retreat from the crowded, bustling city, where "the conveniences peculiar to the finest modern towns" would be combined with "the domestic advantages of a most charming country." Streets, for instance, were at least a foot lower than adjacent properties so that they remained out of view, but under the pavement ran the water, sewer, and gas lines that were becoming essential for a comfortable life.

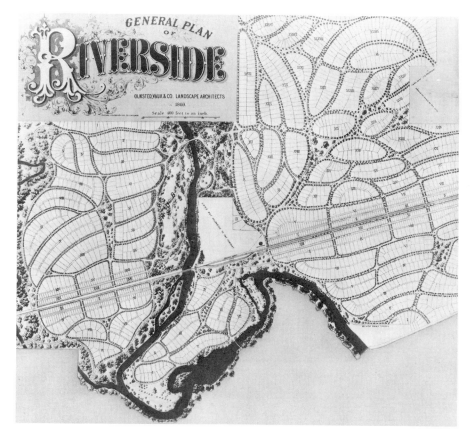

◀ *An 1869 lithograph of Frederick Law Olmsted's plan for Riverside shows the suburb's winding streets and irregular lots.*

▶

Riverside in its early days, looking south from the town's schoolhouse. To the right is Riverside's distinctive water tower, with the railroad station and the suburb's first commercial building behind it.

Unlike Chicago's rigid grid of streets, Riverside's roads followed the natural contours of the land. At intersections, the streets split to form small triangular parks. Seven hundred acres were set aside for open spaces, parks, and trails. Yet, with the Chicago, Burlington & Quincy Railroad running through the site, this oasis would be within easy reach of the city.

The investors, who organized themselves as the Riverside Improvement Company, started to sell lots following Olmsted's plan, but troubles soon clouded the project's pastoral prospects. In 1870, Olmsted and his partner, Calvert Vaux, pulled out because of financial disputes with the investment company. By 1871, about fifty homes were under construction, but the Chicago Fire, in October, diverted efforts to the rebuilding of the central city. The financial panic of 1873 finished the Riverside Improvement Company, which went bankrupt. Construction resumed about a decade later, and about one thousand acres of the original site were completed based on Olmsted's plan. Historians cite Riverside as an early, influential example of a secluded suburb standing apart from the city. In 1970, most of the village was designated a national historic landmark.

—*Anne Little*

▶

Frederick Law Olmsted (1822–1903) wanted Riverside to be a "village in a park."

Marshall Field Moves to State Street

The "Marble Palace" turns a muddy thoroughfare into a great street.

OCTOBER 12, 1868

Crowds packed the sidewalks and streets on this date to watch Chicago's high society pour into Marshall Field's first store on State Street, a grand marble edifice with Corinthian columns. As was frequently the case, Field was on hand to welcome customers to the store that, more than any other emporium, would establish State Street as Chicago's premier shopping district.

By 1868, Field's store was already a civic institution. Field had come to Chicago in 1856 at age twenty-one from Massachusetts, where he had been a dry-goods clerk in a country store. He was polite and earnest, if somewhat taciturn, and had ice-blue eyes. Field immediately got a job in a Chicago dry-goods store, where he listened to his customers, talked knowledgeably about the merchandise, and was

◀ *Marshall Field as a young man: helpful without being unctuous. He was only thirty-three when he and his partner, Levi Leiter, opened the State Street store.*

▶

The first Field and Leiter store on State Street. Previously the store had been on Lake Street, then the commercial heart of the city.

helpful without being unctuous. These were rare qualities among the shopkeepers of the time, and they were to make Field a fortune.

Field and his partner, financial wizard Levi Z. Leiter, bought the enormously profitable Lake Street dry-goods business of Potter Palmer in 1865 and three years later moved into the marble store, which Palmer had built as part of his effort to improve grimy State Street. Field often stood inside the door, white gloves on his hands, and bowed to society ladies and bargain hunters alike as they entered. Encountering a manager arguing with a customer one day, he uttered the admonition that was to become the store's unofficial motto: "Give the lady what she wants." He endeared the store to the public by following the then-remarkable policy of allowing returns.

"When the public goes abroad, it boasts of Field, Leiter and Company just as it does of the Stock Yards," a *Tribune* editorial gushed in 1881, shortly before Field bought out Leiter and the store became simply Marshall Field and Company.

Marshall Field died in 1906, but not before he approved the construction of a new and larger store on State Street, which opened the next year and featured a six-thousand-square-foot Tiffany glass mosaic dome. Since then, countless friends have met under the store's great clock, and generations of children have made annual pilgrimages with their families to lunch under the Christmas tree in the cavernous Walnut Room.

The era of Chicago ownership ended in 1982 when Marshall Field and Company was bought by a British company, which later sold it to Minneapolis-based Dayton Hudson Corporation. It seems unlikely that any modern corporate executive ever will inspire the kind of tribute that a young magazine writer named Theodore Dreiser paid to Marshall Field. This "celebrated Western merchant," Dreiser wrote, "is an example to be studied with profit by every farm boy, by every office boy, by every clerk and artisan—yes, and by every middle-aged business man, whether going along smoothly or confronted by apparently ruinous circumstances, throughout our broad land."

—*Barbara Brotman*

▶

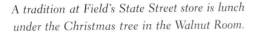

A tradition at Field's State Street store is lunch under the Christmas tree in the Walnut Room.

The Chicago Fire

Out of the ashes, a new city— and a new spirit—rises.

▲ *In its first postfire edition, produced at a small print shop on Canal Street, the* Tribune *told the story of the destruction of Chicago but also prophesied that the city would rise again. The paper resumed publishing the day after the end of the fire.*

OCTOBER 8, 1871

The whole Midwest was parched, caught in the thrall of a mighty drought. Chicago, with its preponderance of wooden buildings, inadequate fire codes, and inferior firefighting equipment, was a conflagration waiting to happen. On this Sunday evening, it did. Blazes had flared up throughout the region that year. One leveled four square blocks along Canal Street the very day before, and on the day of Chicago's disaster, the deadliest fire in American history killed twelve hundred people and destroyed Peshtigo, Wisconsin.

But the Great Fire was without a doubt the *biggest* one, the single most important event in the history of Chicago and one of the most spectacular of the nineteenth century. It changed more than the look of the city, then a bustling metropolis with a population of some three hundred thousand. It changed the city's character forever, infusing its inhabitants with a zealous, can-do spirit.

The fire did indeed begin in the barn behind the O'Leary cottage on De Koven Street, near 12th and Halsted Streets. Despite the familiar legend, the cause of the fire is unknown; Mrs. O'Leary later denied under oath that her much-maligned cow had anything to do with it. Once begun, the blaze was quickly whipped into monster stature by "fire devils," whirling pockets of gas and air that

▼ *No photographs of the Great Fire are known to have survived, but this painting by artist James Session depicts the terror of the fire and the fate of the four-story "fireproof"* Tribune *building on the southeast corner of Dearborn and Madison Streets.*

rolled through the city for two days, knocking down buildings and sending survivors scurrying for safety in the waters of Lake Michigan. The fire jumped the river twice, first crossing the south branch at Van Buren Street and later, after it burned its way across the business district, leaping the main channel to lay waste the North Side. Among its prey: Potter Palmer's hotel, Marshall Field's Marble Palace, the city's brothels, and the *Tribune* building, a spanking-new, four-story, "fireproof" structure.

Fleeing the flames, terrified men, women, and children rushed through the streets. Looters ransacked burning stores. The courthouse bell eerily clanged on, until it, too, succumbed. "The great, dazzling, mounting light, the crash and roar of the conflagration, and the desperate flight of the crowd," a young journalist named J. E. Chamberlain wrote, "combined to make a scene of which no intelligent idea can be conveyed in words." The fire reached Fullerton Avenue

▲ *The fire reduced State and Madison Streets to piles of ash and rubble.*

▶

A workman pours water on a still-hot safe lying in the ruins of the Fifth National Bank.

▲ *The Water Tower and Pumping Station were among the few buildings in the "burnt district" to survive.*

before it petered out on Tuesday morning, October 10. Nearly three hundred Chicagoans were dead, ninety thousand were homeless, and 17,450 buildings were destroyed, with damages totaling $200 million. Many despaired, and many in rival cities gleefully wrote Chicago off. But, in its first postfire issue on October 11, the *Tribune* declared: "CHEER UP . . . looking upon the ashes of thirty years' accumulations, the people of this once beautiful city have resolved that CHICAGO SHALL RISE AGAIN."

And it did. Within a week, six thousand temporary structures were erected. *Tribune* editor Joseph Medill was elected mayor in November as the "fireproof" candidate; before resigning in mid-1873, he oversaw a variety of fire-protection reforms, including a ban on wooden buildings in the business district. Out of the ashes rose new or rebuilt landmarks: a new Palmer House, a new store for Marshall Field, a cavernous exposition building on the lakefront, and, throughout the "burnt district," grander, more elaborate, and taller buildings. But one now-famous structure — "a warped and weather-beaten shanty of two rooms" — did not need to be rebuilt. Mrs. O'Leary's cottage survived the fire.

—*Teresa Wiltz*

◄ *Like many other businesses, the* Tribune *rebuilt on the same site, but bigger and better: the new* Tribune *office, five stories instead of four, was ready for occupancy in 1872.*

◀ *The barn where it all started was gone, but the O'Leary cottage on De Koven Street remained.*

▼ *The intersection of LaSalle and Lake Streets shows the pace of rebuilding in the weeks and months after the fire. Note that no buildings are made of wood. The city banned wooden structures in the business district.*

Montgomery Ward's First Catalog

The mail-order business brings department-store shopping into the homes of rural America.

▼ *An endless stream of packages moves through the Montgomery Ward mailroom. The idea of buying goods sight unseen through the mail was almost unheard of in 1872, but it caught on quickly.*

AUGUST 27, 1872

From a cramped office on North Clark Street, surrounded by hoop skirts, lace curtains, red flannel, wool socks, and more—and with Christmas a mere four months away—Aaron Montgomery Ward launched the nation's first mail-order business. It began with a one-page price list boasting 163 items, which he sent to farmers' cooperatives throughout the rural Midwest. It had not been a particularly easy launch. Less than a year earlier, Ward had been nearly ready to start business when his entire stock of merchandise was destroyed in the Chicago Fire.

Unlike existing mail-order businesses that dealt only in individual items, Ward offered the rural consumer a variety of merchandise and, by eliminating the middleman, kept prices low. His new business found a ready market as homesteaders pushed west across the frontier. By the spring of 1874, his price list had grown to thirty-two pages and was bound into a catalog. Color illustrations, woodcuts, and drawings by Charles Dana Gibson followed. In 1875 Montgomery Ward was the first mail-order business to offer customers the policy of "Satisfaction guaranteed or your money back!"—and peppered the catalog with information from the manufacturer. It was dubbed the Wish Book.

Montgomery Ward was the first but ultimately not the biggest mail-order business in Chicago. In 1887, Richard Warren Sears, who had sold watches in Minneapolis, moved to the city and with the help of Alvah Curtis Roebuck, a watchmaker, began a mail-order business selling watches. By 1893, the Sears catalog, soon to be called the Big Book, was selling furniture, baby carriages, and musical instruments—and carrying some clever advertising. An item described as a sewing machine—price, one dollar—was really a needle and thread.

Over the years, both companies opened stores, and the mail-order business became secondary. In 1985, Montgomery Ward ceased publishing its catalog; Sears ended the Big Book in 1993. Yet the mail-order catalog's place in American life was undeniable. In 1946, a book-lovers' society included a Montgomery Ward catalog on its list of the one hundred American books that had most affected American life, noting "no idea ever mushroomed so far from so small a beginning, or had so profound an influence on the economics of a continent, as the concept, original to America, of direct selling by mail, for cash."

—*Judy Hevrdejs*

GRANGERS
SUPPLIED BY THE
Cheapest Cash House
IN AMERICA.

At the Earnest Solicitation of many Grangers, we have consented to open a House devoted to furnishing

FARMERS & MECHANICS
Throughout the Northwest with all kinds of

Merchandise at Wholesale Prices.

You can readily see at a glance the difference between our Prices and what you have to pay your Retailer for the same quality of goods.

MONTGOMERY, WARD & CO.,
Box 517, Chicago, Ill.

▲ *Montgomery Ward's first catalog in 1872 was printed on a single sheet of paper and listed 163 items.*

Chicago's First National League Baseball Game

The Chicago White Stockings travel to Louisville for their first contest in the new baseball league.

APRIL 25, 1876

In 1876, the nation's centennial year, Alexander Graham Bell was granted a patent for his new invention, something called a telephone. Samuel Clemens, also known as Mark Twain, authored *The Adventures of Tom Sawyer*. At the Battle of the Little Big Horn, General George A. Custer made his last stand. And on this date, the Cubs played their first game in the newly created National League of Professional Base-Ball Clubs. They won it. In Louisville. Unlike Custer, the Cubs did not struggle on the road.

Baseball—or "base-ball"—was already well on its way to becoming the national sport. During the Civil War, Union soldiers had played the game in camp; soon after the war, big cities started organizing teams of professional players. A league of baseball players had been formed in 1871, including members of the Chicago team—the White Stockings, the Cubs' original nickname. But the players' group folded when the new league—an organization of baseball clubs—was founded. In addition to the Chicago and Louisville teams, the charter members were clubs in Cincinnati, St. Louis, Boston, Hartford, New York, and Philadelphia.

William A. Hulbert, the owner of the White Stockings, had put together a solid club, led by manager and pitcher Albert G. Spalding, who would later become a wealthy sporting-goods manufacturer. Hulbert, a wealthy grain broker, was confident he had a pennant winner on his hands, and that confidence proved well grounded when the White Stockings captured the first National League title.

That was still in the future when the Chicagoans took the field in Louisville before a paying crowd of two thousand, plus just as many nonpaying customers who watched from the hills overlooking the park. The game drew a front-page headline in the next day's *Tribune*—"A HANDSOME VICTORY OVER THE LOUISVILLE NINE—SCORE 4 TO 0"—and this account of the White Stockings' first run in the second inning: "Hines hit hard at the first one and sent it to [first baseman] Carbine so briskly that he couldn't hold it, giving Hines a life. Spalding put a corker to centre-field, Hines going to third. After Spalding had been run out and Addy had retired at first, White drove a fierce one to [third baseman] Gerhardt, who gathered it well but threw it wildly to Carbine, letting in Hines with the first tally."

—*Bob Vanderberg*

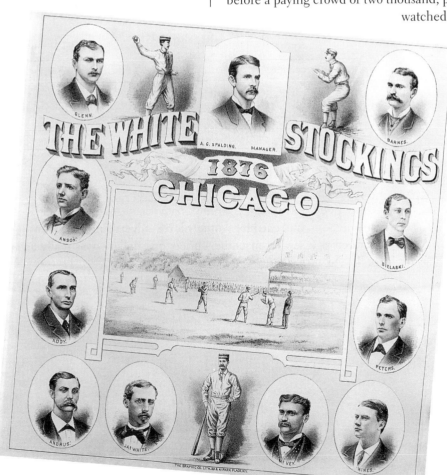

THE WHITE STOCKINGS
A. G. SPALDING, MANAGER
1876 CHICAGO

The Art Institute of Chicago

A commitment to acquiring great artwork establishes the museum as one of the world's finest.

▲ *El Greco's* The Assumption of the Virgin *was the Art Institute's first major purchase, in 1906. The institute's founders hoped that bringing such European masterworks to Chicago would have a civilizing, uplifting influence.*

MAY 24, 1879

On this date five civic leaders incorporated the Chicago Academy of Fine Arts, descendant of the Chicago Academy of Design, which had sprung up in 1866 and had mounted several exhibitions before the Chicago Fire claimed it. Thus, in 1882, when the Academy of Fine Arts changed its name to the Art Institute of Chicago, the organization already had had sixteen years of experience. The institute did not have, however, a home of its own. So trustees purchased a lot on the corner of Michigan Avenue and Van Buren Street, moving into the building at the front of the lot while constructing another building for the school and gallery behind.

Overseeing a series of expansions that took place during the institute's first decade was banker Charles Hutchinson,

▲ *Bequests from Chicago collectors such as Martin Ryerson—shown (left) visiting Claude Monet in the artist's garden in Giverny, France, in 1920—provided the Art Institute with many major works. Monet's art has been the subject of three of the ten best-attended shows in the institute's history.*

who was—for forty-three years—the museum's first president. Hutchinson was also chairman of the committee on fine arts for the 1893 World's Columbian Exposition, and he proposed a new building that would be used by both the fair and the institute. To design a structure in classical style, trustees chose the Boston architectural firm of Shepley, Ruttan, and Coolidge. The result influenced museum design

throughout North America. The bronze lions that flank the entrance to the building arrived in 1894. Wings, courts, and galleries were added in following decades to form a complex that bridges the Illinois Central railroad tracks in Grant Park.

The museum's earliest holdings were five hundred prints and a far larger collection of plaster reproductions of classical sculptures. The first important paintings—by Meindert Hobbema, Jan Steen, and Jean François Millet—entered the collection as gifts in 1894. Trustees made the first major purchase, El Greco's *The Assumption of the Virgin*, in 1906. A commitment to acquiring first-rate works, including many by Impressionist masters, was fulfilled many times over in bequests from Bertha Honore Palmer (1922) and Martin Ryerson (1933), which helped establish the museum among the finest in the world. One of the most admired canvases, Georges Seurat's *A Sunday on La Grande Jatte—1884*, came to the collection in 1926. Other popular works include Grant Wood's *American Gothic*, Edward Hopper's *Nighthawks*, the Thorne Miniature Rooms, and Marc Chagall's *The America Windows*.

—Alan G. Artner

The Palmer Castle

An imposing mansion on the North Side gives fashionable Chicago a new address.

FEBRUARY 22, 1880

Chicago's merchant prince, Potter Palmer, did the unthinkable on this date: He crossed north of the Chicago River and bought part of a filled-in frog pond on what later became a section of Lake Shore Drive, forever changing the fashionable address for chic Chicago. This would be the site of his castle, he proclaimed, as opposed to his house; the Palmer House was the name of his $3.5 million luxury hotel, rebuilt and fireproofed after the Chicago Fire had made ashes of his first such inn just a year after it opened. Anybody could stay at his House; his castle would be for himself and his wife, Bertha, the queen of Chicago society.

Palmer had confounded expectations almost from the day he arrived in town from upstate New York. He had built the nation's most talked-about dry-goods store, with its revolutionary practices of extending credit and offering money-back guarantees. He singlehandedly had shifted the commercial axis of the boom town from east-west Lake Street to north-south State Street. When the Father of State Street, as he came to be known, spotted the frog pond on the North Side, there was reason for the doyens of the Prairie Avenue district, on the near South Side—until then the best address in town—to wonder whether they would soon be migrating north. By the turn of the century, many of them had.

Palmer hired two young architects—Henry Ives Cobb, who would go on to give the University of Chicago its quadrangles, and Charles Sumner Frost, who would give Chicago Navy Pier—to design a three-story manse. Modeled after the castles of the Milwaukee beer barons, the turreted brownstone mansion rapidly overshot its $90,000 budget. When the bill reached $1 million, Palmer told his bookkeeper to stop entering charges against his new home. He had no wish to know the final reckoning. "The age of Pericles seems to be dawning," the *Chicago Inter-Ocean* said of the imposing building. "It belongs in a fishbowl," sniffed others.

All Chicago speculated on the mansion's interior until the day in 1885 when Bertha Palmer gave the first of the many fabled receptions that would be held at

▲ *Chicago's original power couple: Potter and Bertha Palmer. He was a merchant, hotelier, and real-estate magnate. She was the queen of Chicago society and an art collector whose bequest to the Art Institute would form the core of the museum's collection of Impressionist paintings.*

▶

The most famous room in the Palmer castle was the seventy-five-foot-long picture gallery, where Bertha Palmer's latest acquisitions, purchased with the advice of her friend the painter Mary Cassatt, were on display.

the castle. From the gold-leaf outer entrance, visitors stepped into the octagonal great hall, three stories high and domed in stained glass. Cupids in eternal pursuit drifted across the drawing-room ceiling. The dining room, which seated fifty, was paneled in San Domingo mahogany. Nearly every one of the forty-two rooms boasted a huge fireplace of marble and oak. The castle was the first home in the city to have passenger elevators, and no door had a doorknob that could be turned from the outside, which let it be known that a small army of footmen and other servants was there to cater to guests. Chicago's Gold Coast was born.

—*Barbara Mahany*

▲ *The Palmer Castle, at 1350 North Lake Shore Drive, had an eighty-foot tower and the first elevator in a Chicago home. The castle was demolished in 1950.*

The Home Insurance Building

The first skyscraper with a skeleton of steel soars — to nine stories.

MARCH 1, 1884

A permit was issued on this date to build a nine-story structure at the northeast corner of LaSalle and Adams Streets in downtown Chicago. This office building, completed the following year for the Home Insurance Company, was the first large commercial structure to be supported by a skeleton of metal rather than walls of masonry. It was the decisive step forward in the development of the skyscraper, followed in short order by other tall buildings that came to represent a "Chicago School of Architecture." These early office towers pierced the ceiling of the Victorian era, ensuring that cathedrals of commerce would forever dominate the American skyline.

▲ *William Le Baron Jenney, architect of the Home Insurance Building*

It was no coincidence that this innovation took place in Chicago. The booming economy of the 1880s created the need for more floor space, but the business district's compressed area, a mere half square mile, meant that there was nowhere to go but up. Engineering advances derived from bridge construction, the development of hydraulic elevators, and new foundation and fireproofing techniques made skyscrapers possible.

In traditional construction, exterior walls, along with interior columns and beams, bore a structure's weight. Additional floors required heavier, thicker walls, resulting in smaller windows and limited natural light—a significant disadvantage before the widespread use of electricity. To admit the maximum amount of natural light to the Home Insurance Building, architect William Le Baron Jenney used an internal cage of iron and steel to free the exterior from its load-bearing role. The building's outermost iron columns were clad in masonry, but solely to fireproof them. The exterior now could be nothing more than a "curtain wall," made almost exclusively of glass.

◄ *The Home Insurance Building, built in 1884 on the northeast corner of LaSalle and Adams Streets, was the modest beginning of the steel-framed skyscraper.*

◀ *The demolition of the Home Insurance Building in 1931 revealed its revolutionary steel frame. In the background is the Board of Trade building.*

Jenney's facade treatment was ungainly, consisting of stacked horizontal layers. But other Chicago architects, especially John Wellborn Root and Louis Sullivan, took up the challenge not only of building taller steel-framed skyscrapers but also of designing them so that they seemed to soar even higher. Classic Chicago School skyscrapers, such as Holabird and Roche's Marquette Building, at 140 South Dearborn Street, emphasized unadorned vertical lines to carry the eye upward and forthrightly expressed their underlying steel structure with muscular, gridded facades.

For the better part of three decades, the architects of this school produced a remarkable series of tall buildings, but the city has wantonly destroyed many of the gems of its early skyscraper era, such as Root's Masonic Temple. Surviving exemplars include the Marquette and the Reliance Building, at 32 North State Street. The Home Insurance Building itself was demolished in 1931. A plaque inside the structure that replaced it, at 135 South LaSalle Street, marks the spot where the skyscraper took flight.

—Blair Kamin

▶

The twenty-two-story Masonic Temple, at State and Randolph Streets, was an architectural gem from Chicago's early skyscraper era. Completed in 1892, it was demolished in 1939.

The Haymarket Incident

Who threw the bomb that exploded into tragedy? Not the eight men who were convicted.

MAY 4, 1886

Considering the incendiary events of the previous day, the open-air protest meeting on this date at the Haymarket, where Randolph Street widened out for two blocks on Chicago's Near West Side, started out as a disappointingly mild affair. But the evening was destined to become a violent landmark in American labor history.

Throughout the nation, workers were crusading for an eight-hour day. In Chicago, where tensions between labor and management were already high, police had killed two laborers and injured many more on May 3 in a clash at the McCormick Reaper Works. The incident prompted August Spies, who edited an anarchist newspaper, to write that if the strikers had had "good weapons and a single dynamite bomb, not one of the murderers would have escaped his well-deserved fate."

Although fire-breathing in print, Spies watched his words when he spoke at the rally, which began at 7:30 P.M. Because the turnout was much smaller than organizers had hoped for, the speaker's platform was moved to a wagon on Des Plaines Street, a half-block from the Haymarket. As the sky darkened, the crowd dwindled to no more than three hundred people. Mayor Carter Harrison, who had listened to some of the speeches, told Police Inspector John Bonfield that the gathering was "tame."

▶

In this artist's depiction of the Haymarket tragedy, shooting breaks out after a bomb explodes among a group of policemen, many of whom ended up shooting each other in the confusion that followed. The engraving first appeared in Harper's Weekly.

But once the mayor left, Bonfield quick-stepped 178 policemen to the meeting site and ordered the crowd to disperse. Samuel Fielden, who was speaking at the time, agreed to go. Suddenly, as he was stepping down from the wagon, a bomb was tossed over the heads of the crowd and exploded in the midst of the officers. One policeman was killed almost instantly. The others drew their revolvers and opened fire.

In all, eight policemen died and fifty-nine were wounded, but the bomb was only partly to blame. "A very high number of the police were wounded by each other's revolvers," a high-ranking police official told the *Tribune*. At least four civilians, and perhaps as many as ten, were killed, and thirty or more were wounded.

The violence near the Haymarket sparked the nation's first Red Scare. "No effort should be spared until every man engaged in the conspiracy has been clutched," the *Tribune* editorialized. But no bomb thrower was ever found, no conspiracy ever proved. Yet it was unthinkable not to bring someone to trial. Eight anarchists and sympathizers, including Spies, were convicted in proceedings later acknowledged to have been a mockery of the American legal system. Spies and three others were hanged; another committed suicide. Later, in a decision that ruined his political career, Illinois Governor John Peter Altgeld pardoned the remaining three defendants.

—*Patrick T. Reardon*

▲ *Of the eight men convicted of plotting the bomb-throwing, four were hanged in the gallows room of Cook County Jail on November 11, 1887: August Spies (upper left), Albert Parsons (upper right), Adolph Fischer (bottom row, second from left), and George Engel (bottom row, second from right). A fifth man, Louis Lingg (left side, second from top), committed suicide the day before. The rest were pardoned in 1893.*

▲ *The protest meeting at the Haymarket, advertised in this bilingual broadside, was called to denounce the killing of two workers at the McCormick Reaper Works.*

George Streeter's District

For more than thirty years, the colorful captain defended his "deestrick" with dubious documents and a shotgun.

JULY 11, 1886

With the wind picking up off Lake Michigan, the passengers who had traveled to Milwaukee on Captain George Wellington Streeter's homemade steamboat surveyed the darkening skies and Streeter's rickety vessel. They decided to take the train back to Chicago. Their prudence did not stop the irascible "Cap'n" Streeter from defying the advancing storm. Along with his wife, Maria, he pointed the *Reutan* south and headed into Chicago lore as the unlikely founder of one of the city's most exclusive neighborhoods.

At around 3 A.M. on this date, the day after Streeter set out from Milwaukee, his storm-tattered craft rammed into a sandbar that extended about four hundred feet from shore around what is now Superior Street. At daybreak, he noticed he had run aground near the properties of some of Chicago's richest and most influential residents. One of them, N. Kellogg Fairbank, gave Streeter permission to remain until he fixed the boat.

But Streeter, a Civil War veteran who had pieced together a colorful career as a showman, a circus promoter, a Mississippi River steamboat operator, and an excursion guide, stuck around. Over time—with the cooperation of nature's forces, which filled in sand between his boat and the shore, and of contractors who were happy to dump debris around the boat— Streeter found himself in the middle of more than one hundred acres of land that had not existed before he arrived, an area roughly north and east of the streets that came to be called Grand and Michigan Avenues. Streeter could spot a good opportunity, especially one that he had rammed into. The captain declared this territory the "District of Lake Michigan" (the "Deestrick," as he called it) and informed Fairbank and his other dumbfounded neighbors that the land not only did not belong to them but that it was part of neither Chicago nor Illinois. From an office at the Tremont Hotel, he sold parcels to gullible buyers.

For more than thirty years, Streeter defended his shantytown with vague legal arguments—including some dubious documents allegedly signed by President Grover Cleveland—and a loaded shotgun,

◀ *Captain Streeter had plenty of problems with the law that resulted in frequent, though short, stays in jail.*

which he readily pointed at any police officer who tried to evict him. But in 1918, the courts ruled against him. In addition, economic forces overtook him. Development boomed just to the west of his shack on land that even then was called Streeterville. When the Michigan Avenue bridge opened in 1920, commercial and residential construction flooded the area north of the Chicago River, despite legal fights by Streeter's heirs. Their last volley was repelled in 1940, when a federal court dismissed the clan's final claim. But who could blame them for making such a fuss? Consider what came to occupy Streeter's landfill: expensive shops, exclusive restaurants, the Chicago campus of Northwestern University, and some of the city's highest-priced residences.

—*Byron P. White*

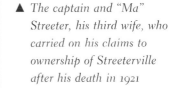

▲ *Captain Streeter's boat, the* Reutan, *after he had repaired it and renamed it for his second wife, Maria. Spelling was never one of his strengths.*

◀ *The Streeter shack looked out on open land in 1906. In this view, to the northwest, the Water Tower can be seen in the distance.*

Adler and Sullivan's Auditorium

A choice commission launches Louis Sullivan on the path to architectural greatness.

▼ *The Auditorium, shown here in about 1890, combined a concert hall, a hotel, and an office building under one roof. Dankmar Adler and Louis Sullivan's offices were on the top two floors of the tower. Roosevelt University took over the building in 1946.*

DECEMBER 22, 1886

The commission to design the Auditorium building went on this date to two men, engineer Dankmar Adler and his partner, architect Louis H. Sullivan, who had shown extraordinary originality in his use of ornamentation and artificial lighting. It was the plum assignment of the year. Ferdinand Peck, an enthusiastic promoter of the arts, had organized a group of wealthy Chicagoans, including Marshall Field and George Pullman, to back construction of a grand concert hall that would cost an astounding $3.2 million. Adler's mastery of acoustics made him a clear choice, but the board had to overcome some doubts about his thirty-year-old partner, who had worked in the office of William Le Baron Jenney but was not well known.

When the building opened three years later, President Benjamin Harrison was on hand for a concert by operatic idol Adelina Patti, who sang "Home Sweet Home." Ever so humble the Auditorium was not. The building, which combined offices, a forty-two-hundred-seat concert hall, and a four-hundred-room hotel under one roof, was a massive, commanding presence along Congress Street between Wabash and Michigan Avenues. Adler solved daunting problems in designing the structure's foundation, and the interior gave free play to Sullivan's intricate ornament and dramatic lighting. In the spirit of Henry Hobson Richardson's since-demolished Marshall Field Warehouse, its exterior had a rugged base and rounded, Romanesque arches.

The Auditorium established Sullivan's reputation, and other important commissions in Chicago and elsewhere came his way. His skyscrapers, including the demolished Chicago Stock Exchange and Garrick Theater, gave physical shape to his belief that the tall office building "must be every inch a proud and soaring thing." Above all other architects of the "Chicago School," he turned the skyscraper into a new work of art, while also creating a highly individual, densely detailed style of ornamentation. This is preserved in one stunning instance in the Chicago Stock Exchange trading room, later reconstructed at the Art Institute.

▲ The heart of the Auditorium is the forty-two-hundred-seat concert hall, where Adler and Sullivan's talents combined to produce a space with excellent acoustics and dramatic ornamentation, notable for its pioneering use of electrical lighting.

The crowning achievement of Sullivan's career was the department store that he designed in 1899 for Schlesinger and Mayer, which was later bought by Carson Pirie Scott and Company. The ornate, cast-iron decoration around the windows on the first two floors serves as a richly flowing picture frame meant to accentuate the merchandise on display. Above, the facade is a spare but precisely proportioned expression of the building's steel frame, illustrating Sullivan's now-famous dictum that "form follows function."

The more business-minded Adler had left the partnership in 1895. Work dried up for Sullivan, a situation that can be blamed on changing tastes as well as on his often abrupt manner with clients. A few Chicago storefronts and bank buildings in small Midwestern towns constituted the bulk of his last designs. Sullivan died penniless, at age sixty-seven, in 1924.

—Stevenson Swanson

◀ The work of Louis Sullivan, who proclaimed that "form follows function," is often seen as a forerunner of the clean-lined modern architecture of the twentieth century.

▲ Sullivan's distinctive style of ornamentation covers the first two stories of the Carson Pirie Scott and Company store, his last great project. The elaborate design over the store's entry incorporates the architect's initials, LHS, to the left and right of the arch.

Frank Lloyd Wright's First House

With a loan from "Lieber Meister," the young architect begins his search for a new style.

AUGUST 19, 1889

His employer had just given him a five-year contract, and yet, already supremely self-confident at the age of twenty-two, Frank Lloyd Wright wanted more. "Mr. Sullivan," he said, "if you want me to work for you as long as five years, couldn't you lend me enough money to build a little house?" Louis Sullivan, his practice flourishing after having designed the Auditorium, agreed to lend his young assistant $5,000. Wright received the money on this date and soon became an Oak Park property owner.

▲ *Frank Lloyd Wright in about 1908, at the height of his Prairie School period.*

Although settled as early as the 1850s, the western suburb of Oak Park had only begun to flourish in the late 1870s. It would develop a reputation for having more churches per capita than any other town in the country. By the time Wright left Oak Park twenty years later, it would also have more houses designed by the pioneering architect of the Prairie School than any other town. Twenty-seven Wright designs have survived into the 1990s, including one at Chicago and Forest Avenues, the first house he designed for his young wife, Catherine, and himself. Its high, steep roof and shingle cladding are hardly typical of the mature Wright designs of later years, but its interior already exhibits the characteristic free-flowing space and sense of repose that were distinctive features of his designs.

Born in Richland Center, Wisconsin, Wright moved to Chicago at age twenty after studying engineering for a year at the University of Wisconsin in Madison. After joining Dankmar Adler and Sullivan's firm in 1888, he soon became Sullivan's chief assistant. Wright always acknowledged his artistic debt to the man he called "Lieber Meister," or "dear master," but in 1893, Sullivan fired Wright for moonlighting. Wright spent the 1890s evolving the ideas that would reach fruition in the first decade of the twentieth century, especially in such houses as the Avery Coonley residence in west suburban Riverside and the Robie House in Chicago's Hyde Park neighborhood. In his search for a style that was modern and appropriate for the Midwest, he emphasized plain surfaces and horizontal lines, often using dramatically cantilevered roofs that also provided a comforting sense of shelter.

◄ *Wright's studio, added to his Oak Park house in 1898, features this two-story, octagonal drafting room, where he designed more than 150 buildings. After he left Oak Park in 1909, he had the studio remodeled as living quarters for his family, and the home was rented out.*

In November 1909 the *Tribune* carried a story with the headline: LEAVE FAMILIES, ELOPE TO EUROPE. Suburban life had become oppressive to Wright, and his work seemed to have reached a turning point. Wright and Mamah Cheney, the wife of a client, spent the next two years in Europe; when they returned to America, they lived at Taliesin, Wright's home in Spring Green, Wisconsin. In 1914 Mamah Cheney, her two children, and four others were murdered at Taliesin by a crazed servant who also set fire to the house. The tragedy nearly crushed Wright.

In later years, he designed such masterpieces as Fallingwater, a house outside Pittsburgh that perches over a brook, and New York's Guggenheim Museum. America's most famous, most original architect died in 1959 at age ninety-one.

—*Stevenson Swanson*

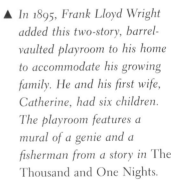

▲ *In 1895, Frank Lloyd Wright added this two-story, barrel-vaulted playroom to his home to accommodate his growing family. He and his first wife, Catherine, had six children. The playroom features a mural of a genie and a fisherman from a story in* The Thousand and One Nights.

◄ *The Robie House, with its dramatically cantilevered roof and strong horizontal lines, is one of the architect's classic Prairie Style residences. The house, designed in 1906, is in Chicago's Hyde Park neighborhood.*

Hull House Opens

Two idealistic young women set out to improve the lot of Chicago's immigrant poor.

SEPTEMBER 18, 1889

Outside the dilapidated mansion at the corner of Halsted and Polk Streets, the neighborhood was choked with immigrants working in sweatshops and sleeping in tenements; smallpox ran rampant, and children amused themselves by fishing for rats beneath the wooden sidewalks. Inside, twenty-nine-year-old Jane Addams and her college friend Ellen Gates Starr set up their household on this date with some "family mahogany" and the vague idea of helping the people around them. The home was called Hull House, after its first resident, Charles Hull, a Chicago real-estate baron who had it built in 1856 for his family.

Under its new tenants, Hull House became the heart of one of the country's most influential social-reform movements. For years Addams, single and college educated, had sought a greater purpose for her life. She found it in an East London slum. There, in the world's first settlement house, Toynbee Hall, educated Englishmen lived and worked among the poor.

The visit inspired Addams to set up a similar settlement in Chicago. A few days after the two women moved in, Hull House started a neighborhood reading group to discuss a George Eliot novel. The following month, the city's first kindergarten opened in the mansion's drawing room.

Over the next two decades, Hull House received worldwide attention for its mix of cultural and educational programs and social-reform efforts. The group of women who lived at the house and its other volunteers built Chicago's first playground and helped create the country's first juvenile court. They fought for landmark child-labor and factory laws. They ran libraries and art exhibits, taught music and painting, opened a theater and bathhouses, organized unions and social clubs. "If it is natural to feed the hungry and care for the sick, it is certainly natural to give pleasure

The Hull House complex once covered a city block on Chicago's West Side; only the original Hull mansion, now a museum, remains.

to the young, comfort to the aged, and to minister to the deep-seated craving for social intercourse that all men feel," Addams wrote in her autobiography, *Twenty Years at Hull-House*.

The settlement did not win universal praise. Some accused the leaders of radical leanings; others dismissed Hull House as paternalistic. Still, with the help of private donors, it prospered. By 1907, Hull House consisted of thirteen buildings covering a city block.

In 1931, Jane Addams became the first American woman to win the Nobel Peace Prize. She died four years later and is buried in her hometown of Cedarville, Illinois. Starr, who had entered a convent in 1930 in failing health, died in 1940. The mansion is now a museum, preserved after most of the original Hull House complex was razed in 1963 to make way for the campus of the University of Illinois at Chicago. Addams and Starr's work continues: the Jane Addams Hull House Association helps an estimated 225,000 people each year.

—*Louise Kiernan*

▲ *Boys at work in the Hull House wood shop in 1911. Teaching immigrant youths useful trades was an important part of the settlement's mission.*

◄ *Jane Addams (opposite, top) and Ellen Gates Starr (left) were college friends who sought a larger purpose to which they could dedicate their lives.*

The 1890 Census

"Everyone had just come from somewhere"— and together they made Chicago the "Second City."

JANUARY 1, 1890

On this date Chicago began its ninety-four-year reign as the nation's "Second City." The 1,099,850 souls the United States Census counted in Chicago represented a 119 percent increase over the city's population just ten years earlier. The landmark tally made Chicago second only to New York in population, a status the city held until it was eclipsed by Los Angeles in 1984.

Not only did the size of Chicago change in that decade; so did its face and its flavor. "Everyone had just come from somewhere—usually from across the ocean—and all the world was going somewhere else," wrote Edith Abbott in *The Tenements of Chicago*. "Here were the most foreign newspapers, the foreign banks, the steamship companies—Italian in one section, Greek in another . . . that made these areas not unlike a series of foreign cities brought together."

A chunk of the city's growth came from annexation. Six months before the census, voters in a 120-square-mile area outside the city announced they wanted in. But the most significant increase came from immigrants, who made up about 40 percent of the city's population in 1890. Immigration from northern and western Europe had been an important factor in the city's population growth for decades, but by the 1890s, many newcomers originated from the countries of central, eastern, and southern Europe.

◀ *An Italian girl and other Italian immigrants in Chicago in the 1870s. In 1890, when Chicago became the second-largest city in the United States, foreign-born residents made up 40 percent of the city's population.*

▶

Although drawn to America for its freedom and economic opportunity, immigrants often brought some of the Old World with them, as this Lithuanian bachelor's residence vividly demonstrates. In the 1890s, Chicago was home to the largest number of Lithuanians, Poles, Greeks, Bohemians, Croats, and Slovaks in America.

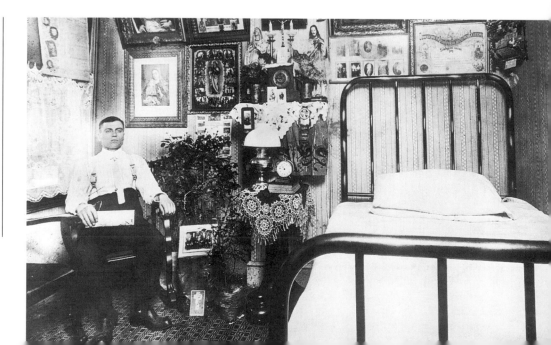

Drawn to Chicago because of its reputation abroad as a place with well-paying industrial jobs or because relatives already lived in the city, immigrants often arrived with notes in English pinned to their clothes asking that they be directed to their brother's or their uncle's address. Others headed from the train station with their small bundles to one of the ethnic churches that became beachheads for all manner of newcomer. Among Catholic churches these included Our Lady of Pompeii, on Taylor Street, which served Italians; Old Saint Patrick's, west of the Loop, for the Irish; and Saint Stanislaus Kostka, on the Near Northwest Side, for the large Polish community.

▲ *In the late nineteenth century, Jewish immigrants started a produce market on Maxwell Street where it crosses Halsted Street. Over the years, Maxwell Street, shown here in about 1905, grew into a vast Sunday-morning flea market. The market moved east to Canal Street in 1994, when the Maxwell Street area was bought by the University of Illinois at Chicago.*

▲ *This Greek grocer, photographed in Chicago in the late nineteenth century, was part of the largest Greek community in the nation. One hundred years later, it was still the largest.*

By 1897 the Greek community, the largest in the nation (and still the largest a hundred years later), had its first permanent Greek Orthodox parish, Holy Trinity Church, on what became known as the Greek Delta, at Halsted and Harrison Streets. The Greeks had either the good fortune or the good sense to center their community in the front yard of Jane Addams's Hull House, the first settlement house in the nation. Other settlement houses soon sprang up to help immigrants adjust to their new lives, including Erie Neighborhood House, which began as a Presbyterian Church in 1870 and served impoverished Germans and Scandinavians in Chicago's West Town neighborhood. Erie was among the settlement houses that survived, and its new clientele, mostly Hispanic immigrants, tells the continuing story of Chicago's newcomers.

◄ *Immigration created a thriving ethnic press—and, in the electronic age, ethnic radio and television stations. A vendor on Milwaukee Avenue on the Northwest Side offers two newspapers for the neighborhood's large Polish population. In the 1990s, Poland remained one of the most important sources of new immigrants to Chicago.*

At the turn of the century, nine out of ten immigrants were from Europe. In the 1990s immigrants to Chicago came from three distinct regions—Latin America, Europe, and Asia. The top countries of origin were Mexico, Poland, and the Philippines. In 1990 the government counted 878,000 immigrants in metropolitan Chicago, only slightly fewer than the 900,000 who lived in the area in 1910. And Edith Abbott, who found ethnic media flourishing at the turn of the century, could just as easily have been writing about 1996, when there were more than one hundred ethnic newspapers and radio and television stations, from African to Ukrainian, whose Chicago-area audience numbered one million.

—*Melita Marie Garza*

▲ *Erie Neighborhood House, established in 1870, serves mostly Hispanic immigrants, helping them adjust to life in Chicago by offering, among other things, lessons in English.*

▲ *Immigration has enriched Chicago's cuisine with a vast range of new foods and flavors. This Vietnamese woman offers grilled kabobs and corn at a neighborhood festival.*

◀ *For many immigrants, religion remains an important link to their native lands. Here a Hindu swami (second from left) performs a ritual for a group of Indians. The countries of Asia were important sources of immigration to Chicago in the 1990s.*

First Concert of the Chicago Orchestra

Theodore Thomas creates an orchestra that becomes one of the world's finest.

▲ From the first, the Chicago Orchestra's concerts drew heavily on the Germanic repertoire.

OCTOBER 16, 1891

The triumphant final chords of Tchaikovsky's First Piano Concerto brought a storm of applause from the audience, most of them young female music students assembled for the first public rehearsal and concert by Chicago's new orchestra. But the sense of triumph that pervaded the Chicago Auditorium on this autumn afternoon was as much a triumph of Chicago-style perseverance as it was of music. At last, the nation's second-largest city would not have to rely on touring orchestras for concerts of symphonic music.

The audience for such music in Chicago, a heavily industrial city, was disproportionately small. But it was growing, and among its number was Charles Norman Fay, a wealthy utilities executive who felt that a resident orchestra could help banish the city's hog-butcher reputation. As Fay saw it, only one man was worthy of leading such an ensemble, and that was Theodore Thomas, already firmly established as an orchestra builder. When the two men met, determination met desire. For the German-born Thomas, the offer to lead a resident orchestra was the fulfillment of a lifelong dream. "I would go to hell if they gave me a permanent orchestra," he told Fay.

Thomas's mandate was to maintain the highest standards of excellence. His orchestra of eighty-six players—twenty-six of them Chicagoans, the remaining sixty from New York—included some of the finest instrumentalists of the time. They performed two concerts weekly during an eight-month season. Reviewing the first "official" concert by the Chicago Orchestra under Thomas's baton on October 17, the *Tribune* extolled "an orchestra which will enable Chicago to take rank in the

music world commensurate with her standing as one of the great cities of the country." Thomas served thirteen seasons in Chicago. He died on January 4, 1905—twenty-one days after leading the dedicatory concert for Orchestra Hall on Michigan Avenue, designed by architect Daniel Burnham to supplant the cavernous Auditorium as the ensemble's home. From 1906 the ensemble was called the Theodore Thomas Orchestra; in 1912 it was renamed the Chicago Symphony Orchestra.

Thomas was succeeded by his assistant conductor, Frederick Stock, whose long tenure (to 1942) solidified the orchestra's reputation as one of the country's finest. Its artistic fortunes then rose and fell until the arrival in 1953 of the tyrannical Fritz Reiner, who transformed the orchestra into an extraordinary precision instrument. Georg Solti's tenure as music director, which began in 1969, secured the orchestra's international reputation with extensive recordings and tours, including its first European trip, in 1971. By the time Daniel Barenboim became the orchestra's conductor in 1991—a century after Thomas raised his baton at the first concert—the Chicago Symphony Orchestra was unarguably a leading source of civic pride for a city that had gone without an orchestra for so many years.

—*John von Rhein*

▶

Four of the symphony's conductors: Theodore Thomas (top), who created the Chicago Orchestra; Fritz Reiner, who transformed the Chicago Symphony Orchestra into an extraordinary precision instrument; Georg Solti, who secured its international reputation; and Daniel Barenboim, who was appointed music director in 1991

◀ *The Chicago Orchestra—as it was known at first—with founder-conductor Theodore Thomas in about 1899 at the Auditorium Theatre, the orchestra's first home*

The First Elevated Opens

Riding high above the crowded streets, a Chicago fixture makes its noisy debut.

▶

The Loop elevated line was completed in 1897, when this photograph was taken. The view is looking east on Van Buren Street from Wabash Avenue. Passenger cars were first pulled by scaled-down steam locomotives, but Chicago pioneered an electrical operating system, with power provided via the famous third rail.

JUNE 6, 1892

This was a banner day in the local history of rapid transit and voyeurism. In the morning, service began on the first section of Chicago's elevated line, a three-and-a-half-mile stretch of track running from Congress to 39th Street above the alley between State Street and Wabash Avenue, a route that put riders at eye level with second-story windows of adjoining buildings.

"Those who made observation runs early in the day were well repaid," noted a *Tribune* reporter, "for the people living on either side of the track had seemingly forgotten the warning about the start, and the passengers saw bits of domestic life usually hidden from the gaze of passing crowds." Besides that fringe benefit, customers of the Chicago & South Side Rapid Transit Railroad Company got commuting times that seemed miraculous: fourteen minutes for a trip that took twice as long by the nearby State Street cable car.

In 1892, Chicago's streets were a mass of carts and wagons and streetcars. Paving was scarce, making travel for even a few blocks an exasperating experience. The promoters of what soon became known as the "el" found a ready market for their proposal to lift commuters above the madding crowd via a railroad supported on a forest of steel stilts. The original route was quickly extended southward to reach the site of the 1893 World's Columbian Exposition. A second "el" was constructed along Lake Street, designed not only to bring commuters in from the West Side but also to enrich its promoter, Charles Yerkes.

Chicago being Chicago, it was not just engineers who brought a creative approach to the building of the elevated. Yerkes once summed up his philosophy of mass transit thusly: "Buy up old junk, fix

◀ *Inside an "el" train, about 1914, leaving Jackson Park, on the city's South Side*

it up a little, and unload it upon other fellows." Indeed, from a ledger-book stand-point, Chicago's rapid transit was perennially suspended between bankruptcy and fraud until the city took it over in 1947. Fares could rarely pay for the expensive technology upon which the "el" was built. Samuel Insull, Yerkes's successor as Chicago's traction magnate, fled the country in 1932, just ahead of indictments for embezzlement.

Still, when the South Side and West Side elevated lines, plus routes running North and Northwest, were joined into trackage circling the business district in 1897, the city got a fitting symbol of Chicago's nitty-gritty style of life. The "Loop" would make an appearance in any number of local scripted and painted works of art. "The dark girders of the El," wrote novelist Nelson Algren, were "the city's rusty heart."

—Ron Grossman

▲ *The elevated line under construction in 1896 on Lake Street in downtown Chicago. This view is looking west from Wabash Avenue. The "Loop" came to refer not only to the downtown elevated structure but also to the central business district.*

The University of Chicago

With its distinguished faculty, the school becomes an instant hotbed of ideas.

OCTOBER 1, 1892

With less celebration than trepidation, the University of Chicago opened its classroom doors on this date. The evening before, its founding president, William Rainey Harper, worried aloud, "I wonder if there will be a single student here tomorrow." In fact, 594 young men and women signed up to hear the lectures of professors who were already distinguished before they set foot on the still-unfinished South Side campus. Eight members of the faculty were former college presidents. Harper was the foremost biblical scholar of the day. Institutions of higher learning generally achieve prominence after a long, slow maturation. The University of Chicago was designed to be an instant hotbed of ideas.

The university had a predecessor and namesake, located at 35th Street and Cottage Grove Avenue, which opened in 1857 and went bankrupt in 1886. Trying to forestall the sheriff, the trustees of the first University of Chicago solicited John D. Rockefeller, citing their mutual membership in the Baptist church. However, the founder of Standard Oil was not interested in bailing out what was, in fact, a failed small college. He subsequently pledged $600,000 when Harper proposed an intellectual partnership—the professor to contribute the brains, the millionaire to supply the cash—with the goal of creating a university to rival Princeton and Yale.

In all, Rockefeller contributed $35 million to the university. When he visited his creation, students serenaded him: "John D. Rockefeller, wonderful man is he/Gives all his spare change to the U. of C." Moved, Rockefeller replied: "The good Lord gave me the money, and how could I withhold it from Chicago?" Department-store magnate Marshall Field contributed land for a campus along Midway Plaisance that became a breeding ground of academic firsts. Professor Albion Small established the world's first sociology department in 1892. In 1907, Professor A. A. Michelson became the first American scientist to win a Nobel Prize—for his work in measuring the speed of light.

At the age of thirty-one, Robert Maynard Hutchins was appointed president in 1929. The boy wonder, per-

▶

John D. Rockefeller (left) and William Rainey Harper in 1901, walking through the campus of the university they created. The millionaire supplied the dollars; the professor contributed the brains.

▲ *The University of Chicago, photographed in 1928, was designed by architect Henry Ives Cobb as a self-contained Gothic university village where the spirit of scholarship ruled. Stagg Field, in the background, was later demolished; the university's main library now occupies the site.*

haps the only college president to double as a celebrity, established an innovative Great Books program as the school's undergraduate curriculum. Hutchins also created the genre of radio-talk show, hosting a popular, but decidedly high-brow, weekly broadcast on the NBC network.

The breakthroughs were not just intellectual in the early days. Coach Amos Alonzo Stagg, whose players were the original Monsters of the Midway, shaped the modern game of football. Still, University of Chicago folk have generally been known more for brains than brawn. Sixty-seven Nobel Prize winners have been either students or faculty members at Chicago, more than any other university can claim. The prize in economics has been a near monopoly for the university, which has had seventeen winners since that Nobel award was inaugurated in 1969.

—*Ron Grossman*

►

Professor A. A. Michelson, the first American scientist to win a Nobel Prize, put his knowledge of physics to practical use during his daily billiards game at the university's Quadrangle Club.

The World's Columbian Exposition

Millions come to gawk and marvel at the "White City" on the South Side.

MAY 1, 1893

The World's Columbian Exposition, which opened on this date, was the most famous world's fair ever held on American soil. The nation's—and the world's—celebration of the four hundredth anniversary of the discovery of the Americas by Columbus, the fair had been the subject of a fierce competition among Chicago, New York, Washington, and St. Louis. Chicago not only won the fight but gained a nickname as well.

In an attempt to turn Congress against the city on the prairie, *New York Sun* editor Charles A. Dana wrote: "Don't pay attention to the nonsensical claims of that windy city. Its people could not build a world's fair even if they won it." But build it Chicago did, on a six-hundred-acre site in Jackson Park on the South Side. And the world came to gawk and marvel. Over its 179-day run, attendance at the fair totaled 27,529,400, or more than one hundred fifty thousand people a day. Most visitors went more than once, but even after multiple visits were accounted for, it was estimated that about twelve million people took part—this in a nation with a total population of about sixty-three million.

Nearly 129,000 people, including President Grover Cleveland, strolled the grounds on the rainy opening day. But it was fitting that the biggest crowd—716,881 people—jammed the exhibits on Chicago Day, October 9, which commemorated the twenty-second anniversary of the Great Chicago Fire. For Chicago, the point of the fair was to prove that the city had risen prosperous and strong from the ashes and was ready to take its place in the front rank of the world's great cities.

▼ *For 179 days, the World's Columbian Exposition created the illusion of a beautiful, orderly White City. The gleam of the fair buildings was due to a plasterlike coating called* staff. *This view is from the roof of the Manufactures and Liberal Arts building.*

◀ Nearly 129,000 people—
"a surging sea of humanity,"
as the title on this stereograph
print describes it—filled the
grounds on the exposition's
opening day.

▼ The architecture of the fair
harkened back to classical
and European models rather
than the modern style that
Chicago architects such as
Louis Sullivan were creating
for the city's skyscrapers.
Architect Daniel Burnham
supervised the design and
construction.

The exposition was really two fairs in one: the official White City, with its grand neoclassical buildings filled with exhibits; and the unofficial Midway, outside the gates, where visitors could ride the world's first Ferris wheel, a gigantic affair with a 264-foot diameter, or watch exotic dancers, such as Fahreda Mahzar, later to be known as Little Egypt. "Your Fair, in spite of its astounding incongruities and its broad border of vulgarities, is a great promise, a great pledge even," Charles Eliot Norton, the nation's foremost expert on the poet Dante, told the *Tribune*. "It at least forbids despair. I have never seen Americans from whom one could draw happier auguries for the future of America than some of the men I saw in Chicago."

▼ Never was the term "White City" more appropriate than at night, when the grounds
glowed with more than one hundred thousand incandescent and six thousand carbon-arc
lights. This view of the Court of Honor looks toward the domed Administration Building.

▶

Civil-rights activist Ida B. Wells objected to the fair's treatment of blacks, particularly its Colored People's Day.

Not everyone was happy. Architect Louis Sullivan, who designed the fair's Transportation Building, complained that the fair's reliance on classical models would set American architecture back by half a century. And blacks, welcomed as paying customers, found that they were vastly underrepresented in the exhibits. One prominent opponent was Ida B. Wells, who, after waging an antilynching campaign in the South, moved to Chicago in 1893. For Wells, the final straw came when, as a sop to blacks (but also as an attendance booster), fair officials scheduled a Colored People's Day, promising two thousand free watermelons.

▶

Many of the exhibits at the fair showed off the potential for industry and technology to improve life. This was especially true of the Electricity Building, shown here, which featured inventor Thomas Edison's tower of light (center of photo), demonstrating how the new technology could be used for interior lighting.

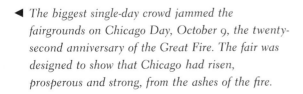

The main attraction on the Midway, outside the fairgrounds, was the world's first Ferris wheel, with a 264-foot diameter. Two twenty-minute revolutions cost 50 cents, as much as admission to the main fairgrounds.

The fair came to a close amid mourning rather than the scheduled speeches and parties. On the evening of October 28, two days before the fair's final day, Mayor Carter Harrison was assassinated in his Near West Side home by a twenty-five-year-old job seeker. Four months later, fire destroyed or damaged six fair buildings and their still-valuable exhibits. Another fire occurred in February, and then in July 1894, a final conflagration leveled nearly all of the remaining structures.

—Patrick T. Reardon

◄ Mayor Carter Harrison, photographed in 1893, was assassinated two days before the fair's closing.

◄ The biggest single-day crowd jammed the fairgrounds on Chicago Day, October 9, the twenty-second anniversary of the Great Fire. The fair was designed to show that Chicago had risen, prosperous and strong, from the ashes of the fire.

The First Heart Operation

A pioneering black surgeon steps into a medical no-man's-land.

JULY 9, 1893

The patient was a young black man named James Cornish. He had been rushed to Provident Hospital, on the South Side, with a knife wound in his chest from a barroom brawl. Dr. Daniel Hale Williams—a founder of Provident, which had opened two years previously as the city's first interracial hospital—knew Cornish was bleeding to death. On this hot summer night, Williams performed a desperate operation that helped set the stage for modern surgery.

Medical textbooks of the time said that operating on a human heart was too dangerous and that there was no precedent for opening the chest. But "Dr. Dan," despite having no x-rays, antibiotics, adequate anesthesia, or other tools of modern surgery, stepped into that medical no-man's-land. With a scalpel, he cut a small hole in Cornish's chest, carefully picking his way past nerves, muscle, blood vessels, and ribs until he reached the rapidly beating heart. Exploring the wound, Williams found a severed artery. He closed it with sutures. Then he discerned an inch-long gash in the pericardium, the tough sac that surrounds the heart. The heart itself had only been nicked and did not need sutures; but the damaged sac had to be closed. With Cornish's heart beating 130 times a minute beneath his nimble fingers, Williams closed the wound with catgut. Cornish survived. He was discharged fifty-one days later as "cured."

▲ *Dr. Daniel Hale Williams (1856–1931), who is generally credited with performing the first successful open-heart surgery. In 1913, Williams was the only black surgeon among the charter members of the American College of Surgeons.*

Williams's operation, which is generally considered the first successful open-heart surgery, contributed to "the emergence of scientific medicine just before the turn of the century," according to a later account. His feat, however, is just one of Chicago's medical milestones. The nation's first demonstration of antiseptic medicine took place in Chicago at the turn of the century; the first diagnosis of a heart attack (1912) and the first use of an incubator (1922) also took place in Chicago. In 1937, the world's first blood bank was established at Cook County Hospital. Surgery became safer, making Chicago a mecca for surgical innovation. At one point, one out of four American physicians received training directly or indirectly from Cook County Hospital doctors. And the tradition of surgical derring-do exemplified by Williams has lived on: in 1989, the first successful liver transplant from a living donor was performed at the University of Chicago.

—*Ronald Kotulak*

◄ *Surgery at Provident Hospital in the 1950s. As a result of Williams's initiative, the hospital opened in 1891 to provide health care for all races and to serve as a training hospital for black doctors and nurses.*

The Pullman Strike

An industrialist's dream of an ideal workers' community dies in a bitter labor dispute.

▼ *Violence in Chicago escalated when federal troops came to break the strike, as illustrated in this drawing from* Harper's Weekly. *More than one thousand rail cars were destroyed, and thirteen people were killed.*

MAY 11, 1894

Workers at the Pullman factory on what became the far Southeast Side of Chicago walked off the job on this date, and, in the protracted strike that followed, one man's dream of a better tomorrow fell apart even as another's was born. In addition to owning a factory that built railroad sleeping cars, George Pullman was a visionary who thought he had solved the problems of modern industrial society. His factory was surrounded by a utopian village—owned entirely by Pullman—and located nine miles south of what were then Chicago's city limits to insulate his workers from the city's baleful influences.

Instead of living in tenement slums, twenty thousand Pullman employees and their families lived in carefully planned row houses and town homes. Nearby were markets, shops, and schools. Taverns were banned. Upon its opening in 1881, Pullman Town was saluted by editorial writers across the nation as a picture-book example of modern city planning. When Chicago was host to the World's Columbian Exposition in 1893, special trains carried international visitors to witness Pullman's handiwork.

But when the 1893 depression caused business to plummet, Pullman sharply reduced wages to cut costs. Yet he held firm on rents, which paymasters subtracted from employees' shrinking paychecks. Desperate, the Pullman workers appealed to the American Railway Union, which was holding its national convention in Chicago. The union voted to support the Pullman strike, instructing its members not to handle any trains containing Pullman cars. By July, sympathy strikes were under way in twenty-three states. Episodes of violence led President Grover Cleveland to order federal troops to intervene, however, and the strike collapsed.

▲ *Eugene V. Debs, leader of the American Railway Union at the time of the strike, makes a speech later in life during one of his five campaigns for president as the candidate of the American Socialist Party.*

Eugene Victor Debs, the railroad union's president, was imprisoned, an experience that radicalized him. Afterward, Debs became a founder of the American Socialist Party, running for president five times on a platform promising working men and women a better society in which to enjoy the fruits of their labor.

George Pullman died three years after the strike and, his name by then synonymous with hostility toward the working class, was buried at Graceland Cemetery under protective layers of concrete and steel. In 1898, the Illinois Supreme Court ordered Pullman Town sold off, ruling that a company town was incompatible with the spirit of America.

—*Ron Grossman*

Chanute's Gliders

Experimental flights at the dunes along Lake Michigan bring mankind closer to powered flight.

▲ *Born in Paris and trained as a civil engineer, Octave Chanute built railroads, designed Chicago's Union Stockyards, and developed a keen interest in flying machines.*

JUNE 22, 1896

Upon their arrival on this date at the windy dunes along the Indiana shore of Lake Michigan, Octave Chanute and his assistants started to unload strange-looking contraptions from the crates they had brought from Chicago. Chanute, who was sixty-four and had made a fortune building railroads, was about to begin a series of critical glider experiments that would culminate seven years later in the first flights of Orville and Wilbur Wright. Augustus Herring, a member of Chanute's team, first tried a bat-winged device invented by German aviation pioneer Otto Lilienthal. "A panic struck when they [spectators] saw Mr. Herring mount the odd-shaped affair and sail through the air," according to a *Tribune* reporter who was on hand. "He succeeded in floating quite a distance."

Chanute had been collecting information about flying machines since the 1850s. He had organized an international conference on aviation in 1893 in conjunction with the Columbian Exposition and the following year had published *Progress in Flying Machines*, a compilation of aviation information and arguably the most influential book in aviation history. By 1895, Chanute had decided to experiment with hang gliders to find a suitable airframe for a flying machine.

Miller Beach, on the site of what became Gary, Indiana, had the advantages of fifty-foot dunes from which pilots could leap, the right winds, and a sandy beach for soft landings. After trying the Lilienthal glider and a twelve-winged device of Chanute's own design—neither of which worked very well—the glider team returned a few months later with more experimental designs. A biplane that Chanute and Herring produced with a truss arrangement similar to the railroad bridges Chanute had built proved most successful. It flew almost 360 feet in one glide. Further tests followed in 1897.

▲ *Chanute's biplane glider, shown here in 1897 during test flights at the Indiana dunes, employed the wing design that evolved into the Wright brothers' first airplane.*

Wilbur Wright wrote to Chanute in 1900 to ask for advice, saying he had read Chanute's book and was experimenting with gliders. That started a correspondence between the elder expert and the young inventor. Chanute later persuaded a dejected Wilbur not to abandon his quest. The Wrights invited him to Kitty Hawk, North Carolina, in 1903 to watch their first attempt at powered flight—in a biplane. But cold weather forced him to leave after a week. He was back in Chicago on December 17, 1903, when he received word of the Wrights' success in a telegram from their sister, Katharine: "The boys have done it."

—*David Young*

The Spanish- American War

Yellow journalism whips up support for a short war that makes the United States a colonial power.

APRIL 21, 1898

The Spanish-American War, which began officially on this date, was a short and thoroughly lopsided affair, but it was long on enthusiasm and colorful characters. Future president Teddy Roosevelt led a charge of cowboys and college students up a hill in Cuba. Future poet Carl Sandburg fought with an Illinois regiment in Puerto Rico. Painter-sculptor Frederic Remington illustrated the war. Novelist-reporter Stephen Crane wrote about it. So did *London Daily Graphic* correspondent Winston Churchill, who later became known for other things.

Whipping up war fever was the era's yellow journalism, marked by exaggeration or just plain lies. William Randolph Hearst, owner of the *New York Morning Journal*, reportedly cabled Remington with directions to illustrate Spanish atrocities in Cuba. "You furnish the pictures," Hearst wrote, "and I'll furnish the war." Many Americans began clamoring for war with Spain after an explosion sank the USS *Maine* in Havana harbor in February. The explosion's source is still a mystery; when a declaration of war came, the official reason was Spain's treatment of Cuba, a Spanish colony.

On May 7, the *Tribune* scored a historic scoop by printing details of Commodore George Dewey's decimation of the Spanish fleet in Manila Bay even before President William McKinley received the news. The *New York World* received a dispatch from its correspondent too late for its final edition, but *Tribune* managing editor James Keeley had kept his staff on alert. When the story came in from the *World*'s press service, the paper was ready to produce an extra. Later, Keeley called the White House to tell McKinley the news.

Spain was defeated in 113 days. America acquired the Philippines, Guam, and Puerto Rico at a cost of fewer than four hundred battle deaths, although because of disease, total fatalities topped five thousand. It had been a popular war, but one who was skeptical about the country's readiness to rule colonies was Mr. Dooley, the fictional saloonkeeper created by Finley Peter Dunne, of the *Chicago Evening Post*. "I know what I'd do if I was Mack," said Dooley's friend Mr. Hennessy, referring to McKinley. "I'd hist a flag over th' Ph'lippeens, an' I'd take in th' whole lot iv thim." "An' yet," said Mr. Dooley, "'tis not more thin two months since ye larned whether they were islands or canned goods."

—*Ken Armstrong*

Reversing the River

Sending the river south means Chicago's drinking water is safe at last.

▼ *The waters of the Chicago River begin to fill the empty Sanitary and Ship Canal on January 2, 1900. The site is at about Damen Avenue on Chicago's Southwest Side.*

JANUARY 2, 1900

The group of dignitaries, clad in heavy overcoats and standing by the side of a new and controversial canal, watched nervously as two men scrambled over mounds of dirt to reach them. Perhaps the men carried a last-minute injunction to stop the work that was so close to completion. The officials—trustees of the Sanitary District of Chicago—had ordered the hurried opening of the waterway on this date after hearing rumors of such legal maneuvers. But no: the men turned out to be newspaper reporters who had been tipped off that the Chicago River was about to be reversed.

They were just in time to see a crane claw away the last few feet of frozen earth that separated the river from the canal. With that, the foul river water began to pour into the canal and run west, toward Lockport and the Des Plaines River, instead of east toward Lake Michigan. The decades-old problem of keeping the city's drinking water safe had at last been solved.

Reversing the Chicago River, polluted with factory discharges, slaughterhouse offal, and sewage, had long been seen as the best way to end periodic epidemics of waterborne diseases, especially cholera. Such outbreaks occurred when rainstorms pushed river water far out into the lake, where cribs collected the city's drinking water. The river had been reversed in 1871, but it had not stayed reversed; a pumping station that emptied river water into the Illinois and Michigan Canal proved inadequate.

Eight years and eighty-five hundred workers had been needed to finish the new twenty-eight-mile-long waterway, one of the great engineering feats of its time. In digging the Sanitary and Ship Canal through earth and limestone, contractors devised new earth-moving methods and new machines that proved invaluable a few years later when the Panama Canal was constructed. But not everyone was in awe of the canal. Cities along the Des Plaines, Illinois, and Mississippi Rivers, especially St. Louis, cringed at the thought of drinking Chicago's sewage. Threats of an injunction by St. Louis caused the trustees to arrange the almost surreptitious opening of the canal.

The spectacle of the westward-flowing river attracted "throngs of people," who, by one account, gathered at bridges and docks to watch "the river current setting briskly upstream instead of lying stagnant as before." Deaths from waterborne diseases plummeted, and towns downstream from Chicago did not suffer. In later years, the North Shore and Calumet Sag Channels were added to take wastewater from the northern and southern suburbs, and treatment plants were built to clean up sewage before it entered the canals. But during especially heavy storms, the area's rivers still backed up into basements and even occasionally into Lake Michigan. Tackling that problem would have to wait for another eighty years.

—*Stevenson Swanson*

▶

A cheap but crowded way to get a bird's-eye view of the project. The men—and one dog—are ninety-five feet above ground in this 1895 photograph.

▲ *These cantilevered cranes were among the new pieces of construction equipment developed for the canal project. They carried excavated rock or earth to spoil piles next to the canal.*

The Everleigh Club

Chicago's famed brothel begins its eleven-year run of luxurious vice.

FEBRUARY 1, 1900

▲ *Ada (left) and Minna Everleigh*

Behind the doors of the twin brownstones at 2131–33 South Dearborn Street, Minna Everleigh gave her final instructions: "You have the whole night before you, and one $50 client is more desirable than five $10 ones. Less wear and tear," she told the women assembled before her. With that, Minna and her older sister, Ada, on this date opened what would become the best little bordello in Chicago and, for a time, one of the best known in the world.

Minna and Ada Everleigh, then twenty-one and twenty-three, took their name from their grandmother's habit of signing her letters "Everly Yours." Raised in a prosperous Southern family, the sisters fled bad marriages to become touring actresses and ended up in Chicago after running a bordello in Omaha during the Trans-Mississippi Exposition.

Amid the grimier brothels of the Levee, Chicago's notorious vice district, the Everleigh Club sparkled like one of Minna's many diamond pins. The *Tribune* described the fifty-room mansion as the world's most richly furnished house of courtesans. Guests were entertained in opulent parlors, among them the Gold Room, which featured gold-rimmed fishbowls, gold spittoons, and a miniature gold piano, and the Chinese Room, where gentlemen could set off tiny firecrackers.

In an era when a beer cost a nickel, the Everleigh sisters charged $12 for a bottle of champagne. Dinners started at $50 a person—without female company. Gentlemen who left without spending at least $50 were advised not to return. Exempt from that rule were newspapermen, for whom the sisters professed a soft spot. If *Tribune* overnight clerks needed to round up reporters quickly, they were told to call Calumet 412, the club's famed telephone number.

Thanks to the protection money the sisters gave police and aldermen, the Everleigh Club operated freely. But its extraordinary success eventually led to its downfall. A brochure advertising the club fell into the hands of Mayor Carter Harrison Jr., and, on October 24, 1911, he ordered it shut down. The sisters left with more than $1 million in cash, jewelry, stocks, and bonds. Ada and Minna resettled on the West Side, but neighbors drove them out. They moved to New York City, and there they led quiet lives under assumed names and started a neighborhood poetry circle. After Minna died in 1948, Ada sold off most of their belongings, including the gold piano, and moved to Virginia. She died in 1960, at the age of ninety-three.

—*Louise Kiernan*

▲ *The Rose Room, one of the opulent upstairs rooms of the Everleigh Club. This photograph is taken from a 1902 brochure advertising the club.*

Sister Carrie

Theodore Dreiser's powerful novel becomes the cornerstone of Chicago's tough-minded approach to literature.

NOVEMBER 8, 1900

Published on this date, Theodore Dreiser's *Sister Carrie* was among the most auspicious debuts in literary history, but only in retrospect. The initial response to Dreiser's first novel, one of the definitive Chicago works of fiction, was largely antagonistic. It was "brought into the world," as Dreiser's biographer W. A. Swanberg noted, "by a publisher who detested both the book and the author." Dreiser's fatalistic outlook and his blunt fictional technique, both shaped by his experiences as a Chicago newspaperman, led to the novel's being condemned for its "immorality" and "philosophy of despair"—as though the author had thrown open the doors to outhouses as well as saloons and tenements.

In an age of lofty literary moralism, Dreiser's unrefined prose, his grubby characters, and his squalid subject matter offended many. But the novelist's chief advocate, critic H. L. Mencken, hailed the novel for capturing "the gross, glittering, excessively dynamic, infinitely grotesque, incredibly stupendous drama of American life." Mencken saw Chicago, the "abattoir by Lake Michigan," as the source of inspiration to the nation's most important new writers at the beginning of the twentieth

▲ *Theodore Dreiser's fatalistic outlook and blunt approach to fiction were shaped in part by his experiences as a Chicago newspaperman. He, in turn, would shape the Chicago literary tradition of fiction in the raw.*

◄ *Harriet Monroe, who founded* Poetry *magazine in 1912, gave crucial early exposure to such poets as Ezra Pound, T. S. Eliot, and Edgar Lee Masters. Carl Sandburg's "Chicago" appeared in the magazine for the first time in 1914.*

century. The city's literary flowering, called the "Chicago Renaissance," included authors Edgar Lee Masters, Floyd Dell, Vachel Lindsay, Sherwood Anderson, and Carl Sandburg as well as vital literary journals, from Margaret Anderson's *Little Review* to Harriet Monroe's *Poetry* to Ben Hecht's *Chicago Literary Times*. Dreiser, in New York by the time he wrote *Sister Carrie*, shared their opposition to the genteel tradition, and his pivotal novel established an enduring Chicago tradition: fiction in the raw, tawdry but compassionate.

Dreiser's novel tells the story of Carrie Meeber, an eighteen-year-old who arrives in Chicago from Indiana, "ambitious to gain in material things," and becomes the mistress of a salesman and manager of a saloon. Rather than punish her for her sins, Dreiser saw to it that she was rewarded. Among the readers aggrieved by *Sister Carrie* was Dreiser's publisher, Frank Doubleday. The book had been accepted by Doubleday's partner, but Doubleday was appalled by what he considered an immoral, crudely written, and potentially uncommercial book and tried to break his con-

▲ *In* Studs Lonigan *and many other novels, the prolific James T. Farrell epitomized the tough-minded Chicago style of fiction.*

▶

Richard Wright, who moved to Chicago as a young man in 1934, set his best-known novel, Native Son, *on the city's South Side. Frustrated by racism, Wright left the United States for France in the 1940s.*

tract with Dreiser. The publisher printed only one thousand copies, of which 456 were sold, bringing the author royalties of $68.40. Seven years later *Sister Carrie* was reissued to high praise and, with such later Dreiser works as *Jennie Gerhardt* and *An American Tragedy*, had a profound influence on the fiction of Upton Sinclair, Willa Cather, Sinclair Lewis, and others. But Chicago writers were Dreiser's chief beneficiaries—notably James T. Farrell, Richard Wright, and Nelson Algren.

Although his cultured prose seems the antithesis of the Dreiserian style, Saul Bellow considers himself a descendant. "When I was young, I read Dreiser very closely and was very much under his spell," said Bellow, winner of the Nobel Prize for literature in 1976. "He showed how you could take the life of the streets and apartment houses and make literature out of them. His prose was crude, but it didn't matter because his stories were so powerful, his characters so staggering. In spite of the language, he was a genius."

—*John Blades*

▲ *Among the Chicago writers who felt Dreiser's influence was Nelson Algren, author of* The Man with the Golden Arm *and* A Walk on the Wild Side. *As with Dreiser, the grim realism of Algren's work offended some readers.*

◄ *Saul Bellow, shown in 1976 when he won the Nobel Prize, is a more elegant stylist than Dreiser, but a literary descendant nonetheless. Among Bellow's novels are* Herzog *and* Humboldt's Gift.

The Iroquois Theater Fire

A fire during a holiday matinee kills hundreds and leads to tougher safety standards nationwide.

DECEMBER 30, 1903

School was out for Christmas, so the Wednesday matinee performance of *Mr. Blue Beard*, a musical starring funnyman Eddie Foy, overflowed with a standing-room audience of nearly two thousand people, mostly women and children, at the five-week-old Iroquois Theater. The richly appointed amusement palace, on the north side of Randolph Street between State and Dearborn Streets, was said to be fireproof. But it would prove as unburnable as the *Titanic* would prove unsinkable nine years later.

In the second act, as the orchestra swung into a dreamy waltz called "Let Us Swear by the Pale Moonlight," an arc light on the left side of the stage sputtered and ignited a strip of paint-saturated muslin on a drape. Unnoticed at first by the audience, the flame ran up the strip and into the flyspace above the stage where scenery hung.

Suddenly, blazing fabric rained down on the stage. The singers raced off, one with a costume on fire, and the audience began to bolt. Foy then ran onstage, raised his hands, and tried to calm the crowd. For a moment, the panic eased. But the draft from an open stage door fed the flames. A fireball leaped across the footlights and engulfed a velvet curtain. Stagehands tried to lower the asbestos curtain to keep the blaze from spreading to the seats, but it stuck a few feet above the stage floor. Then part of the stage collapsed, and the lights went out.

That touched off a stampede for the twenty-seven exits, some of which were hidden by drapes; others were locked to foil gatecrashers. Bodies slammed into bodies. Within minutes, tangles of corpses were piled seven feet high as the living groped for an escape route over the dead, only to succumb themselves to gas, smoke, and flames. By the time firefighters fought their way inside, an eerie silence had fallen over the charred and darkened remains of the theater. "Is there any living person here?" one fire marshal shouted over and over. "If anyone is alive in here, groan or make a sound." No one did.

◄ *A ticket stub from the ill-fated matinee performance* of Mr. Blue Beard

◄ *Decked out in marble, mahogany, and mirrors, and featuring a massive foyer and sweeping stairways, the newly opened Iroquois Theater was "a virtual temple of beauty," according to the* Tribune.

Some 575 people died that day, and hundreds were hurt. Another thirty would die from their injuries in the following weeks. The theater's managers and several public officials were indicted in connection with the fire, but no one was ever punished. The tragedy also spurred a drastic toughening of safety standards for theaters and other public buildings, and the rules became a benchmark for the nation. Henceforth, all theater exits had to be clearly marked and the doors rigged so that, even if they could not be pulled open from the outside, they could be pushed open from the inside.

—Bob Secter

▲ *By the time firefighters fought their way inside, an eerie silence had fallen over the charred and darkened remains of the theater.*

Founding of the *Chicago Defender*

Robert S. Abbott's newspaper is a guiding voice for blacks escaping the oppressive South.

▲ *Robert S. Abbott, founder of* the Defender, *became a scourge of Southern racism.*

MAY 5, 1905

A European visitor observed in 1891 how few blacks there were in Chicago and opined that "the severity of the climate repels the Africans." Robert S. Abbott, who on this date published the first edition of the *Chicago Defender*, recognized that the climate that counted for blacks was not meteorological but social, economic, and political. Abbott not only founded the country's most influential African-American newspaper; through its pages he encouraged the great migration of blacks from oppression in the rural South to relative freedom and economic opportunity in the urban North.

Abbott was born in Georgia to former slaves. He first came to Chicago in 1893, when he sang with a quartet at the World's Columbian Exposition. His stepfather, a minister who also published a small newspaper, instilled in him a belief in the power of the press to improve the lot of black Americans. Although the success of the *Defender* ultimately made Abbott a millionaire, in the beginning the four-page weekly had a one-man staff: reporter, editor, deliverer—he did it all.

Over time, the *Defender* caught on in Chicago's African-American community. Because it was published in the North, the newspaper enjoyed far greater freedom than Southern black newspapers in criticizing the region's racial oppression. Abbott became a scourge of Southern racism. The more vigorously Southern whites tried to suppress the *Defender*, the more ardently Southern blacks sought and responded to it. Said one black leader in Louisiana: "My people grab it like a mule grabs a mouthful of fine fodder."

Abbott urged blacks to abandon the South and move north, where they could "get the wrinkles out of their bellies and live like men." Heeding him—and seizing the opportunity opened by curtailed European immigration as World War I approached—Southern blacks swelled Chicago's black population from about forty thousand at the time of the *Defender*'s founding to almost five hundred thousand by the time the great migration ended in the late 1940s. Other northern cities experienced similar growth. Thanks in no small part to Abbott's *Defender*, America was a radically different nation, and Chicago was a radically changed city.

—*N. Don Wycliff*

▶

This handbill was distributed by the Defender *during the Chicago race riots of 1919.*

Gary, Indiana

As "Steel City" rises on the sandy shores of Lake Michigan, an industrial giant takes shape.

JULY 17, 1906

When the United States Steel Corporation went looking for a vast expanse to hold its new manufacturing complex, a "wasteland" of sand dunes and marshes at Lake Michigan's southern tip seemed the best location. Situated between the iron ore beds of the northern Great Lakes and the southern Indiana coal fields, the area had only one drawback: it was too desolate for anyone to live there. U.S. Steel changed all that, and in doing so took the most dramatic step of any manufacturer in turning the southwestern shore of the lake into one of the greatest concentrations of industry in the world.

In April 1906, U.S. Steel attorney A. F. Knotts and his brother Thomas turned the first shovel of sand—there was little dirt then—and on this date, the city of Gary was incorporated. A. F. Knotts, also a civil engineer who helped lead the project, was called founder, and Thomas was the first mayor. But it was board chairman Elbert Gary who gave his name to the town, which was quickly nicknamed "Steel City." The company had planned everything, from the lakefront harbor to the plot for a government center, to a street grid south of the new steel mill. "Sloughs were filled," the *Tribune* reported later, "towering 60-foot sand dunes leveled, two miles of the Grand Calumet river bed was shifted. Millions of dollars worth of black loam was imported from Illinois to cover the sands of ages."

"Boomtown" is not an explosive enough term to describe Gary during its early years. By the end of 1906, ten thousand people resided in the nation's first "instant city." The following February, steel flowed as liquid fire from the new blast furnaces. In the dense industrial region that developed from Lake Calumet, in Chicago, through northwestern Indiana, Gary Works soon held pride of place. Even in the mid-1990s, it was the largest steel mill in the United States.

Gary had big plans for a northern Indiana metropolis of two hundred thousand citizens, but its population peaked at about 178,000 in 1960 before falling to 116,000 in 1990. In a city where half the jobs were blue-collar and where two-thirds of those were in the steel industry, layoffs and plant closings in the 1970s and 1980s were a severe blow. But to the end it will remain as it was born, the Steel City.

—*Reginald Davis*

▲ *United States Steel Chairman Elbert H. Gary, a judge from the Chicago suburb of Wheaton, was a driving force behind turning the city that was named for him into an industrial giant.*

▼ *The Gary Works of United States Steel had begun to spread across the sands between the Grand Calumet River and Lake Michigan by the time George Lawrence took this photograph from a balloon in 1908.*

The 1906 World Series

In this all-Chicago fall classic, the "Hitless Wonders" seem mismatched against the awesome Cubs.

October 9, 1906

The Cubs had been incredible in the 1906 season, winning 116 games and losing only 36, a record that remained unsurpassed nine decades later. The White Sox, on the other hand, had started off in sixth place. But they won nineteen in a row late in the season, and what had seemed impossible happened: the Cubs and the White Sox were in the World Series, both for the first time. "Last night Chicago was baseball mad," the *Tribune* reported after the Sox clinched the American League pennant. "Men stood and cheered in elevated trains when the news was passed along that the Sox were safe and that Chicago had two pennants—and the world's championship."

Still, baseball's first intracity World Series seemed a pitiful mismatch. Surely the awesome Cubs, led by manager and first baseman Frank Chance, would demolish "the Hitless Wonders." The Cubs exuded quality, starting with the immortal double-play combination of shortstop Joe Tinker, second baseman Johnny Evers, and Chance. The team had been known at first as the White Stockings or White Sox and had many nicknames before becoming the Cubs. At the founding of the American League, in 1900, the new Chicago team took over the Cubs' original nickname. These Sox played in the stench of the stockyards, at 39th Street and Wentworth Avenue, on a soft, spongy surface that was as second-rate as they were thought to be. Owner Charles Comiskey's players had a team batting average of .228, not one .300 hitter, and their pitching was shaky.

Fan rivalry was intense. Tempers flared in bars, and fights broke out between street gangs. On October 9, the opening day of the Series, business stopped, and City Hall closed down. Tickets were $2 for box seats and 50 cents for bleachers. But for nine thousand fans who could not get to the ballpark, the *Tribune* rented the Auditorium and the First Regiment Armory, where the progress of the games would be relayed.

The teams split the first four games, and then the White Sox took Game Five. They needed only one more game to win the Series. Nearly twenty thousand fans jammed the old South Side ball park on 39th Street, and thousands waited in the streets. With Cubs ace Mordecai "Three Finger" Brown on the mound, a seventh game seemed certain. The Cubs scored a run in the first inning, but the Sox, now called "the Hitting Wonders," scored three and then exploded with four in the second. In the Cubs' ninth, with the score 8–3 and two out, Frank Schulte hit a weak ground ball to the mound. Doc White tossed to first and

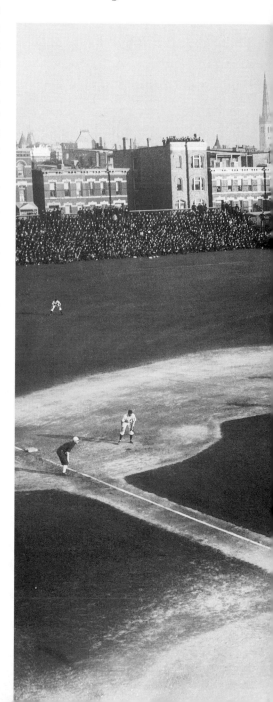

then ran for his life as Sox fans swarmed onto the field and into the streets. That night, bonfires were set for a party that lasted into the morning. Cubs faithful stayed inside and mourned. An embittered Frank Chance said, "There is one thing I will never believe, and that is the Sox are better than the Cubs."

Chance never got his revenge against the Sox, but he did get redemption when the Cubs won the 1907 and 1908 World Series. The Sox ruled the baseball world once more in 1917, but the '06 Series may well remain a unique moment in the city's sports history.

—Ed Sherman

▼ *This remarkable photograph captures Cubs pitcher Jack Pfiester winding up during the key sixth inning of the third game of the 1906 World Series. The game was played at the West Side Grounds, at Polk Street and Wolcott Avenue, then known as Lincoln Street. The score is 0–0, but the Sox have loaded the bases. Although it is unclear who is at the plate in the photo, George Rohe hit a triple later in this inning that scored the only runs of the game, and the Sox won 3–0.*

Essanay Studios

For one brief decade, a pioneering movie studio turns Chicago into Hollywood on the prairie.

▼ *The back lot of Essanay Studios gave the company a way to take advantage of natural lighting, even for interior scenes such as this one.*

AUGUST 10, 1907

Plenty of movies have been made about Chicago. Plenty of movies have been shot on Chicago's streets. But the city itself has never been a center of international studio filmmaking—except for one brief golden age that lasted only a decade. That single ten-year span commenced on this date, when Essanay Studios was formed to enter the new business of making movies. During those years, Chicago had a studio that was the Walt Disney or Warner Brothers of its day.

Essanay boasted among its contract players the world's number-one box-office star (Charlie Chaplin), a great matinee idol (Francis X. Bushman), a glamor queen (Gloria Swanson), and the dean of cowboy stars (studio cofounder Gilbert "Bronco Billy" Anderson). The studio was located in the 1300 block of West Argyle Street in the city's Uptown neighborhood; the peculiar name is an amalgam of the initials of the studio's founding partners: George Spoor and Anderson. Spoor had run a newsstand and, later, a film-and-projector distribution company, National Film Renting. Anderson, a former vaudeville actor, shot to fame playing one of the outlaws in Edwin S. Porter's 1903 hit, *The Great Train Robbery*.

Essanay quickly became a dominant force in westerns and comedies. Its success was due in part to the well-matched talents of its partners. Anderson ground out "Bronco Billy" short westerns at a formidable rate: one a week for 376 straight weeks. (A few were shot in the Rogers Park neighborhood of Chicago, the rest at Essanay locations in Colorado or California). Spoor had a head for business; it was he who introduced Bell to Howell.

Of all the studio's stars, none shone brighter than Chaplin, whom director Jean Renoir would describe as the greatest filmmaker of the century. Chaplin's period at Essanay (1915–16) saw his first real creative flowering. The most important of the fourteen Chaplin Essanay productions was the landmark film *The Tramp*, in which he first endowed his famous character with the combination of humor and pathos that endeared the Tramp to audiences. Other Essanay Chaplin titles include *The Champion*, *The Bank*, *Shanghaied*, and *His New Job*, the only film he shot in Chicago.

But if Chaplin gave Essanay its greatest year, his 1916 departure for the Mutual Company and more money hastened its demise. The defection caused a fatal rupture between penny-pinching Spoor and Anderson. A year later, with the movie industry centralizing in the warmer climes of southern California, Essanay expired. Only the plain brick building on Argyle has remained as a reminder of a period when Chicago was at the center of world moviemaking.

—*Michael Wilmington*

▲ *Gloria Swanson (at the camera) was discovered when she toured the studio with her aunt.*

◄ *Ben Turpin (left) and Charlie Chaplin in* His New Job, *made in 1915. It was the only Essanay film that Chaplin shot in Chicago.*

"Injun Summer"

Like all great editorial cartoonists, John T. McCutcheon found an everyday way to touch readers.

▲ *John T. McCutcheon in the early 1900s, at about the time he drew "Injun Summer"*

SEPTEMBER 30, 1907

Deadlines roll around every day in the newspaper business, whether a writer or an artist is fired by an idea or not. One day in the early fall of 1907, cartoonist John T. McCutcheon found himself groping for inspiration for a drawing to fill his accustomed spot on the front page of the *Tribune*. He thought back to his boyhood in the 1870s on the lonely cornfields of Indiana. "There was, in fact, little on my young horizon in the middle '70s beyond corn and Indian traditions," he recalled later. "It required only a small effort of the imagination to see spears and tossing feathers in the tasseled stalks, tepees through the smoky haze. . . ."

That "small effort of imagination" became McCutcheon's classic drawing "Injun Summer," which was first published on this date. It was accompanied by a lengthy discourse with the plainspoken charm of Mark Twain. McCutcheon's astute folk poetry captured the sere, prickly, enigmatic mood of nature's most puzzling season. The cartoon proved so popular that it made an annual appearance in the *Tribune* beginning in 1912, and over the years ran in many other newspapers.

McCutcheon's long career at the *Tribune* stretched from 1903, when he moved from the old *Chicago Record*, until 1946, when he retired. Over the years, his gentle brand of insight, satire, and nostalgia resulted not only in "Injun Summer" but also in his poignant expression of grief on the death of Pope Leo XIII, showing the world with a mourning ribbon tied around it, and "Mail Call," which depicts a lone soldier without mail in a crowd of happy recipients. A cartoon is worth at least a thousand words: One reader wrote 11,384 letters to men in the service because of it. McCutcheon won a Pulitzer Prize in 1932, the first *Tribune* staff member to receive journalism's coveted award. His death in 1949 earned a front-page obituary.

In tapping his youth to create a drawing with a sense of a shared, almost mythic, past, McCutcheon provided an early and powerful illustration of cartoonists' crucial role in shaping the character of American newspapers and their ability to touch readers in personal, everyday ways. Through the years, Chicago's newspapers have been unusually rich in cartooning talent. At the *Tribune*, Carey Orr (whose career stretched from World War I to the Cold War), Richard Locher, and Jeff MacNelly joined McCutcheon in the Pulitzer ring. Other Chicago newspaper artists to whom Pulitzers were awarded include Vaughn Shoemaker and John Fischetti of the *Daily News*; Jacob Burck of the *Times*; and Jack Higgins of the *Sun-Times*. The drawings of Bill Mauldin, a two-time winner for work done before his arrival in Chicago, enlivened the editorial pages of the *Sun-Times* from 1962 to 1991.

The "Injun Summer" era ended on October 25, 1992, when it appeared for the last time. The drawings may be timeless, but the text had outlived its day. Complaints had been voiced for several years about its offensiveness to Native Americans. Wisps of smoke have continued to rise from those smoldering leaves, however. Every fall, some readers complain that they miss it.

—Sid Smith

INJUN SUMMER

Yep, sonny, this is sure enough Injun summer. Don't know what that is, I reckon, do you?

Well, that's when all the homesick Injuns come back to play. You know, a long time ago, long afore yer granddaddy was born even, there used to be heaps of Injuns around here—thousands—millions, I reckon, far as that's concerned. Reg'lar sure 'nough Injuns—none o' yer cigar store Injuns, not much. They wuz all around here—right here where you're standin'.

Don't be skeered—hain't none around here now, leastways no live ones. They been gone this many a year.

They all went away and died, so they ain't no more left.

But every year, 'long about now, they all come back, leastways their sperrits do. They're here now. You can see 'em off across the fields. Look real hard. See that kind o' hazy, misty look out yonder? Well, them's Injuns—Injun sperrits marchin' along an' dancin' in the sunlight. That's what makes that kind o' haze that's everywhere—it's jest the sperrits of the Injuns all come back. They're all around us now.

See off yonder; see them tepees? They kind o' look like corn shocks from here, but them's Injun tents, sure as you're a foot high. See 'em now? Sure, I knowed you could. Smell that smoky sort o' smell in the air? That's the campfires a-burnin' and their pipes a-goin'.

Lots o' people say it's just leaves burnin', but it ain't. It's the campfires, an' th' Injuns are hoppin' 'round 'em t' beat the old Harry.

You jest come out here tonight when the moon is hangin' over the hill off yonder an' the harvest fields is all swimmin' in the moonlight, an' you can see the Injuns and the tepees jest as plain as kin be. You can, eh? I knowed you would after a little while.

Jever notice how the leaves turn red 'bout this time o' year? That's jest another sign o' redskins. That's when an old Injun sperrit gits tired dancin' an' goes up an' squats on a leaf t'rest. Why, I kin hear 'em rustlin' an' whisperin' an' creepin' 'round among the leaves all the time; an' ever' once'n a while a leaf gives way under some fat old Injun ghost and comes floatin' down to the ground. See—here's one now. See how red it is? That's the war paint rubbed off'n an Injun ghost, sure's you're born.

Purty soon all the Injuns'll go marchin' away agin, back to the happy huntin' ground, but next year you'll see 'em troopin' back—th' sky jest hazy with 'em and their campfires smolderin' away jest like they are now.

The First Ward Ball

When Chicago's most outrageous pols threw a party, it was a lollapalooza.

DECEMBER 15, 1908

Nearly twenty thousand drunken, yelling, brawling revelers filled the Coliseum on South Wabash Avenue and clogged the street by the time the Honorable John J. Coughlin arrived by carriage on this December night. It was a satisfying sight to the alderman, better known as "Bathhouse" John. A loud, year-long campaign by reformers had failed to stop the annual festivities. "A real description of [last year's] ball is simply unprintable," Arthur Burrage Farwell, the fiery president of the Chicago Law and Order League, had thundered. "[We] must stop this disgrace to Chicago." This "disgrace" was the First Ward Ball, for more than a decade the city's most notorious party, hosted by Coughlin and Michael "Hinky Dink" Kenna.

The reformers were rarely a match for these masters of political shenanigans, the first names on a long list of characters in Chicago's history who have made public service a lucrative calling. The tiny, cigar-chomping Kenna was a genius at political organization and the owner of the Workingman's Exchange, a popular saloon at Clark and Van Buren Streets. Coughlin had been a bathhouse masseur, wrote terrible poetry, and wore garish clothes. He blustered while Kenna said little. They shared the aldermanic duties of the ward, an area that includeds dwellings of the rich, tenements, and the notorious Levee, home of pimps, prostitutes, and pickpockets. They conceived the First Ward Ball as a way of further stuffing their pockets, already bulging with graft, through imposed ticket and liquor sales. The first ball, held at the Seventh Regiment Armory on South Wentworth Avenue in 1896, had attracted a wild mix of society thrill seekers, police captains, politicians, prostitutes, and gamblers.

The 1908 ball made that affair look tame. During the course of the evening, revelers slurped up ten thousand quarts of champagne and thirty thousand quarts of beer. Riotous drunks stripped off the costumes of unattended young women. A madam named French Annie stabbed her boyfriend with a hat pin. "It's a lollapalooza! . . . There are

▲ *The hosts of the First Ward Ball, "Hinky Dink" Kenna (left) and "Bathhouse" John J. Coughlin, at the 1924 Democratic National Convention, in New York City*

◄ *Another of Chicago's colorful politicians, Alderman Mathias "Paddy" Bauler (in the top hat), coined that durable maxim "Chicago ain't ready for reform." He hosted parties in the 1950s and 1960s in his office and saloon on North Avenue.*

THE GRAND MARCH AT BATHHOUSE JOHN'S BALL.

◄ *"Bathhouse" John J. Coughlin and Michael "Hinky Dink" Kenna monitor admissions at their First Ward Ball in this 1908 editorial cartoon by the* Tribune's *John T. McCutcheon.*

more here than ever before. All the business houses are here, all the big people," Kenna proudly proclaimed. "Chicago ain't no sissy town."

The reformers inevitably triumphed—the next year's affair attracted only three thousand—and soon the gambling houses and brothels of the Levee were closed. Coughlin and Kenna remained powerful for decades, though, their influence apparent in that blustery Coughlin protégé and former cowboy, Mayor William "Big Bill" Thompson. And their political philosophy was embodied by Forty-third Ward Alderman Mathias "Paddy" Bauler, who coined that durable maxim "Chicago ain't ready for reform." Bauler hosted parties at his North Avenue office and saloon in the 1950s and 1960s—pale but perky reminders of the First Ward's scandalous soirées.

—*Rick Kogan*

◄ *The Coliseum, at 1513 South Wabash Avenue, hosted national political conventions and other grand events. Its stone walls had once been the front of Libby Prison, a notorious prison for Union soldiers in Richmond, Virginia, during the Civil War. In 1908, it was the site of the notorious First Ward Ball.*

Plan of Chicago

Burnham inspires civic improvements with his vision of a city of beauty and reason.

JULY 4, 1909

O n the 133rd anniversary of the nation's birth, Daniel H. Burnham issued his *Plan of Chicago* as a declaration of independence from the ugliness and confusion that characterized the city after more than a half century of explosive—yet haphazard—growth. The internationally famous architect and city planner wrote, "The time has come [for Chicago and other world cities] to bring order out of chaos incident to rapid growth."

Burnham's 164-page plan, executed with the help of Edward H. Bennett and strikingly illustrated with watercolors by Jules Guerin, was his vision of Chicago as a city of beauty and reason. Commissioned by the Commercial Club of Chicago, the plan distilled ideas that Burnham had preached since the conclusion of the World's Columbian Exposition of 1893. Burnham, the fair's chief designer, wanted to re-create Chicago to match the splendor of the

▲ *"The time has come," Daniel H. Burnham wrote, "[for Chicago and other world cities] to bring order out of chaos incident to rapid growth."*

White City, as the exposition was called, and he addressed any group that would listen.

"As he talked on quietly, easily," Hamlin Garland wrote of one gathering, "describing his vision of a great front park, harbors and lagoons, indicating here and there on a roughly drawn map, the civic centers and the great architectural plazas . . . I, for one, came to think of him with surprise as a poet, a

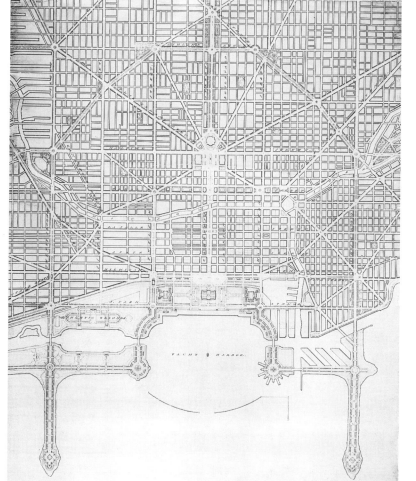

◄ *One of the most impressive features of the plan was its comprehensive sweep, including railway stations, parks, radial arterial streets, piers, and a yacht harbor in one integrated, rational urban landscape. At the heart of the plan was a civic center at the intersection of Halsted and Congress Streets, which became the site of the Chicago Circle expressway interchange.*

dreamer, one who was dwelling in the far future." It was a dream that captured the imagination of even such a rough-edged politician as "Bathhouse" John Coughlin. According to Thomas S. Hines, Burnham's biographer, Coughlin argued in an impassioned speech that if Chicago could not come up with the funds to pay for the improvements Burnham envisioned, it was "a city of pikers and deserved to take a back seat."

Much of Burnham's plan was eventually carried out in one form or another: the creation of an unbroken string of lakefront parks, the straightening of the Chicago River on the Near South Side, the transformation of Michigan Avenue into "a high-grade shopping street," the creation of a landscaped boulevard system, a double-decked Wacker Drive, and the construction of a wide thoroughfare (the Eisenhower Expressway) running west from downtown. The plan also gave impetus to existing proposals, such as the move to create a ring of forest preserves around Chicago. One of its key, yet often ignored, results was the creation of the Chicago Plan Commission, which has a hand in shaping all major projects in the city.

Burnham, whose architectural firm designed such important projects as the Reliance Building, the Field Museum, and the Marshall Field store, supposedly said, "Make no little plans. They have no magic to stir men's blood." No exact account exists of Burnham's uttering what became the most famous statement in urban planning; he likely said it in a speech, a conversation, or now-lost correspondence. In any event, he made no little plan, but he did not live to see its implementation. Burnham died in 1912 while on one of his many European tours.

—Patrick T. Reardon

▲ *This view from the Plan of Chicago shows Grant Park and a proposed harbor in the lake. Much of Burnham's plan was implemented. The island at the top of the drawing, for example, is Northerly Island, the future site of Meigs Field. In addition to being an important planning document, the 1909 plan was a beautiful work of art, thanks to the watercolors of Jules Guerin.*

The Lakefront

Montgomery Ward's twenty-year fight protects a "breathing spot" on the lake.

DECEMBER 21, 1910

For the fourth time, Montgomery Ward was entangled in a lawsuit over the destiny of the lakefront. For the fourth—and, as it turned out, the last—time, the Illinois Supreme Court upheld Ward's position. Grant Park must remain clear of buildings, the court ruled on this date, and the officials who had wanted to build the Field Museum in the park had no choice but to look elsewhere. The ruling was crucial in protecting Chicago's breathtaking lakefront, one of the city's chief glories.

Ward's lawsuits were based on a few words written in 1836, when the three commissioners of the Illinois and Michigan Canal set aside a soggy stretch of lakefront east of Michigan Avenue that was to remain "forever open, clear and free." That noble declaration was put aside in 1852, when the new Illinois Central Railroad built a trestle in Lake Michigan so its trains could reach the Chicago River. The trestle and its breakwater were unsightly, but they protected Michigan Avenue and its mansions from fierce lake storms.

▲ *Montgomery Ward, the "watchdog of the lakefront," in a 1907* Tribune *caricature.*

▼ *The unsightly condition of Lake Park, the strip of land between Michigan Avenue and the Illinois Central railroad tracks, provoked retailer Montgomery Ward to fight for the preservation of Chicago's lakefront. In this 1894 photograph, troops who were called in during the Pullman strike have pitched tents in the park.*

Over the years, the water between the shore and the trestle was filled in with such things as debris from the 1871 fire. The resulting scruffy patch was called Lake Park. Stables, squatters' shacks, mounds of ashes and garbage, and the Illinois Central tracks cluttered the landscape. Ward, who looked down on this mess from the Michigan Avenue skyscraper where his mail-order empire was based, filed suit in 1890 to have it cleaned up and kept open and clear. That was the beginning of a twenty-year fight with city and park officials over the future of the land.

At first, few could believe that Ward wanted to keep such valuable land open. A downtown lakefront was no place for a park, one alderman snorted: "It should be used to bring revenue to the city." Then officials embraced the idea and started to fill in the lake to make the park bigger. But park officials wanted to put buildings on this open land, renamed Grant Park in 1901. Ward counted twenty proposals at one point, including Marshall Field's natural history museum.

▲ *The landscaping of Grant Park, shown in about 1950, followed Daniel Burnham's 1909 plan, which called for formal, symmetrical gardens. Burnham's plan, however, placed the Field Museum at the heart of the park. After Ward defeated that proposal in court, Buckingham Fountain was constructed there instead.*

◀ *By 1907, Lake Park had been renamed Grant Park, and it was being expanded east of the Illinois Central tracks. But park officials and Ward were still fighting in court over the park's future.*

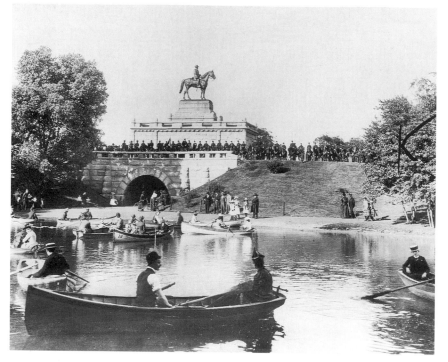

In the 1890s, Ward had agreed to the construction of the Art Institute in the park, but he later regretted it. "I fought for the poor people of Chicago," he told the *Tribune* in the only interview he ever gave on the subject. "Here is a park frontage on the lake, comparing favorably with the Bay of Naples, which city officials would crowd with buildings, transforming the breathing spot for the poor into a showground of the educated rich. I do not think it is right."

The Field Museum was eventually built on the lakefront outside Grant Park, and after World War I, Daniel Burnham's *Plan of Chicago* fueled an ambitious series of landfill projects.

▲ *Lincoln Park was already twenty-eight years old by the time of this 1892 photograph. The park, created in 1864, was located on part of the old city cemetery. Landfills later expanded it along Chicago's North Side.*

Burnham Park was created on the South Side to link Grant and Jackson Parks, and Lincoln Park, on the North Side, was expanded farther north, reaching Hollywood Avenue after World War II.

▼ *Navy Pier, completed in 1916, was one of two long piers envisioned in Burnham's plan, but the second was never built. Although it failed as a pier, it has served as a focal point of lakefront activities, such as in 1931, when thousands gathered to watch United States Army air maneuvers. After renovation, it reopened in 1995 with a variety of amusement and entertainment attractions.*

The debate about the lakefront did not end with Ward's court victory. A large water filtration plant next to Navy Pier, the soaring Lake Point Tower residential building, and the McCormick Place exhibition hall were built over the objections of lakefront preservationists. Grant Park, however, fulfilled Ward's hopes and became the city's front yard. Music festivals, symphonic concerts, fireworks displays, and the Taste of Chicago food festival annually attract huge summertime crowds to Grant Park, the gem at the center of a twenty-mile-long necklace of lakefront parks and beaches.

—Stevenson Swanson

▲ *Buckingham Fountain, shown in 1935, was built in 1927 with $500,000 donated by Kate Buckingham in memory of her brother Clarence, a director of the Art Institute. The fountain is modeled on one at Versailles, except that, in true Chicago fashion, it is twice as big.*

◀ *Lake Shore Drive was laid out in 1875 to connect Oak Street with North Avenue, at the south end of Lincoln Park, but it grew into the thoroughfare that runs the length of Chicago's lakefront parks. This view, from the 1920s, looks north from about Oak Street.*

Market Square in Lake Forest

The nation's first shopping center is designed to be "sound, sanitary, and picturesque."

January 13, 1913

Evergreen Plaza, in the southern suburbs, opened in 1952. Old Orchard, in the northern suburbs, dates from 1956. Compared with Market Square in Lake Forest, both are newcomers. Four decades earlier, the business district of the North Shore community became the first planned suburban shopping center in the United States. Areas in Baltimore and Kansas City make the same claim, but the National Register of Historic Places awarded the title to Market Square. A board of trustees was formed on this date to provide the necessary capital of $225,000. Construction started in 1915, and shop doors opened in 1916.

Inspiration for Market Square came from Lake Forest resident Arthur T. Aldis, a real-estate investor and patron of the arts who sought something "sound, sanitary, and picturesque" to replace the ramshackle buildings of the business district, which ill suited the rest of the community. Lake Forest, a haven for Chicago's wealthy as early as 1856, was from the first a town of winding streets and wooded lots with large homes.

Aldis engaged Howard Van Doren Shaw, a Lake Forest resident whose landmark projects include the Fourth Presbyterian Church on Chicago's North Michigan Avenue, to design a U-shaped square. Shaw blended Italian Renaissance, Tyrolean, Bavarian, Flemish, and English architecture in the three sides of the U, which enclose a grassy square with a fountain in the middle. Shops are on the ground

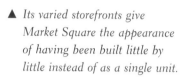

▲ *Its varied storefronts give Market Square the appearance of having been built little by little instead of as a single unit.*

◄ *Market Square, shown shortly after it was constructed in 1916, had the essential element of all shopping centers that would follow: it was planned, built, and operated as a unit. But it remained more an ideal than an example for later shopping centers.*

floors of the buildings; above are offices and apartments. The open end of the U faces the train station, and two towers frame the sides of the square.

The varied storefronts give Market Square the appearance of having been built little by little, and the intimate scale creates a comforting charm. In 1931, Marshall Field's moved into the entire west building. Local merchants, such as a sporting goods store and a stationery shop, have remained magnets for locals over the years. "The first time I saw Market Square," wrote Lake Forest resident Susan Dart, "I had never seen a place I liked so much, and I knew that I felt happy there."

As a model shopping center, it remained more an ideal than an example. In the years following World War II, shopping centers sprouted in suburbia like dandelions, starting small and simple like Evergreen Plaza but growing into sprawling complexes, such as Woodfield Mall in northwest suburban Schaumburg, with hundreds of stores, surrounded by acres of parking lots. Still, they shared a common element with Market Square: they were planned, built, and run as a unit. In 1984, a management company purchased the square from descendants of the original investors, but the green in the middle has remained a focal point for community events, such as book fairs, art shows, and Christmas-tree lighting ceremonies.

—*Mike Conklin*

◀ *The north side of the square in the 1960s: "I knew I felt happy there," a resident wrote.*

Robert R. McCormick

For more than four decades, the Tribune *spoke with the Colonel's voice.*

▼ *The cartoons of Carey Orr were one of the editorial weapons the Colonel used in the* Tribune's *long-running battle with President Franklin Roosevelt and his New Deal.*

MAY 13, 1914

His name was Robert R. McCormick, a president but not yet the colonel. He was thirty-three and had been president of the *Tribune* for three years. On this date, McCormick embarked on an arrangement with his cousin, Joseph Patterson, to share editing and publishing duties. In time, Patterson moved to New York, but McCormick spent more than four decades putting his distinct and unbendingly conservative personal stamp on the *Tribune*.

At first, McCormick was known primarily as the aristocratic grandson of the late Joseph Medill, the *Tribune*'s esteemed editor and publisher. "The family knew I didn't know anything about the newspaper business," McCormick said, "but also they knew that I wasn't a socialist." But after returning from World War I with the rank of colonel, McCormick presided over a circulation increase that made the newspaper the largest in the Midwest and one of the most profitable in the country. The Colonel built his own paper mill in Canada, created marketing and advertising innovations, and, in early recognition of the potential of broadcasting, expanded into the new medium in 1924 with radio station WGN. A champion of press freedom, he underwrote the cost of winning a landmark Supreme Court case that found a Minnesota gag law unconstitutional.

▲ *Colonel Robert R. McCormick, shown in the 1920s, played as important a role in the development of the* Tribune *in the twentieth century as his grandfather, Joseph Medill, had in the preceding century.*

To make the paper speak with his voice, McCormick met daily with editors and editorial writers, and he peppered his staff with memos and telephone calls from Cantigny, his estate near west suburban Wheaton. "Colonel McCormick's xenophobic 'World's Greatest Newspaper' is one of the last, anachronistic citadels of muscular personal journalism," *Time* said. The Colonel waged his fiercest campaign against President Franklin Roosevelt's New Deal, in his view as monolithic a threat to individual freedom as Mussolini's fascism and Hitler's totalitarianism. The enmity was mutual. Roosevelt once told John Boettiger, the *Tribune*'s Washington correspondent: "John, you tell Bertie he's seeing things under the bed."

Perhaps the most enduring of his sometimes eccentric campaigns was his attempt to simplify the English language. "Tho," "thru," "iland," and "frate" were among the eighty words that were spelled the Colonel's way in the *Tribune*, even nineteen years after his death in 1955. But, as the Colonel's powerful influence faded, the paper declared in 1974, "Thru is through and so is tho."

—*Tim Jones*

AFTER ALL, THEY ARE ONLY THE WHEELS' OF INDUSTRY

World War I Begins

Europe slides into a grisly war that Americans hope will not entangle them.

JULY 28, 1914

A month after a Serbian nationalist murdered Archduke Francis Ferdinand, son and heir of the Austrian emperor, the Austro-Hungarian Empire declared war on this date against Serbia. That led Austria's ally Germany to declare war on August 1 against Russia, Serbia's protector. More declarations of war soon followed.

The United States quickly asserted its neutrality. Most Americans wanted no part of a European war that seemed to confirm the belief that the troubles of the Old World never changed. On August 2, the *Tribune* published one of its most memorable editorials, "The Twilight of the Kings." Written by Clifford Raymond, it captured American disquietude toward the injustice of a war declared by the ruling classes but fought by those they ruled:

"Before establishing hell on earth the pietistic kings commend their subjects to God. Seek the Lord's sanction for the devil's work.

"'And now I commend you to God,' said the kaiser from his balcony to the people in the street. 'Go to church and kneel before God and pray for His help for your gallant army.'

"Pray that a farmer dragged from a Saxon field shall be speedier with a bayonet thrust than a winemaker taken from his vines in the Aube; that a Berlin lawyer shall be steadier with a rifle than a Moscow merchant; that a machine gun manned by Heidelberg students shall not jam and that one worked by Paris carpenters shall. . . .

"And the pietistic czar commends his subjects to God that they may have strength of arm in a quarrel they do not understand. . . .

"The pietistic emperor of Austria commends his subjects to God, to seek divine assistance to crush the peasants of Serbia, dragged from the wheat field when it was ready for the scythe and given to the scythe themselves.

"This is the twilight of the kings. Western Europe of the people may be caught in this debacle, but never again. Eastern Europe of the kings will be remade. . . .

"If Divinity enters here it comes with a sword to deliver the people from the sword.

"It is the twilight of the kings. The republic marches east in Europe."

—*R. Bruce Dold*

THE SPORT OF KINGS.

[Copyright: 1914: By John T. McCutcheon.]

The *Eastland* Disaster

A summer excursion turns into the worst accident in the annals of Great Lakes shipping.

JULY 24, 1915

For an hour, while passengers were boarding the steamship *Eastland* on this rainy but otherwise calm Saturday, the ship slowly rocked back and forth from starboard to port. The motion of the boat, which was scheduled to take employees of the Western Electric Company on an excursion to Michigan City, Indiana, did not alarm the crew.

At 7:25 A.M., the list to port became more severe. A refrigerator behind the bar toppled over with a crash, and the 2,573 passengers and crew suddenly realized that disaster was upon them. As it was being cast loose from its moorings on the south bank of the Chicago River between LaSalle and Clark Streets, the *Eastland* slowly settled on its side. The ship was only a few feet from the wharf, where a large crowd of horrified spectators watched, and it was in only twenty feet of water. That, however, was deep enough to drown 844 people who were trapped or trampled below decks. Although most were young factory workers from Berwyn and Cicero, twenty-two entire families were wiped out.

"The screaming was terrible," one man told the *Tribune*, which devoted eleven pages of coverage to the disaster. "I watched one woman who seemed to be thrown from the top deck. . . . I saw her white hat float down the river, and that was all."

▼ *The* Eastland *lies on its side in the Chicago River. While rescue workers try to reach passengers trapped inside the boat, survivors line up in the background to cross over to the safety of a tugboat.*

▲ *The Second Regiment Armory, on Washington Boulevard, served as a temporary morgue for victims of the* Eastland. *Some were never identified.*

Of all Great Lakes shipping accidents, the *Eastland* was by far the worst; the sinking of the *Lady Elgin* in 1860, in which 279 people died, is a distant second.

   Court decisions blamed improperly weighted ballast tanks for the disaster. But transportation historian George W. Hilton argued in a 1995 book that the reaction to the sinking of the *Titanic* three years earlier ultimately doomed the *Eastland*, which had almost capsized in 1904 with 2,370 people aboard. Because there were lifeboats and rafts for less than half the *Titanic's* licensed passenger capacity, an international furor arose. Senator Robert M. La Follette of Wisconsin introduced a bill requiring ships to have enough lifeboats for 75 percent of their passengers.

   On July 2, 1915, the owners of the *Eastland* added three lifeboats and six rafts, weighing fourteen to fifteen tons, to its top deck. A boat that had already exhibited stability problems became top-heavy. Three weeks later, the next time it was loaded to capacity, the *Eastland* capsized.

—David Young

▲ *Scenes of weeping survivors were common along the river following the disaster.*

◀ *The tugboat* Kenosha *served as a floating bridge to let survivors reach safety.*

"The Gumps"

An editor with a common touch creates a new kind of comic strip.

FEBRUARY 12, 1917

Who could believe that America would carry on a forty-two-year love affair with Andy Gump—a bald, toothless, chinless chap whose biggest claim to fame was that he invented the flowerpot and introduced the polka-dot tie to America?

Maybe *Tribune* coeditor Joseph Medill Patterson, who introduced Andy and the rest of "The Gumps" to Chicagoans on this date. As Patterson saw it, his brainchild would be quite unlike the one-gag comic strips then filling newspapers. Besides delivering a daily dose of laughter at the American breakfast table, the strip would tell a continuing story, and the characters in "The Gumps" would mirror the lives of *Tribune* readers.

This creation was so perfectly Patterson, the sometime playwright, sometime farmer, who possessed a keen newspaperman's instinct for what would appeal to the common people. Patterson's cousin, the starched and formal Robert R. McCormick, recognized these talents and urged Joe to join him in running the *Tribune*. Although the two men could hardly have been more different—McCormick was a Republican, Patterson a former avowed Socialist—they worked well together. McCormick focused on the newspaper's business affairs, while Patterson shaped daily features and put his stamp on the Sunday paper. They took monthly turns running the editorial page.

Patterson frequently wrote story lines for "The Gumps," but it was artist Sidney Smith who brought Andy and his family to life on the page. The strip soon prompted passionate responses from readers across the country, thanks to newspaper syndication. When Uncle Bim almost married the conniving Widow Zander, the Minneapolis Board of Trade suspended operations briefly so its members could find out what happened. And thousands called the *Tribune* and other newspapers to protest the death of a character named Mary Gold. The *New York Times* commented when Smith was killed in a car accident in Octo-

▲ *Joseph Medill Patterson wanted comic strips to mirror readers' lives as well as be funny. Patterson moved to New York in 1925 to run another of his creations, the* New York Daily News. *He died in 1946.*

The Gumps (S. Smith), 1917

ber 1935: "The death of Sidney Smith, creator of Andy Gump . . . will be felt by literally millions of Americans."

In 1925, Patterson moved to New York to devote his attention to the *New York Daily News*, which had begun publication in 1919. It was another classic Joe Patterson product: a tabloid newspaper that was easy to read and loaded with pictures common people would find appealing. (Tribune Company sold the newspaper in 1991.) The move did not stop Patterson from developing more story strips, securing his reputation as one of the most influential figures in the annals of American comics. He is credited with bringing to life such legendary titles as "Winnie Winkle," "Moon Mullins," "Little Orphan Annie," "Terry and the Pirates," and "Dick Tracy," which debuted in the *Daily News* in 1931 and in the *Tribune* the following year. While many of Patterson's story strips have survived into the 1990s, the Gump family went to comic-strip heaven on October 17, 1959.

— *Judy Hevrdejs*

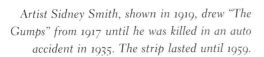

Artist Sidney Smith, shown in 1919, drew "The Gumps" from 1917 until he was killed in an auto accident in 1935. The strip lasted until 1959.

America Enters World War I

Chicago does not go willingly into the great conflict.

APRIL 6, 1917

When President Woodrow Wilson asked for a declaration of war against Germany on April 2, 1917, it surprised no one. When Congress issued the declaration on this date, it was a matter of course. America's entry into World War I had been building for months following the German declaration of unrestricted submarine warfare and publication of the Zimmermann telegram, in which German foreign minister Arthur Zimmermann proposed that Mexico become Germany's ally in case America entered the war.

In Chicago, patriotic fervor did not take easily. The city's population of 2.1 million included more than 225,000 residents born in Germany or Austria and many more who traced their lineage to those countries. "Chicago," noted first-term Mayor William Hale Thompson—later derided as "Kaiser Bill" for his softness toward the war—"is the sixth-largest German city in the world." There also were tens of thousands of Russians who had fled the czars and their armies, Irish who held no love for the English, and socialists and pacifists (including Jane Addams of Hull House) who opposed the war on philosophical grounds.

A *Tribune* advertisement urged volunteers to sign up with Major Robert R. McCormick or his cousin, Lieutenant Joseph M. Patterson, the newspaper's coeditors

▼ *Recruits practice marching in Grant Park in 1917 with the Art Institute in the background. Despite such scenes, Chicago did not respond enthusiastically to the outbreak of war.*

and publishers. But an editorial bemoaned the reality: "More men are applying for marriage licenses to avoid the service than are enlisting." Two months after the United States joined the Great War, and with voluntary enlistment stalled, the nation's young men were ordered to sign up for a new draft. Of the three hundred thousand who signed up in Chicago, two-thirds sought exemptions.

The city seemed consumed by other things. In 1917, a White Sox team ranked among baseball's all-time best would capture the American League flag and then beat the New York Giants in six games to win the World Series. War stories competed for attention with reports of race-related clashes over housing as war work accelerated the growth of the city's black population. In the end, the war came home. World War I would take 4,266 Illinois lives and leave 13,794 injured. Also wounded: the public face of Chicago's rich German heritage.

◄ *The Tribune joined in efforts to drum up volunteers with advertisements such as this. By the end of the war, McCormick was a colonel, and his cousin was a captain.*

► *Even in a city with a large German population, anti-German sentiment was evident. This sign was posted in Edison Park in 1917.*

◄ *To finance the war, the federal government held campaigns to boost sales of government bonds. Bond drives would become an even more familiar part of the home front during the next world war.*

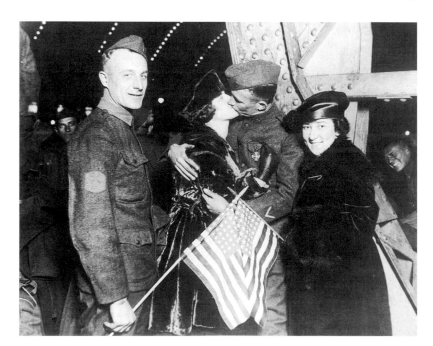

▲ *Chicagoans jam the intersection of State and Madison Streets on Armistice Day, November 11, 1918, to celebrate the end of the great war.*

Frederick Stock, the German-born conductor of the Chicago Symphony Orchestra, felt compelled to resign briefly over his failure to pursue naturalization. The Bismarck Hotel for a time became the Hotel Randolph. The Goethe statue in Lincoln Park was vandalized (though attempts to change Goethe Street's name were unsuccessful). The Germania Glub became the Lincoln Club,

Nineteen months after joining the fight, and just three weeks after a flu epidemic killed 381 Chicagoans in a single day, the riven city—for it was not nearly as whole as it had been, wartime prosperity notwithstanding—celebrated. It was November 7, 1918. News of the war's end turned out to be just rumor. Four days later, it was true. The *Tribune* received the Associated Press confirmation of the war's end at 1:55 a.m. "The *Tribune* set off its giant sirens . . . at least five minutes ahead of any other noise-producing instruments in informing the public of the news," the paper boasted. And Chicago got out of bed. "Showers of paper poured from the windows."

—*Alan Solomon*

◄ *Home from the war, a soldier of the Black Hawk Division receives the time-honored welcome.*

The 1919 Race Riots

Thirty-eight people are killed after an invisible line is crossed.

▲ *Police remove the body of a black man killed in the rioting. Twenty-three blacks and fifteen whites were killed.*

▼ *Many houses in the predominantly white stockyards district were set ablaze during the five days of violence.*

JULY 27, 1919

They were separated by a line unseen and a law unwritten: the 29th Street beach was for whites, the 25th Street beach for blacks. An invisible boundary stretched from the sand into Lake Michigan, parting the races like Moses' staff parted the Red Sea. On this stifling hot summer Sunday, Eugene Williams, a black teenager, drifted south of that line while swimming with friends. Whites picked up rocks and let fly. Some accounts say Williams was hit on the head and went under. Others say he became tired and was too afraid to come ashore. Either way, he drowned, touching off the deadliest episode of racial violence in Chicago history.

For five days it raged, mostly on the city's South Side. White mobs attacked isolated blacks. Blacks attacked isolated whites. John Mills, a black stockyards worker, was riding home when a mob stopped his streetcar and beat him to death. Casmero Lazeroni, a white peddler, was pulled from his horse-drawn wagon and stabbed to death. Thirty-eight people died—twenty-three blacks and fifteen whites. By the time the National Guard and a rainstorm brought the riots to an end, more than five hundred people had been injured, wounded blacks outnumbering whites by about two to one.

Several factors had heightened tension between the races. Blacks, drawn by the promise of employment and dignity, had been moving to Chicago in rapidly increasing numbers; the city's black population more than doubled between 1916 and 1918. "Chicago is a receiving station that connects directly with every town or city where the people conduct a lynching," wrote Carl Sandburg. Blacks had balked at joining white-controlled unions, and in the face of violence, black leaders had begun preaching self-defense instead of self-control. But, most important of all, housing in the city's narrow "Black Belt," which stretched south of the Loop, had not kept pace. When blacks began moving into white neighborhoods, whites responded violently, bombing twenty-six homes in the two years preceding the riot.

One of the riot's great mysteries is whether the city's future boss of bosses, Richard J. Daley, participated in the violence. At the time, Daley belonged to the Hamburgs, a Bridgeport neighborhood club whose members figured prominently in the fighting. In later years, Daley repeatedly was asked what he did during the riots. He always refused to answer.

—*Ken Armstrong*

The Black Sox

A fixed World Series casts a shadow over the national game.

▼ *Before the fall: the ill-fated 1919 White Sox strike relaxed poses for a team picture.*

October 1, 1919

The 1919 White Sox—the White Sox of Eddie Collins, Eddie Cicotte, Dickie Kerr, Ray Schalk, Buck Weaver, and "Shoeless" Joe Jackson— are considered by baseball historians to be one of the greatest teams ever to take the field. But there were rumors about these Sox even before Cicotte's second pitch hit Morrie Rath, the leadoff batter for the underdog Cincinnati Reds, in the first game of the World Series, played on this date. "I don't know yet what was the matter," Sox manager Kid Gleason told the *Tribune*'s James Crusinberry the day the Reds won the Series. "Something was wrong. I didn't like the betting odds."

Those betting odds, in fact, had been a story even before the Series started. Bookies had made the Sox 7–5 favorites to win it all, and there was speculation those odds could go as high as 2–1 by game time. But in New York, a sudden and unusually large amount of cash was bet on the underdog Reds, sending odds there crashing toward even money. After the Game One loss, White Sox owner Charles A. Comiskey told intimates he suspected a fix. The intimates suspected sour grapes, but the Reds went on to win the best-of-nine Series in eight games. Gleason was right: something was wrong.

On September 28, 1920, the indictments came from a Cook County grand jury. Eight players were charged with conspiracy to commit fraud: Cicotte, Weaver, Jackson, Fred McMullin, Swede Risberg, Chick Gandil, Happy Felsch, and Lefty Williams. Cicotte, whose plunking of Rath signaled that the fix was in, said he got $10,000 from gamblers. Jackson, promised $20,000, got only $5,000. When he com-

plained, he said, Risberg threatened to kill him if he went public. "Swede," he said, "is a hard guy." So Jackson had kept his mouth shut—and hit .375 in the Series. Defense lawyers argued that although the players admitted to taking money to throw baseball games, they had not intended to defraud the public.

"I guess I'm through with baseball," said Shoeless Joe. They all were. The jury acquitted them, but new baseball commissioner Kenesaw Mountain Landis banned the eight "Black Sox" from the game forever. The suspected fixers got off clean. The man thought to be the power behind the fix, New York gambler Arnold Rothstein, never went to trial.

The White Sox, who won ninety-six games in 1920 to finish second in the American League, were a shambles. The next year, they went 62–92 and wound up seventh. It would be 1959—forty years after baseball's biggest scandal had destroyed a marvelous team and shaken the national game—before they would win another pennant. "I wish," a suspicious but circumspect Kid Gleason had said the day the Reds savored their Series victory, "no one had ever bet a dollar on the team."

—Alan Solomon

▲ *Sympathetic fans packed the courtroom during the trial. Although a boy is supposed to have pleaded with Shoeless Joe, "Say it ain't so, Joe!" the story is considered apocryphal.*

◄ *Eddie Cicotte (from left), Joe Jackson, and Lefty Williams at their 1921 trial. All the Black Sox were acquitted, but they were banned from baseball.*

Prohibition Begins

Despite an attempt to legislate morality, the drinks keep flowing during the "dry" years.

JANUARY 17, 1920

Even as the Volstead Act went into effect at 12:01 A.M. on this date, only the naive really thought Prohibition would do away with alcohol consumption. Chicago's gangsters, crooked cops, corrupt politicians, and the booze-consuming public all conspired to keep the drinks coming. The combination of flamboyant characters and flagrant lawbreaking made the Prohibition era the most notorious in Chicago's history and left the city's reputation with a whopping hangover for decades.

In the 1870s, Evanstonian Frances Willard, a power in the Prohibition Party and a founder of the WCTU (Women's Christian Temperance Union), laid much of the groundwork that led to the Eighteenth Amendment, but she died nearly twenty-two years before this experiment in social reform came to pass. Bootleggers and other criminals should have been building

▲ *Temperance leader Frances Willard of Evanston did not live to see Prohibition—or its aftermath.*

shrines to Willard's memory, because Prohibition ushered in a bonanza for the
underworld. By 1924, there were fifteen
breweries in the city going full steam and
an estimated twenty thousand saloons.

These speakeasies (a term that originated in the dry states of the 1880s meaning "speak softly when ordering") and the
gangs that supplied them operated more
or less openly, because William Hale "Big
Bill" Thompson, who was mayor during
much of Prohibition, was a master of the
broad wink. His police chief, Charles Fitz-
morris, complained that "60 percent of
my police are in the bootleg business."
His successor, Morgan Collins, said cops
earned $5 every time they ignored a beer
truck. Which was hard to do. Beer trucks
were everywhere.

Hundreds of bars brazenly kept their
doors open and conducted business as
usual. Slightly more discreet "blind pigs"
proliferated. Customers would mutter a
code phrase at the door ("Joe sent me"),
undergo peep-hole scrutiny, and then join the crowd inside. Countless restaurants,
snack shops, ice cream parlors, and private dwellings housed handcrafted distilleries
or hidden barrooms. Women, previously relegated to a side entrance at most drinking establishments, could enter these illicit saloons through the same door as the
men, risking neither arrest nor a sullied reputation.

In his book, *The Dry and Lawless Years*, Prohibition-era judge John H. Lyle
noted that inflated drink prices hardly discouraged the consumption of illegal hooch.
"Whiskey highballs that sold for 15 cents in 1919 shot up to 75 cents now that they
were forbidden," Lyle wrote. "If you went to a cabaret with your own pint of gin,
you paid $1 for a pint of ginger ale and $1 for ice." Most of these profits, of course,
ended up in the coffers of organized crime.

▲ *It took a major underground operation to supply the city's twenty thousand speakeasies. This distillery, discovered by Prohibition agents on the city's West Side in 1931, produced five thousand gallons of liquor a day.*

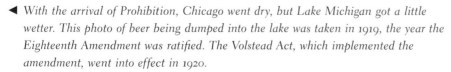

◀ *With the arrival of Prohibition, Chicago went dry, but Lake Michigan got a little wetter. This photo of beer being dumped into the lake was taken in 1919, the year the Eighteenth Amendment was ratified. The Volstead Act, which implemented the amendment, went into effect in 1920.*

▲ *North Side gangster Dion O'Banion was gunned down in his flower shop in 1924 as part of the gang war over control of Chicago's bootlegging business.*

Cops also took a laissez-faire attitude toward the gang wars that frequently broke out over the control of alcohol-distribution territories. At first, Johnny Torrio, a New York import, dominated the mobster scene. He called in a Brooklyn thug named Alphonse (Al) Capone, a former brothel bouncer who was blowing out the candles on his twenty-first-birthday cake the very day Prohibition took effect. Capone, nick-named "Scarface" because of the evidence of a brawl on his left cheek, helped Torrio open a string of suburban vice-and-booze roadhouses. As Torrio—badly wounded in a bump-off attempt—faded from the picture, Capone muscled in on the Chicago saloon trade. Federal authorities estimated the Capone-Torrio mob pulled in $70 million a year, while rivals scrapped over another $40 million or so.

Dion O'Banion, the North Side gang kingpin, was gunned down by Capone's men in 1924 at O'Banion's flower shop, across from Holy Name Cathedral. Two years later, O'Banion's loyal former partner, Earl "Little Hymie" Weiss, staged a vengeance raid on Capone's headquarters in west suburban Cicero. But Big Al escaped. Within a month, Weiss succumbed to a hail of Capone-gang bullets in front of Holy Name, leaving George "Bugs" Moran as Capone's only serious rival. For the time being, Capone wanted peace. Ten days after Weiss's death, at a meeting of gang leaders Capone had convened at the Hotel Sherman, the city was split into territories. Capone, of course, got the lion's share—everything south of Madison Street. "There's plenty of beer business for everybody," Capone declared later. "Why kill each other over it?"

—*Robert Cross*

▶

As his power and wealth increased, Al Capone became a Chicago celebrity. Here he enjoys a front-row seat—and a visit with the Cubs' Gabby Hartnett—at a Wrigley Field charity game. Seated to Capone's right, smoking a cigar, is Roland Libonati, a state representative.

▲ Despite raids on speakeasies and stills, the city's thirst for alcohol far outstripped local government's ability — or inclination — to enforce the Volstead Act.

▲ Mayor William "Big Bill" Thompson, master of the broad wink, set the tolerant tone that allowed speakeasies and bootleggers to operate more or less openly.

▼ Thompson's lax approach to the mayhem in the city led the Tribune, never keen on either Thompson or Prohibition, to broaden its attacks in editorials and cartoons, such as this John T. McCutcheon drawing.

The Michigan Avenue Bridge

This landmark "Chicago-style" span opens the way for humble Pine Street to become magnificent.

▼ *The richly decorated piers of the Michigan Avenue bridge were still under construction on its dedication day.*

MAY 14, 1920

Just before the Michigan Avenue bridge was dedicated on this date, a bridge-tender began to open a portion of the span for a passing boat, unaware that four cars were parked on the bridge. Policemen fired their pistols to get the worker's attention before the cars were dunked in the Chicago River. A more serious mishap occurred on September 20, 1992, as work neared completion on a major renovation. The structure's southeast section flew open, sending a seventy-foot crane crashing to the street and slightly injuring several passersby.

And yet such odd incidents cannot detract from the significance of the Michigan Avenue bridge. Inspired by the monumental Seine River bridges in Paris, designer Edward Bennett crafted a marvel of architecture, engineering, and urban planning. The span's pioneering double deck, for example, carried two levels of traffic—automobiles above, heavy commercial vehicles below.

More important, the bridge provided a link between the Loop and Pine Street, previously an unpaved thoroughfare of soap factories, breweries, and dwellings north of the river. Developers poured billions of dollars into the newly dubbed North Michigan Avenue, transforming it into an elegant shopping, office, and residential district that real estate developer Arthur Rubloff nicknamed the Magnificent Mile.

A premier example of what would become a Chicago trademark, the trunnion bascule bridge, Bennett's 256-foot span has two leaves that pivot up and down (*bascule* is the French word for "seesaw") to let boats pass under quickly and efficiently. The design proved so well suited for Chicago that the city had fifty-two movable bridges by the 1990s—forty-nine of which were trunnion bascules.

—*Gary Washburn*

Birth of the National Football League

For six decades, George Halas was the father figure of a team and a league.

▲ *George S. Halas in the 1930s, a pioneer prodding the Bears and the National Football League toward popularity*

▶

In 1920, they were the Decatur Staleys. Later, they would become the Chicago Bears, the most storied team in professional football history.

SEPTEMBER 17, 1920

As the 1920 football season began, professional teams faced three pressing problems involving players: salaries were rising quickly, players were jumping from one team to another, and teams were using college players who had yet to graduate. These issues brought together representatives of ten pro teams, who gathered on this day in the Jordan and Hupmobile auto showroom in Canton, Ohio. Out of the meeting came a new league, the American Professional Football Association (APFA). Ultimately, one man would stand above all others at the gathering: the representative of the Decatur Staleys, George S. Halas. The very name resonates with the history of professional football.

Between the administrations of Presidents Warren Harding and Lyndon Johnson, Halas's teams won nine titles and galvanized the public's growing interest in pro football with the play of such electrifying stars as Red Grange, Bronko Nagurski, and Sid Luckman. He was not, however, an easy man to work for. His unwillingness to part with dollars during salary negotiations was legendary. During his forty years as head coach (with a record of 324 victories and 151 losses), Halas also was known for kicking players and threatening referees.

In 1921, starch and syrup manufacturer A. E. Staley turned the Decatur franchise over to Halas and the team moved to Chicago, where it played in Cubs Park (later called Wrigley Field). The Staleys won the APFA title with a 9–1–1 record. Two significant name changes took place the next year: the Staleys became the Chicago Bears and the APFA became the National Football League.

Among early championship games, one standout is the 9–0 victory over the Portsmouth Spartans (later the Detroit Lions) in December 1932. An early-winter snowstorm forced the contest to be played indoors at Chicago Stadium, where, on an eighty-yard field, the Bears won the NFL's first postseason game. And in 1940, Halas's Bears came out on the right side of perhaps the most famous score in sports history, the 73–0 championship humiliation of the host Washington Redskins. Early in the game, a Redskins receiver dropped a sure touchdown pass from Washington quarterback Sammy Baugh. After the game, Baugh was asked what difference that touchdown would have made. "The score," said Baugh, "would have been 73–7."

—*Richard Rothschild*

The Field Museum

Its new home on the lakefront becomes a destination for scholars and schoolchildren alike.

▼ *Many of the first-day visitors to the Field Museum trudged across a narrow wooden walk that spanned a dirt plain to reach the regal neoclassical building.*

May 2, 1921

Without fanfare, the doors at the new quarters of the Field Museum of Natural History were opened at 2 P.M. on this date. "Speeches and music," noted one report, "would have been superfluous." Despite the lack of pomp and circumstance, some eight thousand people ventured out on a blustery, drizzly day to tour the museum.

The collection that awaited the opening-day crowd was already well on its way to becoming one of the most extensive of any natural history museum in the world. Over the years, Field Museum scientists have launched expeditions to far corners of the globe, from Mesopotamia to Peru, in search of new specimens for its collection, which numbers over twenty million items. But one of the museum's most enduringly popular exhibits, a forty-foot-tall brachiosaurus that dominates the main hall, was found closer to home. A researcher unearthed the fossilized bones during a trip to the western United States at the turn of the century.

The museum began in 1893 as a result of the World's Columbian Exposition. Frederick Ward Putnam, the chief ethnologist for the exposition, argued that the huge collection of human and animal artifacts that had been gathered for the fair needed a permanent home. That led Edward Ayer, a railroad-tie mogul, to appeal to Marshall Field for funds. Field proved less than eager. "You can sell dry goods until hell freezes over," Ayer finally shouted at the merchant prince of State Street, "but in twenty-five years you will be absolutely forgotten." Field threw him out of his office but later relented and gave the museum astounding sums—more than $9 million.

▲ *Schoolchildren examine a dinosaur fossil. Countless classes
have followed them over the years to view one of the
museum's most popular exhibits.*

At first, the old Palace of Fine Arts, on the grounds of
the Columbian Exposition, housed the museum's collections. But the temporary structure, which was far from
downtown, soon started to fall apart. A proposal to build a
permanent home in the middle of Grant Park led Montgomery Ward to file—and win—one of his most important
lakefront-protection lawsuits. Eventually, the Illinois Central Railroad donated the land on which the museum now
stands, and in time, the Shedd Aquarium and Adler Planetarium were built adjacent to the Field to form a "museum
campus" on the lakefront.

—*Jon Anderson*

▶

*Stanley Field, a nephew of Marshall Field, shaped the museum
into one of Chicago's most important and popular institutions
during the more than fifty years that he served as museum
president. He is shown here at the museum in 1941.*

The Chicago Theatre

With the opening of this Loop showplace, the golden age of movie palaces begins.

OCTOBER 26, 1921

In a city once filled with enormous and elaborate movie houses, none has lasted longer or been more revered than the Chicago Theatre, a structure that in concept and design defines the golden age of movie palaces in the United States. The first downtown theater built for the Balaban & Katz theater chain by the brother architects George and Cornelius W. Rapp, the Chicago dazzled its customers when it opened on this date. In time, it came to be a Chicago icon, its marquee and overhanging sign as much a symbol of the city as the Water Tower or, in later years, the Picasso sculpture.

The Chicago Theatre had everything: a location at 175 North State Street that dominated the Loop, an exterior ablaze with electric lights, a lobby with towering marble columns and a grand staircase, and a 3,880-seat auditorium, decorated in the French-regal style of the Court of Versailles that the Rapp brothers favored. It was an environment that was guaranteed to send twentieth-century urbanites into what George Rapp called "a celestial city—a cavern of many-colored jewels, where iridescent lights and luxurious fittings heighten the expectation of pleasure."

The Chicago's opening day fare was typical of the entertainment that these shrines to movie fantasies were to offer for many years. There was a feature film (the long-forgotten *The Sign on the Door*, starring Norma Talmadge), a stage show with a star headliner (Buster Keaton), and, of course, a miniconcert on the mighty Wurlitzer pipe organ, played in the Chicago's glorious early years by the legendary Jesse Crawford.

◀ *Unlike most movie palaces, the Chicago Theatre survived and reopened in 1986 as a performing arts center. The chandelier, which weighs twenty-two hundred pounds, is made of hand-cut Czechoslovak crystal.*

Other movie palaces soon rose above the storefronts and sidewalks of Chicago's neighborhoods. The West Side had the Paradise. The Tivoli was a South Side landmark. On the North Side stood the vast Uptown, a Spanish Baroque fantasy that opened in 1925 with almost forty-four hundred seats, the largest of the Balaban & Katz palaces. There were many others, including the Central Park, Marbro, Riviera, Picadilly, Norshore, Palace, Oriental, Granada, and Avalon, and they were unparalleled for more than two decades. But in post–World War II America, the old palaces faced hard times. The advent of television, the growth of the suburbs, and the development of multiscreen theaters forced most to close. Many fell into disrepair and were demolished, their splendor never to be re-created.

The landmark Chicago, threatened with destruction in the mid-1970s, survived and, like dozens of other old movie palaces around the country, was converted into a performing-arts center for musicals, concerts, and dance events. Restored and brought back to something like its original luster, it opened again on September 10, 1986. Despite some rocky financial patches and changes in management, it has continued to function as an important part of Chicago's downtown life, its "celestial city" still able to pop the eyes of new generations of audiences.

— *Richard Christiansen*

▲ *At night, with its lights aglow, the Chicago Theatre became "a celestial city." The lights form the outline of the Arc de Triomphe in Paris.*

◀ *The luxurious interiors of the movie palaces, such as the grand staircase at the Chicago, were intended to "heighten the expectation of pleasure," according to architect George Rapp.*

Tribune Tower Competition

A Gothic vision of the American skyscraper rises on Michigan Avenue.

JUNE 10, 1922

Tribune Tower is the product of the most famous architecture competition of the twentieth century. On this date, the seventy-fifth anniversary of the *Tribune*, copublishers Robert R. McCormick and Joseph Patterson announced an international design contest for the newspaper's new quarters. In their words, it was to be "the world's most beautiful office building." They offered $100,000 in prize money.

The hype drew considerable skepticism. But then the entries came pouring in, 263 of them from twenty-three countries. Most relied heavily on the architecture of the past; others anticipated the austere forms of Bauhaus modernism. Some included billboards and radio towers suggesting that the building housed a newspaper. First prize of $50,000 went to New York architects Raymond Hood and John Mead Howells, who designed a soaring Gothic skyscraper with a spectacular topside treatment.

Completed in 1925, the tower rises thirty-six stories (460 feet) above North Michigan Avenue. Indiana limestone sheaths its steel frame. Structural piers shoot upward to the flying buttresses that form the Tower's ornamental crown. Elaborate Gothic carvings adorn the top and bottom of the building, and fragments from more than 120 structures, including the Great Wall of China, are embedded in the base. Many of the pieces were gifts to Colonel McCormick; some were brought back to Chicago by foreign correspondents, such as one recent addition, a chunk of the Berlin Wall. The lobby is inscribed with patriotic passages and ringing defenses of press freedom, including some words by the Colonel. No American newspaper is more closely associated with the building that houses it.

Striking though the Tower is, the second-prize entry proved to be more influential. It came from Finnish architect Eliel Saarinen, who never had designed a skyscraper. Saarinen's tower had the same telescoping profile of the American entries, but it rose more gracefully because of its refined

◀ *Tribune Tower, shown under construction in 1924, was built in front of the newspaper's existing printing plant on a stretch of Michigan Avenue that was far from magnificent at the time.*

▲ *Nighttime illumination highlights the Tower's flying buttresses and delicate Gothic ornamentation.*

▲ *Eliel Saarinen's design came in second but proved more influential.*

setbacks and delicate vertical projections. Louis Sullivan called it "a voice, resonant and rich, ringing amidst the wealth and joy of life." Its trim vertical look influenced a generation of skyscrapers, including the Empire State Building.

Nonetheless, Tribune Tower quickly became a major architectural and urban presence. Along with the neighboring Wrigley Building and the Jazz Age skyscrapers at 333 and 360 North Michigan Avenue, it dramatically frames the Michigan Avenue bridge, helping define one of the city's great urban spaces.

—*Blair Kamin*

▶

This stone from Reims Cathedral is one of the more than 120 fragments from structures around the world that are embedded in the base of the tower and printing plant.

Louis Armstrong Moves to Chicago

The hot new music from the South called jazz finds a new home up North.

AUGUST 9, 1922

At 11:30 P.M. on this date, the Illinois Central train from New Orleans eased into Chicago's 12th Street Station carrying an unknown twenty-one-year-old trumpeter who soon would turn the city—and the rest of the world—on its ear. "When the conductor came through the train hollering, 'Chicago, next stop' at the top of his voice, a funny feeling started running up and down my spine," Louis Armstrong recalled later. "I was all eyes looking out of the window when the train pulled into the station. Anybody watching me closely could have easily seen that I was a country boy."

Within a few months, this "country boy" would begin releasing—with Joe "King" Oliver's Creole Jazz Band—the most brilliant jazz records yet made. Never before had the world heard such hot trumpet playing, with high notes that reached the stratosphere and crying, blue-note phrases more eloquent than the human voice. Chicago's concentration of nightclubs, record companies, publishing houses, and national radio broadcasts made Armstrong an international star.

More than that, his ascent put jazz music on the map for good. Jazz had started as a somewhat crude folk music in turn-of-the-century New Orleans; Armstrong's glorious Chicago recordings with his Hot Five and Hot Seven bands in the late 1920s transformed the music into a bona fide art form by giving it the vocabulary it

◄ *Benny Goodman, shown sitting in on a public school band concert, was one of the best-known native Chicago jazz musicians. The conductor in this 1954 photo is James Sylvester, Goodman's Hull House clarinet teacher.*

needed to develop. His improvised vocals on "Heebie Jeebies" inaugurated the art of scat singing; his sublime improvisations in "West End Blues," "Struttin' with Some Barbecue," and others established jazz forever as a soloist's art.

To be sure, Armstrong did not achieve this alone. The earlier migration of New Orleans musicians, including Oliver, Jelly Roll Morton, and Sidney Bechet, had made the city a hothouse for new ideas in music. As early as the mid-1920s, the Austin High Gang—an informal group including cornetist Jimmy McPartland and tenor saxophonist Bud Freeman—began to transform the New Orleans sound. The Chicagoans' exuberant rhythms and big-city sound set the stage for the ascent of Benny Goodman, who had studied clarinet at Hull House and, by the late 1930s, would be known worldwide as the King of Swing.

But it was Armstrong who lit the fuse. From his breakthroughs came such Chicago contributions to jazz as Earl Hines's piano innovations at the Grand Terrace Ballroom in the '30s; Nat "King" Cole's revolutionary trio of the '40s; the South Side's tough-tenor tradition of saxophonists, including Gene Ammons, Johnny Griffin, and Von Freeman; Sun Ra's outlandish "free jazz" musings with his Arkestra; and the birth, in 1965, of the Association for the Advancement of Creative Musicians (AACM), which gave the world such innovators as Muhal Richard Abrams, Anthony Braxton, and Henry Threadgill.

—*Howard Reich*

▲ *Tenor saxophonist Bud Freeman was a member of the Austin High Gang in the 1920s.*

◄ *Louis Armstrong (kneeling in front with trombone) came to Chicago to join King Oliver's Creole Jazz Band, shown here in 1922. From left, Honore Dutrey, Baby Dodds, Joe "King" Oliver, Armstrong, Lil Hardin (who married Armstrong in 1924), Bill Johnson, and Johnny Dodds.*

The Leopold and Loeb Case

Two precocious college boys horrify the city with their "perfect crime."

MAY 21, 1924

Bobby Franks, fourteen, was heading home for supper on this date in the elegant South Side neighborhood of Kenwood, near the University of Chicago. But only a block and a half away from his dinner table, little Bobby Franks simply disappeared. The boy had vanished into a car rented under a phony name by two precocious University of Chicago graduate students. Ten days later, there would not be man, woman, or child in Chicago who did not know the names of the murderous lads: Leopold and Loeb.

Nathan "Babe" Leopold Jr., nineteen, and Richard "Dickie" Loeb, eighteen, neighbors and lovers, were the pampered sons of prominent Kenwood families. The young men set out to commit the "perfect" slaying because they thought it would be exciting. They chose their victim at random, a fact that added to the unique horror of the crime.

On May 22, the day after he disappeared, Bobby Franks's naked body was found in a ditch along the Illinois-Indiana border. The killers had hit him over the head with a tape-wrapped chisel and suffocated him with a rag stuffed down his throat. A pair of tortoise-shell eyeglasses was found near the body. Those and the typewriter that had been used to produce a $10,000 ransom note were the killers' undoing.

► *Nathan Leopold (left) and Richard Loeb, brilliant graduate students at the University of Chicago, thought it would be exciting to kill someone at random.*

The glasses were quickly traced to Leopold, who told police he lost them while bird-watching near the murder scene days before Franks's death. Industrious reporting by two young newsmen—products of a cutthroat and rollicking era of Chicago journalism—cracked the case. *Chicago Daily News* reporters Jim Mulroy and Alvin Goldstein located Leopold's school notes, typed on the same Underwood portable as was the ransom note. Confronted with the evidence, Leopold and Loeb confessed in the early hours of May 31. Goldstein and Mulroy won a Pulitzer Prize.

The killers' wealthy parents hired legendary attorney Clarence Darrow. "Great crowds of disappointed men and women rioted and howled and attempted to fight, slug or push their way into Chief Justice [John R.] Caverly's courtroom yesterday afternoon for Clarence Darrow's opening plea to save Nathan Leopold Jr. and Richard Loeb from the rope's dangling end," said the *Tribune*. The boys pleaded guilty, but Darrow successfully persuaded the judge to spare their lives.

Less than twelve years later, thirty-year-old Loeb was murdered in prison, his throat slashed by a fellow prisoner who claimed he was fending off Loeb's homosexual advances. Loeb's murder led to one of the most famous lead paragraphs in the history of journalism, written by *Chicago Daily News* reporter Ed Lahey: "Richard Loeb, a brilliant college student and master of the English language, today ended a sentence with a proposition." Leopold spent thirty-three years in prison until his parole in 1958. He died of natural causes in Puerto Rico in 1971. He was sixty-six.

—*Ellen Warren*

▲ *Leopold's Underwood portable typewriter, a key piece of evidence in solving the case. Leopold twisted off many of the keys with pliers in an attempt to prevent it from being traced to him.*

▲ *Even in an era when murder and mayhem splashed onto the front pages of Chicago's newspapers every day, the Leopold and Loeb case stood out. Chicago's newshounds filled the press gallery of the courtroom where the trial was held.*

The Golden Age of Radio

For two decades, the radio programs that entertained America were broadcast from Chicago.

JANUARY 12, 1926

"Sam and Henry" were not the names that would make Freeman Gosden and Charles Correll famous, but they were the names of Gosden's and Correll's characters when their show was first broadcast on radio station WGN on this day. In the vaudeville tradition of white actors performing in blackface, Gosden, a former Virginia tobacco salesman, and Correll, a onetime Peoria bricklayer, performed comedy in an exaggerated black dialect.

The daily fifteen-minute show was so popular that in two years Gosden and Correll were wooed away by WMAQ and its national network at the time, Columbia Broadcasting. But the *Tribune*-owned WGN, whose call letters reflected the paper's boast to be the "World's Greatest Newspaper," retained rights to the "Sam and Henry" name. Gosden and Correll simply renamed their characters. They became "Amos 'n' Andy."

"Amos 'n' Andy" was just one of the shows that marked Chicago's golden age of radio production. In addition to a prodigious number of soap operas, "The National Barn Dance," "The Breakfast Club," "Little Orphan Annie," and "Fibber McGee and Molly" were among the other national favorites to originate from Chicago, largely because the city was home to the advertisers that sponsored the shows.

"Fibber McGee and Molly," in which Jim Jordan played the hapless, dissembling Fibber and his wife, Marian Jordan, portrayed Fibber's long-suffering wife, became the most popular show in the nation by 1941, ten years after the show began in Chicago as "Smackout" and two years after its stars took their program, along with its famous 79 Wistful Vista address, to Hollywood. WLS's "National Barn Dance," a weekly, country-theme variety show, debuted in April 1924 and remained popular for two decades before NBC dropped it in 1946.

◀ *Charles Correll (left) and Freeman Gosden in their "Sam and Henry" days, before they jumped from WGN to a national network and became "Amos 'n' Andy."*

"Amos 'n' Andy," which left the city for the West Coast in 1937, survived in a variety of formats until 1968, but as it became more popular it also became controversial. Defenders said its white actors' portrayals of underachieving blacks were little different from other ethnic humor. But critics, especially black groups, charged that the program bolstered stereotypes among the ignorant and prejudiced. Some radio historians argue that the inferior television version was the real target of protests.

After World War II, television took over radio's function of providing entertainment programs for the nation, but by then Chicago had already lost its status as a radio capital. Most shows had moved to New York or Los Angeles. Don McNeill's "The Breakfast Club," however, continued to broadcast its quintessentially Midwestern assemblage of pleasant morning banter and gentle humor from Chicago until it went off the air in 1968.

—*Steve Johnson*

▶

Jim and Marian Jordan, from Peoria, Illinois, played Fibber McGee and his long-suffering wife, Molly. McGee was famous for his overstuffed closet, while Molly's sharp rebuff, "T'ain't funny, McGee," usually silenced her mate.

◀ *Don McNeill (at the microphone) stayed on the air until 1968, long after radio's heyday.*

Municipal Airport Opens

After almost banning aviation, Chicago builds an airport that becomes the busiest in the world.

▲ *Early air-traffic controllers at Municipal Airport directed airplanes with signal flags.*

MAY 8, 1926

Chicago's first municipal airport commenced operations on this date with considerable fanfare but very little business. The first plane to land there was flown from the western suburb of Maywood by National Air Transport (later United Airlines), and immediately after the opening ceremonies it went back to Maywood Field to fly some mail to Dallas. It would be several years before Chicago could claim that Municipal Airport, which was renamed Midway Airport after World War II, was the world's busiest. In fact, it would be a couple of years before Municipal Airport would become the busiest in the Chicago area.

From the time adventurous types first took to the air in powered machines, Chicago had used just about any open space to accommodate them. White City Amusement Park, on the South Side, served as a center for airships until well after World War I. Beginning in 1909, shows, demonstrations, and races of heavier-than-air machines were held in Grant Park and at several suburban racetracks that could hold the huge crowds of curious onlookers.

Chicago almost banned aviation within its borders after the city was the site of the world's first commercial aviation disaster, in 1919. The Goodyear blimp *Wingfoot Air Express* caught fire and crashed through the skylight of Illinois Trust and Savings Bank in the Loop, killing thirteen people. By the 1920s, when the United States Post Office Department had made Chicago a center for its airmail service, the city had changed its mind about aviation. The service first used Grant Park as an airport but eventually settled at Maywood Field.

In 1922, the city opened its first permanent flying field, Chicago Aero Park, on part of the site that would become Midway, a tract of prairie on the city's Southwest Side. When it became obvious that the federal government was going to contract with private airlines for its airmail operation, Chicago decided to build a first-class facility on a square mile of land leased from the Board of Education. After its dedication, Municipal Airport remained largely deserted for a year and a half until all airmail flights were transferred there from Maywood. Within a few years, however, civic boosters were describing it as the busiest airport in the world, a position it held until the 1960s.

—*David Young*

▼ *By the late 1920s, the time of this photograph, Chicago's Municipal Airport was already being described as the nation's busiest. Eleven airmail, cargo, and passenger lines operated forty flights daily.*

The Dempsey-Tunney Fight

A championship heavyweight contest lives on as the legendary "long count" bout.

SEPTEMBER 22, 1927

It was instantly dubbed "the long count." And it has been recounted in tales both true and tall ever since the heavyweight championship fight this night in Soldier Field. Amid a screaming crowd of 104,943 spectators, reporters at ringside said it took champion Gene Tunney somewhere from twelve to fifteen seconds to regain his feet after being knocked down by former champion Jack Dempsey. It should have taken referee Dave Barry ten seconds to count out Tunney, making Dempsey a winner by knockout in the seventh round.

But Dempsey ignored the rule that he first had to go to a neutral corner. He thereby transformed those few seconds into legend. Barry escorted Dempsey to a corner and then began a delayed count. Tunney rose before it reached ten. In his autobiography,

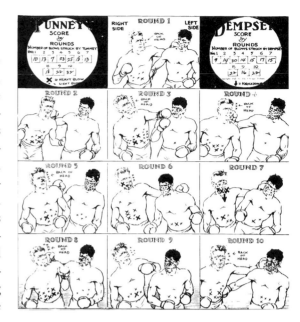

▲ Tribune *cartoonist Carey Orr drew this "scorecard" of the big fight, indicating with X's where the fighters landed blows on each other. Tunney is on the left, Dempsey on the right.*

Dempsey conceded that he forgot all about the rule: "It's hard to stop what you're doing, standing over a guy and waiting for him to get up. . . ." Tunney, who floored Dempsey briefly in the ninth, won the ten-round fight and retained the title he had won from Dempsey the year before.

In the 1920s, peacetime revelry following the devastation of World War I spawned intense love of sport. Babe Ruth in baseball, Red Grange in football, Bill Tilden and Helen Wills in tennis, Bobby Jones in golf, Gertrude Ederle and Johnny Weissmuller in swimming, and Dempsey and Tunney all emerged as "golden athletes." Seventy-four radio stations carried the Dempsey-Tunney bout to a potential audience of fifteen million listeners. Boston and Washington were among the cities where the fight was broadcast over amplifiers in public places. Throughout the fight, more than twenty-five thousand callers sought updates from the *Tribune*'s special telephone setup of one hundred trunk lines.

The paper chartered a speedboat so reporters and photographers could bypass the throng of exiting fans and hustle from the stadium to Tribune Tower in a few minutes. The day after the fight, the *Tribune* devoted most of the first twelve pages of its fifty-six-page newspaper to the story. "The verdict was accepted as sound by a majority of the vast assemblage present," the paper reported, but added, "a great cry arose from the Dempsey camp that Jack had been robbed by a slow count." Thus the "long count" began its long ride through history.

—*Michael Hirsley*

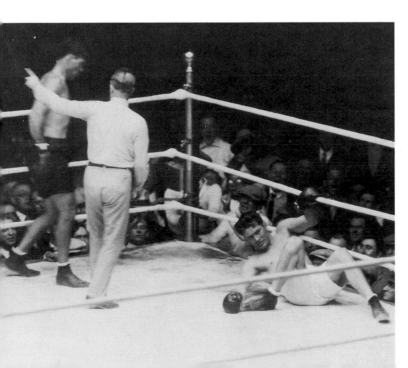

▼ *The "long count": with Gene Tunney down in the seventh round, referee Dave Barry motions Jack Dempsey to a neutral corner before he begins his count. Tunney got back up and went on to win the fight.*

The St. Valentine's Day Massacre

With one ruthless stroke, Al Capone assumes undisputed leadership of Chicago crime.

▼ *The grisly scene inside the SMC Cartage Company after gunmen dressed as policemen mowed down members of the Moran gang*

FEBRUARY 14, 1929

On this frigid morning, in an unheated brick garage at 2122 North Clark Street, seven men were lined up against a whitewashed wall and riddled with ninety bullets from submachine guns, shotguns, and a revolver. It was the most infamous of all gangland slayings in America, and it savagely achieved its purpose— the elimination of the last challenge to Al Capone for the mantle of crime boss in Chicago. By 1929, Capone's only real threat was George "Bugs" Moran, who headed his own gang and what was left of Dion O'Banion's band of bootleggers. Moran had long despised Capone, mockingly referring to him as "The Beast."

At about half past ten, four men burst into the SMC Cartage Company, a garage that Moran used for his illegal business. Two of the men were dressed as policemen. The quartet presumably announced a raid and ordered the seven men they had surprised inside the garage to line up against a wall. Then they opened fire. Witnesses, alerted by the rat-a-tat staccato of submachine guns, watched as the gunmen sped off in a black Cadillac touring car that looked like the kind police used, complete with siren, gong, and rifle rack.

The victims, killed outright or left dying in the garage, included Frank "Hock" Gusenberg, Moran's enforcer, and his brother, Peter "Goosy" Gusenberg. Four of the other victims were Moran gangsters, but the seventh dead man was Dr. Reinhardt Schwimmer, an optician who cavorted with criminals for thrills. Missing that morning was Capone's prize, Moran himself, who slept in.

Capone missed the excitement, too. Vacationing at his retreat at Palm Island, Florida, he had an alibi for his whereabouts and disclaimed knowledge of the cold-blooded killings. Few believed him. No one ever went to jail for pulling a trigger in the Clark Street garage, which was demolished in 1967. But gangland justice caught up with the suspected head of the hit team, "Machine Gun" Jack McGurn, who was gunned down in 1936 in a Milwaukee Avenue bowling alley, apparently to avenge the murders of Moran's men.

Although Moran survived the massacre, he was finished as a big criminal. For decades to come, only one mob, that of Capone and his successors, would run organized crime in Chicago. But the St. Valentine's Day Massacre shocked a city that had been numbed by "Roaring '20s" gang warfare over control of illegal beer and whiskey distribution. "These murders went out of the comprehension of a civilized city," the *Tribune* editorialized. "The butchering of seven men by open daylight raises this question for Chicago: Is it helpless?" In the following years, Capone and his henchmen were to become the targets of ambitious prosecutors.

—*John O'Brien*

▲ *The massacre finished George "Bugs" Moran as a Capone rival.*

▲ *Onlookers watch police remove the bodies from the garage on North Clark Street. The St. Valentine's Day shootings shocked a populace that had grown numb to gangland killings.*

The 1929 Stock Market Crash

The Roaring Twenties grind to a halt, and a new era of hard times begins.

▼ *A long line forms outside Al Capone's free lunchroom in 1930 on the near South Side. Throughout the 1930s, such scenes made up the gray, grim backdrop of life.*

OCTOBER 29, 1929

Bankers and brokers on LaSalle Street thought the town's hoodlums were shooting their way into brokerage offices and promptly called police. The noise reverberating in the canyon of office towers turned out to be a boy's firecracker. All the police found were law-abiding citizens with nerves rubbed raw by the October stock market crash. No one living through the market break, which began in earnest a week earlier and reached its biggest one-day loss on this date, realized what was happening. The market had peaked in early September and days of wild selling often were followed by equally frenzied "bargain-hunting" rallies.

Chicago, a town built—and rebuilt—on speculation, was neither deterred by speculative excesses nor cowed by speculative losses. For weeks before the crash, investors who on one day jammed brokerage offices to sell crowded in the next day to buy. The Railroad Shares Corporation, a sort of mutual fund for railroad stocks traded on the Chicago Stock Exchange, advertised on October 31 that the crash presented "the best opportunities for Chicago people to lay the foundation for fortunes since they bought real estate from the Indians."

The *Tribune* banner headline of October 30 read STOCK SLUMP ENDS IN RALLY. The next day, the paper declared MARKET SCARE OVER. But the market slump was not. Share prices slid through mid-November. Prices rebounded in early 1930, but the rout resumed. When it ended in 1932, stocks had fallen by 85 percent. During the October shocks, utilities magnate Samuel Insull and Julius Rosenwald, chairman of Sears, Roebuck and Company, helped employees meet brokers' demands for payment for stocks bought on margin. Comedian Eddie Cantor joked that he asked Rosenwald for a job so that he, too, could cover his stock loans. As Cantor told it, Rosenwald agreed to hire him but he could not afford the train fare to Chicago.

▲ *Newspaper headlines reflected the uncertainty of the days leading up to October 29, "Black Tuesday," the day of the stock market's biggest loss. The next day,* Variety *carried its classic headline.*

▼ *A young woman buys an apple from an unemployed veteran on South Wells Street in 1930. With the onset of the Great Depression, unemployment hit 25 percent nationally.*

By the fall of 1929, the farm belt was already in a depression; and the market break signaled that the downturn was spreading to the cities. Nationally, unemployment reached 25 percent. More than 160 banks in the Chicago area failed, and in the first half of 1931 alone, nearly 1,400 families were evicted. Jobless men slept along lower Wacker Drive and renamed it the Hoover Hotel in honor of the country's president. A new form of political spoils, handed out by corrupt judges, was receiverships awarded to oversee—which meant "loot"—bankrupt real estate. Al Capone sponsored soup lines. Chicago's boom times—for the 1920s had roared not just in the speakeasies and stock markets but also in real estate and industry—had come to an abrupt end. For the next dozen years, the Great Depression would be the gray, grim backdrop of life.

—Bill Barnhart

A WISE ECONOMIST ASKS A QUESTION

"I DID"

"BUT WHY DIDN'T YOU SAVE SOME MONEY FOR THE FUTURE, WHEN TIMES WERE GOOD?"

VICTIM OF BANK FAILURE

◄ Tribune *editorial cartoonist John T. McCutcheon won the Pulitzer Prize in 1932 for this depiction of the country's economic plight.*

HELP A VET BUY AN APPLE 5¢

The Shooting of Jake Lingle

A reporter who always got the story, Lingle had better sources than he should have.

▲ *Alfred "Jake" Lingle was a $65-dollar-a-week reporter, but he had $1,400 in his pocket when he was slain.*

JUNE 9, 1930

Alfred "Jake" Lingle was part of the crowd that filled the pedestrian walkway underneath Michigan Avenue on the afternoon of this late spring day. Lingle, a *Tribune* police reporter, was heading for the Illinois Central station at Randolph Street to catch the 1:30 P.M. express to the Washington Park racetrack, in south suburban Homewood. An ace at covering sensational crime stories, he was about to become one. A tall, blond man walked up behind him and put a bullet through his head. Lingle's killer paused over the body. Then he dropped the murder weapon, a .38 caliber revolver, and got away.

Lingle epitomized the journalism of his day, cavorting with cops and robbers and working his sources in speakeasies. A street reporter, he never rolled paper through a typewriter. As in *The Front Page*, the Ben Hecht–Charles MacArthur play about Chicago journalism, Lingle phoned in scoops to rewrite men. The popular play was a work of fiction, but it was based on fact. The world of Chicago newspapers was viciously competitive, frequently unscrupulous, and not too worried about the truth.

But even in that era, Lingle turned out to be exceptional. In the aftermath of his shooting, Chicago newspapers decried the slaying as a mob attempt to silence the press. But as the reporter's mysterious private life came to light, a different picture developed. He was paid $65 a week but had an annual income of $60,000. When he was killed, he had $1,400 in his pocket. Lingle's friends ranged from politicians and city payrollers to the henchmen of crime boss Al Capone. "Big Al" himself thought enough of Jake to give him a diamond-studded belt buckle. Lingle, as the *Tribune* reported, had been a middleman for a variety of characters seeking favors from Capone and the police commissioner, who resigned after the story broke. "A newspaper," *Tribune* city editor Robert M. Lee wrote with an almost audible sigh, "is the least likely to hear bad news about its own."

As for Lingle's killer, police rounded up 664 minor hoodlums. Nothing but headlines came of it. Then, in January 1931, Chicago detectives got a tip and arrested a St. Louis gunman, Leo V. Brothers. Seven witnesses fingered him as the shooter; seven others swore he was not the man. Brothers was convicted, but he received the minimum sentence for murder then—fourteen years. He served eight of them, his mouth shut the whole time. The questions of who wanted Lingle killed and why were never answered.

—*John O'Brien*

◄ *The scene in the tunnel under Michigan Avenue leading to the Illinois Central train station at Randolph Street shortly after Lingle was shot. He died clutching a copy of the* Racing Form.

Bushman Comes to Chicago

He was Lincoln Park Zoo's most popular resident, but not always its best tempered.

AUGUST 15, 1930

In 1930, most African animals were exotic creatures that few Americans had seen. When an orphaned infant gorilla named Bushman arrived at Lincoln Park Zoo on this date, he was said to be the first one west of the Potomac River. He quickly became an international attraction. He appeared in newsreels. The nation's zoo directors voted him "the most outstanding animal in any zoo in the world and the most valuable." A Marine Corps reserve battalion named him the gorilla that would be most welcome in establishing a beachhead.

Taken from the Cameroons, in West Africa, Bushman was sold to the zoo for $3,500 by a Presbyterian missionary and an animal trader. He looked, *Tribune* writer Edward Barry wrote in 1947, "like a nightmare that escaped from darkness into daylight and has exchanged its insubstantial form for 550 pounds of solid flesh. His face is one that might be expected to gloat through the troubled dreams that follow overindulgence. His hand is the kind of thing a sleeper sees reaching for him just before he wakes up screaming."

Photographed often, the solitary animal was a temperamental subject, often hurling food and his own dung at photographers. Those who had been pelted claimed the gorilla's aim was more accurate than that of any Cubs or Sox pitcher.

Although he may not have always enjoyed the limelight, Bushman was a publicity godsend to the zoo, which had opened in 1868 with a pair of swans donated by New York's Central Park. Hemmed in on just thirty-five acres, Lincoln Park Zoo became an international center for gorilla breeding as well as a popular city attraction. Its suburban counterpart, Brookfield Zoo, which sprawls over 216 acres, has emphasized naturalistic surroundings since its opening in 1934.

No other animal in a Chicago zoo has ever drawn the crowds as Bushman did in his stark steel cage. On a single June day in 1950, about 120,000 people flocked to see Bushman when he was thought to be dying. The gorilla rallied and in October 1950 escaped from his cage through an unlocked door. He roamed a kitchen and corridor for nearly three hours before a harmless garter snake frightened him back into his cage. Bushman died on New Year's Day 1951, and for weeks mourners filed past his cage. His mounted remains are displayed at the Field Museum.

—*Cindy Schreuder*

◀ *Bushman in 1942, looking like the star that he was*

Capone's Downfall

He got away with murder, but taxes trip up "the flower of the noble experiment."

OCTOBER 24, 1931

By the time he turned thirty-two in 1931, Alphonse Capone virtually owned Chicago. So great was his power—bought and paid for in police stations, courtrooms, and at City Hall—that even the president of the United States was taking notice. Herbert Hoover had quietly unleashed Treasury agents on "Scarface," telling them, "Remember, now, I want that Capone man in jail."

For Capone, dubbed "Public Enemy Number One" in June by the Chicago Crime Commission, 1931 was pivotal. That year, the gangster chieftain was put on trial and convicted—not of murder and mayhem, but of evading $182,000 in taxes on income of $915,000 for the years 1925, 1926, and 1927. The prosecution's evidence was developed with the help of an obscure Treasury agent named Eliot Ness and his squad of federal revenue investigators, later known as the "Untouchables" because they could not be bribed. They produced various bills that showed Capone's presumed income. For example, the mob boss ran up $3,141.50 in charges on his Miami telephone in one seven-month period, spent up to $250 a week on meat when sirloin steak cost thirty-three cents a pound, and gave $58,000 to a police widows' and orphans' fund in 1925.

"I guess it's all over," Capone muttered on this date, when he was sentenced to eleven years by U.S. District Judge James Wilkerson, who also imposed a $50,000 fine. It was. But, noted the *Tribune* in an editorial, the law that produced him was not. "Without the Volstead act [the law that enforced the provisions of the Eighteenth Amendment, which prohibited the manufacture and sale of alcoholic beverages], he could not have existed. With it he was a predetermined product. For any one who could see, he was the flower of the noble experiment."

Capone vanished behind prison walls. When he got out in 1939, ill and despondent, he headed for his winter home on Palm Island, Florida. There he remained until his death in 1947 from the lingering effects of syphilis. Capone's downfall was the start of a long series of crackdowns and jailings aimed at breaking up the Chicago crime family that he and his henchmen founded in the 1920s. But it remained a part of the city's fabric, and over the years Capone's successors diversified their territory to include a large piece of Las Vegas gambling. Even in the 1990s, Chicago gangsters remained active in gambling, extortion, and loan-shark rackets as well as in bankrolling, if not actively dealing in, illegal drugs.

—*John O'Brien*

▲ *Still free—but looking nervous—Al Capone, flanked by his attorneys, leaves court during his trial for income tax evasion.*

▶

Eliot Ness led a squad of federal agents, later known as the "Untouchables," who developed the evidence for the prosecution.

FDR's Nomination

In a crucial election year, Roosevelt flies to Chicago and calls for a New Deal.

JULY 1, 1932

Chicago was the center of the American political universe in the summer of 1932, hosting both the Democratic and Republican presidential nominating conventions. "For the next three weeks Chicago will be in the spotlight," the *Tribune* declared. "By newspaper and radio the American audience will follow with breathless interest the unfolding of the plot of the quadrennial thriller."

With the nation mired in its worst economic crisis, the election would be one of the most crucial in the country's history, and the two parties would offer dramatically different candidates. A dispirited GOP trooped into the new Chicago Stadium to renominate President Herbert Hoover, who preached "rugged individualism" as a way for Americans to see themselves through the bad times. Two weeks later, eight candidates turned up at the Democratic convention—also held in the Stadium—to challenge the early frontrunner, New York Governor Franklin Delano Roosevelt, who called for massive government intervention to end the Depression.

The biggest threat to FDR came from Al Smith, who had been the 1928 Democratic nominee. Smith's strategy was to deadlock the convention and give control of the nomination to party leaders, many of whom were wary of Roosevelt's ideas about social and government reforms. Roosevelt, Smith asserted, "can't get elected."

Through three tedious roll calls, the Roosevelt forces bartered with delegations and finally put their man over the top on the fourth try when House Speaker John Nance Garner of Texas folded his candidacy in exchange for the vice-presidential nomination.

After winning the nomination on this date, Roosevelt boarded a trimotor plane in Albany, New York, and flew to Chicago for a tradition-breaking address to the convention. "These are unprecedented and unusual times," Roosevelt said. "May this [appearance] be the symbol of my intention to be honest and to avoid all hypocrisy or sham." Roosevelt, who would trounce Hoover and be nominated in Chicago again in 1940 and 1944, summoned the nation to battle back from despair. "I pledge you, I pledge myself, to a New Deal for the American people," he said, introducing the name for the wide-ranging government programs that would be created to fight the Depression. "Let us all here assembled constitute ourselves prophets of a new order of competence and courage."

—*Thomas Hardy*

◄ *After winning the nomination, Roosevelt broke precedent and flew to Chicago to address the convention. Here he accepts congratulations from the Democratic donkey. Seated next to Roosevelt is Chicago Mayor Anton Cermak.*

The Birth of Gospel Music

A double tragedy leads blues pianist Thomas Dorsey to create a music of faith.

AUGUST 26, 1932

Were it not for the tragedy that befell Thomas A. Dorsey on this date, the world might never have known the glorious sound of gospel music. Dorsey, who was born outside Atlanta in 1899 and moved to Chicago as a teenager, already was a popular blues pianist around town. He had toured with Ma Rainey throughout the Roaring Twenties and sold millions of copies of his blues song, "It's Tight Like That." Then his life was shattered. While on the road, Dorsey was informed that his wife had died during childbirth. Rushing home, he learned that their child, too, had died.

"My wife died and the baby died, and I had my life's hope in the baby," Dorsey said later. "I lost quite a bit of trust. I lost a lot of confidence in the Lord or somebody. It was quite a while before I could get myself together." When he did, Dorsey cast aside the blues life and poured his musical gifts into writing songs of faith. He had dabbled in religious music before, but now it became his passion, prompting him to write a type of religious song never heard before. By introducing syncopated rhythms, lamenting vocal lines, and other blues elements to religious music, Dorsey invented the gospel song—a music neither totally sacred nor wholly secular.

Just one month after his personal disaster, Dorsey penned "Take My Hand, Precious Lord," which would become one of the most popular of all gospel songs. Over the years, he wrote such anthems as "Peace in the Valley," "Today," and "Search Me, Lord." Some churchgoers balked at Dorsey's steeped-in-blues, Jazz Age church songs, but the music eventually caught on in churches across the South Side. For years the radiant tunes simply were called "Dorseys." After establishing gospel music at Pilgrim Baptist Church, at 33rd Street and Indiana Avenue, he created the National Convention of Gospel Choirs and Choruses. He started the first gospel publishing company and staged the first

◄ *Thomas Dorsey, photographed in about 1929, was a popular blues pianist before his life was shattered in 1932. He devoted the rest of his life to gospel music, writing such anthems as "Take My Hand, Precious Lord" and teaching the first generation of gospel singers.*

commercial gospel concerts—all in the 1930s. Soon the South Side was the epicenter of gospel music.

It was Dorsey who coached, trained, and inspired the first generation of gospel singers, with Chicago greats such as Roberta Martin, Sallie Martin, Clara Ward, and Mahalia Jackson all taking the Dorsey sound to churches and concert halls around the world. The gospel stars who followed—including James Cleveland, the Edwin Hawkins Singers (who hit the pop charts with "Oh, Happy Day" in 1969), the Soul Stirrers, Albertina Walker's Caravans, the Barrett Sisters, Shirley Caesar, Inez Andrews, and Bessie Griffin—all built upon Dorsey's innovations. Gospel music today is an international industry, its sound having evolved into something considerably more high-tech than the sweet, piano-and-tambourine settings of Dorsey's youth. Yet the music owes its origins and its flowering to Dorsey, who created an entire genre of music and taught the world how to sing it.

—*Howard Reich*

▲ *Dorsey sent Sallie Martin, called the "Queen of Gospel," on solo tours around the country. Her charismatic performances won gospel converts coast to coast. In turn, Martin, shown performing in Chicago's Grant Park in 1980, persuaded Dorsey to publish his works.*

◀ *The Soul Stirrers, a pioneering Chicago gospel group, set the stage for the sweet-toned vocal quartets of popular and swing music in the 1940s and 1950s.*

The Called Shot

Babe Ruth hits the most argued-about home run of his career.

OCTOBER 1, 1932

Despite the decades, the debate will not die. Did Babe Ruth call his shot or not? It happened—if it really did happen—while Ruth was at the plate at Wrigley Field in the third game of the 1932 World Series. The score was 4–4. The New York Yankees had won the first two games in New York and would sweep the series in four.

The famous slugger was fighting off intense heckling from the Cubs' bench and assorted fruits and vegetables from the stands when he took a strike from the pitcher Charlie Root in the fifth inning. Ruth held up an inoffensive finger and said to Chicago catcher Gabby Hartnett, "It only takes one to hit it." Ruth watched a second called strike.

Here's where things get fuzzy. According to many players and eyewitnesses, Ruth then pointed toward Root and hollered something unpleasant. Or he held up two fingers and hollered something unpleasant at the Cubs' dugout. Or he held up one finger and pointed directly to center field. Or he first held up two fingers and then thrust dramatically with one finger toward the bleachers in center field.

Westbrook Pegler, who thought Ruth was reacting to riding from Cubs pitcher Guy Bush on the bench, saw it this way in his *Tribune* column the next day: "Then, with a warning gesture of his hand to Bush, he sent him the signal for the customers to see. 'Now,' it said, 'this is the one. Look!' And that one went riding in the longest home run ever hit in the park."

Root went to his grave scoffing at the "called shot" story. And Ruth? "The ball just went on and on and on," he said in his 1948 autobiography, "and hit far up in the center-field bleachers in exactly the spot I had pointed to." On the other hand, he also said he did not call the shot. "Hell no," he said in a 1933 interview. "Only a damned fool would do a thing like that."

"As memory dimmed," wrote baseball writer Tom Meany, who was there, "the Babe wasn't sure whether he called his shot or not, but he had no doubt that night [after the game] that he had hit the ball where he pointed."

So did Babe Ruth call his shot? It's your call.

—Alan Solomon

▲ *Babe Ruth is at the plate in these stills, taken from a home movie shot by spectator Matt Kandle at Wrigley Field. At the critical moment of the "called shot" (above), he is gesturing with his right hand. But what does the gesture mean? Ruth then hits the next pitch for a home run (below).*

The Shooting of Anton Cermak

The mayor who created the city's Democratic machine takes an assassin's bullet intended for Franklin Roosevelt.

FEBRUARY 15, 1933

Two notable immigrants stood in the crowd when President-elect Franklin D. Roosevelt emerged from a yacht in Miami on this date after a fishing trip in the Bahamas. One was Chicago Mayor Anton J. Cermak, a Bohemian-born politician who was the master builder of the city's Democratic Party. The other was Giuseppe Zangara, an Italian immigrant with a ferocious hatred for politicians and their governments. After a short speech, Roosevelt sat atop the backseat of a convertible and motioned Cermak to his side.

As the two spoke privately, Zangara raised a handgun and began shooting. He was aiming for Roosevelt, but he hit Cermak and four others. The crowd collapsed on Zangara, wrestling the gun from his hands and beating him. Cermak was helped into Roosevelt's car, which sped to the hospital. During that ride, with Roosevelt at his side, Cermak uttered his famous line: "I am glad it was me instead of you." Cermak died on March 6. Zangara, who laughed when he was sentenced to die, was executed on March 20.

Cermak, a man who once sold firewood out of a wagon, had climbed his way up the political ranks, beginning in 1902 when he was elected to the state legislature. He went on to win posts as alderman, municipal bailiff, and Cook County Board president. In 1931, he was elected Chicago's thirty-sixth mayor, defeating scandal-plagued Republican William Hale "Big Bill" Thompson and establishing a Democratic stranglehold on the mayor's office. Cermak built the strength of the Democratic Party by bringing together diverse factions, using clout and patronage to punish and reward. He could be ruthless but also conciliatory.

His own rewards, it is widely held, came from real-estate deals and bootlegging. While Cermak was in the hospital after the shooting, the *Tribune* wrote: "We think he faced his problems courageously and did the best that was in him to put this punch drunk city back on its feet, to restore its reputation in the eyes of the world, to reestablish its credit, to relieve its taxpayers and to pay its debts." Edward J. Kelly, president of the South Park Board, was selected to succeed Cermak by his fellow Democrats in the City Council. Kelly won his first full term in 1935 and, fully in charge of the powerful Democratic machine Cermak had bequeathed him, ruled City Hall for another twelve years.

—*Peter Kendall*

▲ *Assassin Giuseppe Zangara, an Italian immigrant with a ferocious hatred for politicians, strikes a defiant pose in a Miami jail. He was executed two weeks after Cermak's death.*

◄ *Chicago Mayor Anton Cermak is helped after being shot in a Miami park while talking to President-elect Franklin Roosevelt.*

"A Century of Progress"

Science and show biz come together to revive a city worn weary by the Depression.

MAY 27, 1933

"A Century of Progress," Chicago's second World's Fair, opened on this date with standard pageantry: a parade with marching bands, smartly uniformed policemen, and a beauty queen from Racine, Wisconsin, glowingly reported to have been blessed with violet eyes. In the evening came the dramatic touch: rays from the star Arcturus sparked floodlights that illuminated the cloudy, drizzly night sky.

Arcturus had been chosen because its light takes about forty years to reach the Earth, and forty years had passed since Chicago's Columbian Exposition in 1893. Harnessing the energy of a star to switch on the fair's lights was meant to symbolize the exhibition's theme of scientific progress, but the stunt also had that dash of show biz that made the fair a wildly popular attraction for a city frayed and fractured by the Depression.

It had been one hundred years since a muddy patch of wild onions on the banks of the Chicago River had been incorporated. The exhibition was meant to show what that city had made of itself. Or, as the *Tribune* put it, "A community which, 100 years ago, numbered but 250 Yankees, Indians and halfbreeds . . . today is a world metropolis with a population of 3½ millions drawn from the wide, wide world."

The exhibition's gleaming Art Deco buildings, made of such inexpensive materials as sheet metal and prestressed concrete, were constructed on new land that had been created by filling in Lake Michigan. For 50 cents admission, fairgoers could wander among eighty-two miles of exhibits that ranged from highbrow—the chemistry of sulfur in the Hall of Science—to decidedly lowbrow—trained fleas on the midway. For the brave of heart, a sky ride stretched between two spidery towers, one on the mainland and one on Northerly Island. In a Buck Rogers vision of what future travel might be like, streamlined cars shot back and forth along steel cables two hundred feet above the fairgrounds.

◀ The "Century of Progress" fairgrounds, shown here in 1933, stretched along the lakefront from the Adler Planetarium to 37th Street. In the left foreground is the Travel and Transport building, which featured a roof that "breathed."

◀ Unlike the Columbian Exposition, whose architecture looked back to the Classical Age, the buildings at "A Century of Progress" were meant to represent the architecture of the future.

▶ *Rides and scientific
exhibits were fine, but
the most popular
attraction at the fair
was fan dancer
Sally Rand.*

Throughout the fair, the emphasis was on the modern and futuristic. The roof of the Travel and Transport building was the "dome that breathes." Held up by a dozen cables attached to towers, the roof could rise or sink by a foot and a half, depending on air pressure or the weight of snow.

Along the midway was much traditional carnival fare, such as Jo-Jo the Dog-Faced Boy. It was also the scene of an instant fair sensation: fan dancer Sally Rand, who appeared nightly in nothing but strategically placed feathers. Rand, who noted that she had not been out of work since taking her clothes off, was hauled into court, but Judge Joseph B. David refused to issue an injunction against her. "Lots of people in this community would like to put pants on horses," he said. Still, the judge did not have much use for Sally's audience, either. "If you ask me, they are just a lot of boobs come to see a woman wiggle with a fan or without fig leaves. But we have the boobs and we have a right to cater to them."

*Barney Ross, a boxing champion
of the 1930s, enjoys some
low-tech fun and an ice cream
cone at the futuristic fair.* ▶

▲ *With one hundred thousand people streaming into the fairgrounds daily, the Midway,
shown here during the fair's second year, was almost always crowded.*

Judged a resounding success in 1933, the fair reopened for a second year. In its
two seasons, it drew 38,867,000 visitors and turned a profit, a remarkable feat for
any World's Fair. When the gates closed for the last time, the buildings came down,
and the Depression was still on. But while it lasted, "A Century of Progress" was a
much-needed diversion and a shining symbol of what the future might be.

—*Ellen Warren*

The Museum of Science and Industry

A grand reminder of the past becomes home to an ever-changing tribute to technology.

MAY 27, 1933

A director of the Museum of Science and Industry once told the nation's industrial leaders that he hoped the museum "would never be finished." And indeed, since its official opening on this day, this homage to the Industrial Revolution, by necessity, has constantly changed to keep up with the times. Because the museum evolves and has such a vast variety of exhibits, it keeps Chicagoans and tourists coming back. Year in and year out, it has remained one of the most popular destinations in the metropolitan area.

The vast Greek classical structure in Jackson Park is the only surviving building from the 1893 World's Columbian Exposition. Designed by Charles B. Atwood, it was then called the Palace of Fine Arts. Architects of the day said that its copper-clad domes and graceful lines rivaled the Parthenon. Because it housed valuable artworks, it was the only fireproof building at the fair. After the exposition, it housed the early collections of the Field Museum of Natural History, but the Field moved to Grant Park in 1921 and the building deteriorated rapidly.

Its savior came in 1926 in the form of industrialist and philanthropist Julius Rosenwald, president of Sears, Roebuck and Company. Rosenwald spearheaded an $8 million campaign—using both private and public funds—to refurbish the build-

▲ *Sears mogul Julius Rosenwald spearheaded an $8 million campaign to establish the museum.*

ing into a world-class industrial museum. It was completed in time for the opening of the 1933 "Century of Progress" World's Fair.

Since then, the museum's vast halls have echoed loudly with the clanking of gears, screeching of horns, and other mechanical moving parts of the more than two thousand exhibits on display. Visitors have paused in front of a giant black locomotive, circa 1893; crept through the inner workings of a dark coal mine dating to 1933; and jostled one another inside the claustrophobic U-505, a captured German submarine from World War II.

A metal capsule that dates from 1934 served as the gondola of a balloon that allowed scientists to penetrate the stratosphere 11.5 miles above the earth. And a sixty-five-foot-high version of Foucault's pendulum offers mysterious proof of the rotation of the earth. Uncounted feet have worn a path through a giant model of a beating human heart large enough to serve a body twenty-eight stories tall. People have stepped gingerly aboard a simulated flight deck of a navy aircraft carrier and explored a Boeing 727 jet, its ninety thousand pounds suspended from a balcony. Up-to-the-minute scientific exhibits provide insights into the workings of the human brain, genetic diseases, and the HIV virus.

In the mid-1990s, the museum announced plans for a modern underground parking garage. The concrete parking lot that for decades has sprawled in front of the museum's north side was to be turned back into an inviting expanse of green, the way its original designers planned it.

—*LeAnn Spencer*

▲ *The museum's many hands-on exhibits, such as this 1940s-era scale-model steam shovel, have proven popular with children.*

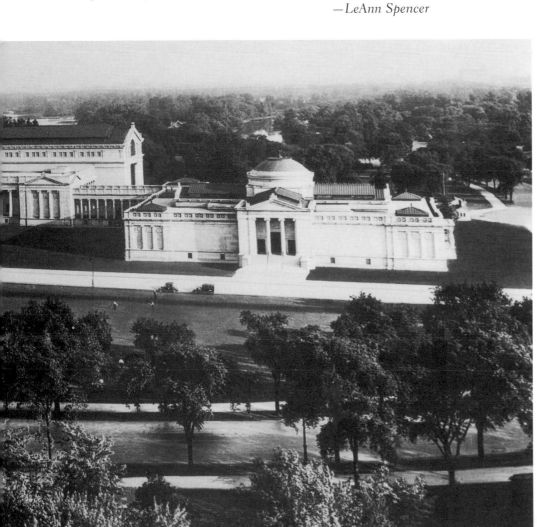

◄ *The classical Greek building, erected as a temporary structure in 1893 for the World's Columbian Exposition, had to be rebuilt of permanent materials before the Museum of Science and Industry could move in. This view dates from the 1930s, before the lawn was replaced with a parking lot.*

The First All-Star Game

Arch Ward creates baseball's annual showcase, and Babe Ruth christens it.

▼ *Lou Gehrig (left) and White Sox batboy John McBride congratulate Babe Ruth after his home run, the first in All-Star history.*

JULY 6, 1933

While the "Century of Progress" World's Fair was in full swing, an event occurred on this day that changed baseball history: the first All-Star game. A few months earlier, Chicago Mayor Edward J. Kelly had gone to Colonel Robert R. McCormick, publisher of the *Tribune*, with an idea. He wanted to arrange a sports event as an adjunct to the fair. "'We've got the man right here,' McCormick said. Ten minutes later sports editor Arch Ward was in McCormick's office," as Ward's biographer, Tom Littlewood, recounted the meeting.

Ward knew what he wanted: a matchup of the best players in the American and National Leagues. In April, he went to the Michigan Avenue headquarters of American League President Will Harridge. The office of baseball commissioner Kenesaw Mountain Landis was four blocks closer. Ward walked the extra half-mile. Landis was an autocrat, and Ward was wise enough to realize that if it was not Landis's idea, more than likely it would die aborning. Harridge had a more agreeable personality and would give the editor a better reception. The *Tribune* would underwrite the game against loss, Ward told Harridge, and its sports department would tabulate the votes from fans to select the starting teams. Harridge agreed to place it on the agenda of the next American League owners' meeting. All eight supported the idea.

Ward immediately began cultivating the National League owners, but he had to pressure three holdouts—the St. Louis Cardinals, New York Giants, and Boston Braves. According to Littlewood, Ward told the Boston owner, the last holdout, "We're going to announce this game the day after tomorrow, and either we're going to say there is a game or that we almost had one because of you. Can you and the National League stand that kind of publicity?"

The game, played at Comiskey Park in ideal weather, brought out a capacity crowd of 47,595 fans to see such players as Lou Gehrig, Gabby Hartnett, Al Simmons, and Jimmy Foxx. Appropriately, Babe Ruth, baseball's greatest player, was the star in a 4–2 American League victory. Wild Bill Hallahan, pitching for the National League, walked Charlie Gehringer in the third inning. Ruth, the next batter, stroked a line drive into the right-field seats, the first home run in All-Star history. Arch Ward's game has been an annual fixture ever since.

—*Jerome Holtzman*

▲ *With a combination of diplomacy and arm twisting,* Tribune *sports editor Arch Ward got both baseball leagues to agree to the All-Star game.*

Repeal of Prohibition

The city celebrates the death of America's "noble experiment."

December 5, 1933

Chicago was never thirstier than at a few minutes before 4:32 P.M. on this date, as thousands waited for the repeal of the Eighteenth Amendment to end a drought that had lasted thirteen years, ten months, and nineteen days. Though a number of neighborhood taverns—mostly former speakeasies—jumped the gun by a few hours, many large downtown establishments kept patrons waiting until the exact minute the new law went into effect. Huge crowds lined up five and six deep along bars, and they had stamina, staying into the early morning hours.

An obvious flop, Prohibition nonetheless continued to hang on until the onset of the Depression and the election of Franklin Roosevelt. Its final undoing came at the hands of Utah, which became the thirty-sixth state to ratify repeal in the form of the Twenty-First Amendment.

▲ *The throng at the Palmer House bar welcomes the return of legal liquor. Oscar Mayer, the meatpacking tycoon, was said to be the first person served when the bar reopened.*

The celebration was relatively sedate. Only twenty-seven people were arrested for intoxication, including a lawyer named Raymond Canady, who was fined $1 for punching a waiter. Downtown hotels such as the Congress and the Sherman House served hundreds of cases of alcohol to thousands of unbridled drinkers—both male and female. The increase in female customers troubled many older bartenders, with one complaining, "If the talk gets rough, we'll have to defend the ladies."

If the day had a star it was Oscar Mayer. The seventy-five-year-old meatpacking tycoon was cited by newspapers as the first person served when the Palmer House bar reopened. He also was featured in a photo taken somewhat later, happily drinking champagne with friends at the Red Star Inn on North Clark Street.

Repeal may have ended Prohibition, but the "noble experiment" had left its mark. Organized crime had grown fat on huge profits from its illicit trade in outlawed alcohol, and in doing so it extended its reach deeper into American life.

—*Rick Kogan*

John Dillinger's Death

The brazen bank robber, betrayed by "The Woman in Red," is gunned down in a North Side alley.

JULY 22, 1934

Twenty-three people died of the heat on this date, but the death that drew by far the most attention was that of a thirty-one-year-old Indiana man who, on his birthday a month earlier, had been declared Public Enemy Number One by the Federal Bureau of Investigation. At the time of his death, handsome, daring bank robber John Herbert Dillinger was as famous as anyone in America.

In little more than a year, Dillinger robbed several banks, escaped from two jails, eluded police traps, and killed at least one policeman. Despite Justice Department rewards totaling $15,000, he lived an unnoticed and relatively normal life on Chicago's North Side. He often had dinner at the Seminary Restaurant, at the corner of Lincoln and Fullerton Avenues. He once went to a Cubs game at Wrigley Field and pulled one of his trademark bravado stunts by saying hello to his lawyer, who was chatting with a policeman. His girlfriend was a redheaded waitress named Polly Hamilton; Polly's landlady, Anna Sage, who was to become known legendarily though inaccurately as "The Woman in Red," was Dillinger's confidante and knew his identity.

In the heat of that July, movie houses advertised that they were "air cooled." Perhaps that's what made Dillinger decide to take Polly and Anna to a movie in the evening. Dillinger told the women he wanted to go to the Biograph Theater, on Lincoln Avenue, to see *Manhattan Melodrama*, starring William Powell and Clark Gable. Anna Sage told the law.

▼ *The scene on Lincoln Avenue shortly after Dillinger died in a shootout. He and two women had seen* Manhattan Melodrama *at the Biograph Theater.*

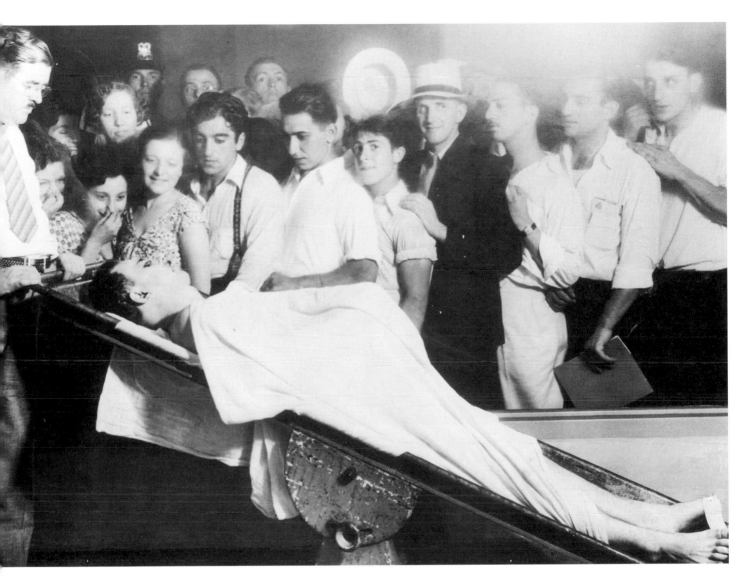

Sage, who had come to the United States from Romania as Ana Cumpanas, was a successful operator of houses of prostitution. Deportation proceedings had been started against her, but when Dillinger admitted his identity to her, she must have thought she had been given a ticket to remain in this country.

Dillinger and the two women—Anna Sage in an orange skirt that looked red in the light of the marquee—left the Biograph at about ten-thirty. More than twenty lawmen were waiting. As the three walked south on Lincoln Avenue, Dillinger realized he was walking into a trap and bolted for the alley. Shots rang out. One bullet hit Dillinger in the back of the neck and exited through his right eye. That shot killed him.

"His insouciance, his cynical attitudes, his put-on good humor . . . were as much a part of the legend of this super-criminal as his uncanny ability to shoot his way out of traps or his unfaltering courage in battle," according to the *Tribune*.

Dillinger was buried in a cemetery in Crown Point, Indiana, resting with President Benjamin Harrison, three vice presidents, two governors, and poet James Whitcomb Riley. Anna Sage died in 1947 in Romania, to which she had been deported.

—*Charles Leroux*

▲ *Public Enemy Number One on display at the Cook County Morgue. Coroner Frank J. Walsh shows off John Dillinger's body to a crowd of curious Chicagoans, who are standing on the other side of a glass panel.*

The Republic Steel Strike

A bloody chapter in the movement to unionize workers unfolds outside a Chicago steel mill.

▼ *The confrontation between strikers and police turns violent as strikers throw bricks and stones and the police fire tear gas.*

MAY 30, 1937

Carrying American flags and singing union songs, the marchers—men, women, and a few youngsters—formed a long line as they crossed the grassy field. Their destination was the main gate at Republic Steel's South Chicago plant on the city's Southeast Side, but facing them were about 150 Chicago policemen. It was a hot and sticky Memorial Day afternoon that soon would get even hotter.

Beyond the police was the massive steel plant, the only one in the Chicago area that had stayed open during a bitter nationwide showdown between a number of steel companies and the Steel Workers Organizing Committee, which was trying to unionize the plants. A combative mood was in the air. The nascent steelworkers union was determined to win a contract with the steel firms. The owners were equally determined not to surrender to the union. Swinging riot clubs, the police had turned back another group of demonstrators two days earlier. Eighteen marchers had been injured, three seriously.

This time, as about two hundred of the marchers approached the police, angry words were exchanged. Rocks and bricks thrown by the strikers brought a flurry of tear gas from the police. Gunfire then broke out, and the marchers scattered as the police charged into their line. By the time things calmed down, ten marchers lay dead. Forty police were injured. At least sixty marchers were hurt or wounded, some of them shot from behind. Police said they were fired upon by the strikers first, but hospital reports showed no gun wounds among the policemen.

In the aftermath, charges and countercharges flew back and forth. Police said the march had been well orchestrated. The demonstrators said they had acted spontaneously, stirred by anger over the number of persons hurt by police during the prior confrontation. City and police officials denied charges of police brutality and blamed the whole incident on Communists and radicals. A Paramount photographer captured some of the mayhem, but the company refused to release the newsreel, saying it might incite audiences to riot. The *St. Louis Post-Dispatch* published an account of someone who had seen the suppressed film, describing the police firing on the marchers without warning and beating them up in a "businesslike" way. A congressional investigation later condemned the police for using excessive force.

Shortly after Memorial Day, the strike folded as workers streamed back to their jobs in Chicago and elsewhere. Ultimately, however, the union won its contract. But in all of the nation's labor wars, those few minutes of violence in front of a Chicago steel mill rank among the bloodiest.

—*Stephen Franklin*

▲ *Strikers flee or fall down to escape blows from police clubs.*

▼ *Police carry a wounded striker from the field.*

Mies Arrives in Chicago

Despite a chilly introduction, the architect firmly plants the International Style in America.

▼ *Ludwig Mies van der Rohe, the master modernist, looms over a model of his highly regarded design for Crown Hall, built in 1956 to house the Illinois Institute of Technology's College of Architecture.*

OCTOBER 18, 1938

Ludwig Mies van der Rohe, former head of the Bauhaus School of Design and a recent emigrant from Nazi Germany, was to be honored this evening on his appointment as director of the Armour Institute of Technology's department of architecture. But at a dinner in the Red Lacquer Room of the Palmer House another architect upstaged him, presaging a struggle that would leave its imprint on American architecture for the remainder of the twentieth century.

The scene-stealer was Frank Lloyd Wright, who introduced the guest of honor as "my" Mies van der Rohe and told the audience, "But for me there would have been no Mies—certainly none here tonight." Then, according to Franz Schulze's biography of Mies, Wright "strode out of the room, followed by a train of acolytes, even as Mies was taking his place at the dais."

The master modernist was fifty-two, spoke no English, and had been in Chicago for only two months. He spent the next twenty years at what became the Illinois Institute of Technology, training a generation of architects and influencing countless others with the buildings and homes he designed in the austere Bauhaus International Style. He never commented on Wright's behavior that night, but in the years that followed disciples of each man did their best to discredit the other camp. The Mies camp championed buildings constructed without ornamentation; Wright dismissed such structures as "flat-chested architecture." The Miesian designs that "made poetry of technology" for his admirers were so cold and mechanical to his detractors as to be downright un-American.

▶ *The apartment buildings at 860 and 880 Lake Shore Drive,
completed in 1952, ushered in a new age in architecture.
Their influence can be seen in countless steel-and-glass
towers around the world.*

Mies, who coined the famous phrase "less is more,"
is credited with ushering in "a new age of architecture"
with his glass-and-steel high-rise apartments at 860 and
880 Lake Shore Drive in Chicago. Completed in 1952,
they were the first to be built without mortar and were
free of exterior decoration. Their influence can be seen
in countless steel-and-glass towers that sprang up in cities
around the world. Other hallmark designs that continue
to grace Chicago are the IIT campus, the Federal Center,
and the IBM building.

Though Mies shared with the native-born giants of
Chicago architecture—Louis Sullivan and Wright—what
biographer David Spaeth describes as technological roots
and a concern for structural expression, he was determined to remain his own man. "I really don't know the
Chicago School," he told an interviewer, referring to the
work of turn-of-the-century Chicago architects. "You see,
I never walk. I always take taxis back and forth to work.
I rarely see the city." Although the stark but elegant
approach that put him in the forefront of modern architecture reached its zenith with the Seagram Building in
New York City in 1958 (the "Whiskey Building," Wright
called it), Mies lived and worked in Chicago until his
death in 1969.

—William Rice

▼ *The architect's stark yet elegant approach extended to
residential projects, such as the house he designed for
Edith Farnsworth on the Fox River near Plano, west of
Chicago.*

World War II

Pearl Harbor brings a unified America into the war, and Chicago does its part.

DECEMBER 7, 1941

Abruptly ending months of debate, the sneak attack on Pearl Harbor left no more doubt. America was in the war, and it would be a fight to the end. Most Chicagoans talked with bravado in public. "We'll whip 'em in two weeks," prophesied a Notre Dame junior over a glass of beer at a Loop bar. "Don't be silly," the man on the next stool said. "It'll take a few months." But there were telltale signs of underlying shock and dread. Among the fifty thousand calls that flooded the *Tribune* switchboard on this day of infamy and the day after, several hundred callers asked how to prepare for a blackout. One man wanted to know where he could buy a gas mask.

Many had believed that the United States should stay out of the war, which had begun with the German attack on Poland in September 1939. The *Tribune's* Colonel Robert R. McCormick had been such an influential exponent of isolationism that President Franklin D. Roosevelt encouraged Marshall Field III to start an opposition newspaper. Field's *Sun* (which later became the *Sun-Times*) had been on the newsstands less than a week when the attack on Pearl Harbor convinced nearly everyone—McCormick included—that America must fight.

Tribune correspondents covered the war from the front lines. Robert Cromie contracted malaria in the jungles of Guadalcanal and flew in a bomber that was crippled by German antiaircraft fire. John H. Thompson parachuted into Sicily and stormed ashore on D-Day with the troops at Omaha Beach. A *Tribune* story about the Battle of Midway drew intense scrutiny from the Roosevelt Administration on the grounds it might alert the Japanese that the United States had cracked their code. The Japanese continued to use the code, and a grand jury determined the paper had not violated espionage laws.

Chicago became a major hub for the war effort. The Stevens Hotel (later the Chicago Hilton), then the world's largest with three thousand rooms, became a barracks. So did the neighboring one-thousand-room Congress. Together, they crammed in fifteen thousand troops. Twelve bowling alleys for GIs debuted on the stage of the Auditorium Theater. Sailors attended spe-

▶

A USO volunteer teams up with a sailor for a game of Ping-Pong at a Loop USO club in 1942. Chicago had a reputation with the troops as a wonderful "liberty town."

▼ *The USS* Sable, *shown cruising along the Chicago lakefront in 1945, and the USS* Wolverine *were based in Chicago for the training of navy pilots. Both ships were converted lake steamers.*

▶ *Draftees preparing to march off to war in June 1942 get a send-off from the Austin High School band.*

▲ *In one of the odder moments of Chicago wartime life, Montgomery Ward chairman Sewell Avery was carried out of his office in April 1944, when he balked at an order from the War Labor Board.*

cialty schools on Navy Pier, and navy pilots trained on makeshift carriers in the lake. Word got around that Chicago was a wonderful "liberty town." Servicemen, it was said, weren't allowed to pay for anything, including cab rides. The United Service Organizations (USO) established lively outposts at all six train stations and a hospitality center in the Loop—fourteen stories of dorms plus a ballroom where top-name entertainers appeared and the hostesses were lovely.

▶

Edward "Butch" O'Hare, who was raised in Chicago, became an early war hero in 1942, when he single-handedly shot down five Japanese planes. O'Hare, who was awarded the Congressional Medal of Honor for his feat, was killed in 1943. The city later renamed that out-of-the-way airport on the Northwest Side in his honor.

▲ *Scrap drives proved a popular way for the home front to show support for the troops. These southwest suburban Bridgeview children show off the old tires they collected as part of a rubber-salvage drive.*

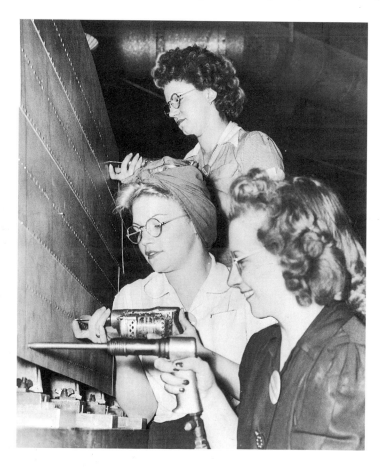

The majority of women who did war work had to handle jobs more rigorous than USO jitterbugging. They poured into factories to supplement the depleted male labor force, which was also buttressed by approximately 100,000 black workers who had migrated north. All over Illinois, defense plants sprang up. Dodge built a $100 million factory on the Southwest Side, considered the largest in the world, where thirty thousand workers assembled engines for B-29 Superfortress bombers. The Douglas plant on the site of what became O'Hare International Airport churned out C-54 Skymaster cargo planes, while Western Electric in Cicero—with twenty-nine thousand workers—developed radar systems.

With all that going on, the city still managed to complete construction of the State Street subway, which opened in October 1943. However, the Dearborn line, started early in 1939, would not be finished until 1951. The materials were needed elsewhere. There was a war on.

—*Robert Cross*

◀ *With millions of men inducted into the armed forces, women flooded into factories to do "men's work" here at home.*

Birth of the Atomic Age

Beneath the stands of an old football stadium, the power of the atom is unleashed.

▲ *Italian physicist Enrico Fermi, shown in 1951,* led the team that achieved the first controlled atomic reaction, depicted years later by Tribune *artist Gary Sheahan.*

DECEMBER 2, 1942

After months of preliminary work, the scientists at the University of Chicago's new Metallurgical Laboratory were ready to run their first experiment on this date. The experiment did not involve metallurgy. In fact, there were no metallurgists in the Metallurgical Laboratory. The name was a screen to disguise a key part of America's vast effort to beat Nazi Germany in the race to build an atomic bomb.

An early hurdle in that race was to prove that a nuclear chain reaction could be turned on and off, something that had never been done before. That was the dangerous job of the forty-three physicists who crowded onto a freezing squash court beneath the stands of Stagg Field, where the first nuclear reactor had been built.

Considering the sophisticated science involved and the risk of conducting such an experiment in a city neighborhood, the materials that the scientists used in building "Chicago Pile No. 1" were laughable. Spheres of a uranium compound were placed between layers of solid graphite bricks, which were held together by a wooden frame. The chief researcher, Italian refugee and Nobel Prize–winner Enrico Fermi, relied upon a six-inch slide rule. Most incredible of all, three young physicists stood by at the top of the pile. In case the reaction started to run out of control, they were to pour a cadmium solution over the pile and hope for the best.

Throughout the day, a control rod was withdrawn from the reactor a few inches at a time. Shortly after 3:30 P.M., a measuring device finally traced a steep line on a piece of graph paper. "The pile has gone critical," Fermi said, signifying that the reaction had figuratively caught fire. With that laconic announcement, the Atomic Age was born.

From that beginning grew not only the atomic bombs that destroyed Hiroshima and Nagasaki but also peaceful uses of nuclear power, such as nuclear medicine. The early reactor work at the University of Chicago led to the establishment of the Argonne National Laboratory in a forest preserve southwest of the city. Fermi, who died of cancer in 1954, was commemorated in the 1960s when another national laboratory, Fermilab, was built in the Chicago area. In 1995, Fermilab scientists announced they had discovered what is believed to be the last remaining piece of the subatomic jigsaw puzzle, the long-elusive "top" quark.

—*Stevenson Swanson*

Pizzeria Uno Opens

A thick crust and plenty of cheese: Chicago-style pizza is born.

DECEMBER 3, 1943

Chicago-style pizza may owe its existence to a bad enchilada. When partners Ike Sewell and Ric Riccardo planned to open a restaurant, Sewell, a native Texan, wanted to feature Mexican food. But one of the sample meals the partners tested made Riccardo so sick that he rejected Mexican food entirely.

Riccardo suggested pizza, which he had encountered in Italy—as many American servicemen were doing during World War II. Sewell's complaint with pizza was that it was insubstantial—little more than an appetizer—and was already readily available in Chicago's Little Italy neighborhood.

▲ *It takes both hands to hold a Chicago pizza. Aldine Stoudamire had been making pizzas at Uno's for twenty years when this photograph was taken in 1976.*

Sewell wanted a substantial, meal-sized pizza. After some experimenting, the partners devised something with a thick crust and plenty of cheese. Their restaurant, Pizzeria Uno, opened on this date at the corner of Ohio Street and Wabash Avenue.

Chicago has contributed many dishes to American cuisine, among them shrimp DeJonghe, chicken Vesuvio, and the Italian beef sandwich. But none has been so widely imitated, nor so closely identified with the city, as Chicago-style pizza. Pizzeria Uno, however, was not an overnight success. In the early days, bartenders distributed free sample slices to introduce customers to the new pizza. "Fortunately," Sewell said, "we had a very good bar business."

Sewell, a regional vice president of Fleischmann's Distilling Corporation, left the day-to-day operation of the restaurant to manager and future partner Rudy Malnati and his son, Lou. (Lou later would break away to establish Lou Malnati's Pizzeria.) But Sewell promoted Pizzeria Uno at every opportunity, even stopping strangers on the street to tell them about the new restaurant.

Business slowly increased, and in 1955 the partners opened Pizzeria Due, on the corner of Wabash and Ontario Street. Pizzeria Uno became synonymous with Chicago, and the gregarious Sewell, eventually the last surviving partner, became one of Chicago's best-known restaurateurs. Imitators sprang up throughout the city, sparking a never-ending debate as to which restaurant made Chicago's best pizza. People even debated the relative merits of Uno and Due, though the restaurants theoretically were serving the identical fare.

—Phil Vettel

▼ *Ike Sewell, shown here in 1987 at Pizzeria Due, stopped strangers on the street to promote his restaurant in the early days. Sewell died in 1990.*

World War II Ends

Soldiers and civilians jitterbug in the streets at the news of Japan's surrender.

▼ *A joyous crowd celebrates the end of World War II at State and Madison Streets. Some five hundred thousand people jammed Loop streets. The servicemen hold a copy of the* Chicago Herald and American.

AUGUST 14, 1945

World War II, which began for the United States with a day of infamy, ended with one of ecstasy. After Germany's surrender in May, all attention had turned to the Pacific theater, where Japan was expected to continue fighting to the death. But Japanese resistance crumbled with stunning speed after atomic bombs mushroomed over Hiroshima, on August 6, and Nagasaki, on August 9. At 6 P.M. Chicago time on Tuesday, August 14, President Harry S Truman gathered reporters in the Oval Office of the White House to announce that Emperor Hirohito had agreed to surrender.

Within minutes of Truman's declaration, the nation went wild. In New York, two million revelers poured into Times Square and watched the news flash across a huge electronic bulletin board. In Washington, about seventy-five thousand people massed in front of the White House as face powder and pillow feathers showered down from office windows after the ticker tape and shredded paper ran out.

By prior arrangement, bars closed immediately upon word of the surrender, but in Chicago that did little to dull the spirits of the five hundred thousand people who crammed into the Loop, shouting, singing, and jitterbugging down State, Clark, and Dearborn Streets. The crowd included thousands of sailors, soldiers, and marines, many with lipstick-smeared faces. At State and Madison Streets, "thirty sailors formed a line, grabbed pretty girls as they passed, kissed them, and passed them from one to another," the *Tribune* reported.

Elsewhere in the city, worshippers by the thousands filed into churches to celebrate the war's end with prayers of thanksgiving and perhaps to remember loved ones among the 22,283 Illinoisans who died in the service during the war. In the backyard of his home at 2330 Washington Boulevard, J. A. Beauparlant climbed a ladder to light an eighteen-foot-tall, 2,250-pound solid wax victory candle that had taken him three months to make. An effigy of Hirohito was run up a flagpole and set ablaze by the fire department in downtown Evanston, where five thousand people had gathered. And ten minutes after Truman spoke, the area's first postwar baby was born to Mr. and Mrs. Dan Severino at Mother Cabrini Hospital. They named her Philomina Victoria.

—*Bob Secter*

The Planned Suburb: Park Forest

Postwar suburbanization of the Chicago area takes off with "GI Town."

▼ *With suburbanization, countryside gave way to ranch houses and winding streets. Here couples inspect new homes in Park Forest in 1952.*

AUGUST 30, 1948

This was moving day for the new residents of one of the first planned communities in the United States built after World War II. In its formative stages, the area was dubbed "GI Town," and, true enough, returning soldiers with wives and children were given top priority on the waiting list for this landmark town. But when the first occupants unpacked, they settled into a place officially christened Park Forest.

The fledgling community set the standard for many Chicago-area municipalities in the widespread suburbanization of the metropolitan area. Park Forest developers, led by Philip M. Klutznick, had a straightforward goal: to create a "complete" community for middle-income families with children. The new town would have plenty of open space and parks, a shopping center, churches and public buildings, and schools within walking distance. "Homes, laid out in staggered clusters around a cul-de-sac, are being arranged so that every mother from her kitchen window can keep an eye on her youngster in centrally located and fenced-in 'tot yards,'" the *Tribune* reported in an article that year.

By 1950, Park Forest had become a haven for young families: Nine out of ten couples living there were parents, and nine out of ten children were under thirteen years of age. The plans called for a population of twenty-five thousand, living in fifty-five hundred rental, cooperative, and single-family units. Four decades later, Park Forest was remarkably similar: the 1990 population was about 24,660, and only a few homes had not been in the original plans for the town.

As the baby boom swelled the population in the decades after the war, millions of people moved to what were once the prairies and farmlands surrounding urban Chicago. They sought the same things as those first Park Forest residents: bigger or more affordable homes, bigger yards, quieter neighborhoods, and safer streets. Sprawling growth at the Chicago region's fringes gobbled up land. From 1970 to 1990, developed acreage increased by about 50 percent, while the region's population grew only 4 percent.

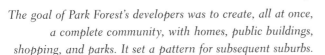

▲ One of the selling points of the planned suburb of Park Forest and of the suburbs that followed was that they were good places to raise families. By 1950, about the time of this photograph, nine out of ten couples in Park Forest had children.

The dispersal of the population brought changes not only to the land but also to the way people lived and worked. Travel times of two hours—one-way—into Chicago's Loop were not unusual, but neither were commutes to jobs in one of suburbia's major business centers, such as Schaumburg, in the northwestern suburbs, or Du Page County, west of Chicago, home to many high-technology companies. And many newer subdivisions were walled off and guarded with gates, which ensured greater privacy and security but also further fractured the sense of a larger community. Even by 1996, the pace of suburban sprawl still seemed relentless. Six new municipalities had been incorporated on the outskirts of the Chicago region since the 1990 census.

—Sue Ellen Christian

▶

The goal of Park Forest's developers was to create, all at once, a complete community, with homes, public buildings, shopping, and parks. It set a pattern for subsequent suburbs.

Dewey Defeats Truman

Well, everyone makes mistakes.

NOVEMBER 3, 1948

As a presidential candidate, Governor Thomas Dewey of New York was not a glad-hander, not a flesh presser. He was stiff and tended toward pomposity. "The only man who could strut sitting down" was the crack that made the rounds. But on November 2, Election Day, an overwhelming sense of inevitability hung about the Republican nominee. The polls and the pundits left no room for doubt: Dewey was going to defeat President Harry S Truman. And the *Tribune* would be the first to report it.

Arguably the most famous headline in the newspaper's 150-year history, DEWEY DEFEATS TRUMAN is every publisher's nightmare on every election night. Like most newspapers, the *Tribune*, which had dismissed Dewey on its editorial page as a "nincompoop," was lulled into a false sense of security by polls that repeatedly predicted

a Dewey victory. Critically important, though, was a printers' strike, which forced the paper to go to press hours earlier than it would have under normal circumstances.

As the first-edition deadline approached, managing editor J. Loy "Pat" Maloney had to make the headline call, although many East Coast tallies were not yet in. Maloney banked on the track record of Arthur Sears Henning, the paper's longtime Washington correspondent. Henning said Dewey. Henning was rarely wrong. Besides, *Life* magazine had just carried a big photo of Dewey with the caption "The next President of the United States."

The ink was hardly dry on 150,000 copies of the paper when radio bulletins reported that the race was surprisingly close. The headline was changed to DEMOCRATS MAKE SWEEP OF STATE OFFICES for the second edition. Truman went on to take Illinois and much of the Midwest in this whopping election surprise. Radio comedian Fred Allen noted Truman was the "first president to lose in a Gallup and win in a walk." The *Tribune* blamed the pollsters for its mistake.

The headline might well have been quickly forgotten but for a chance encounter two days later in St. Louis. Truman, traveling by rail to Washington, stepped to the rear platform of the train and was handed a copy of the *Tribune* early edition. He had as low an opinion of the *Tribune* as it did of him. Truman held up the paper, and photographers preserved the moment for history.

—*Tim Jones*

The Bi-level Commuter Train

A new passenger car design enters the lives of commuters worldwide.

SEPTEMBER 6, 1950

The first bi-level commuter train made its appearance on this date on the Aurora line of the Chicago, Burlington & Quincy Railroad. Along for the inaugural ride were Pops Hanna and Horace B. Hench, both of Hinsdale, who had been riding Burlington trains for nearly half a century. The new air-conditioned design was an instant success with old-timers and younger passengers alike, according to a *Tribune* story the following morning. Since then, the bi-level car has spread to cities around the globe and become a regularly scheduled presence in the life of that most clock-conscious of creatures, the commuter.

Shortly after World War II, the Burlington developed the dome car in its Aurora shops for intercity passenger routes; the dome section sat atop a modified coach. From that bi-level arrangement, it was a short step a few years later to extend the concept to commuter cars. Designed to let the Burlington handle its growing suburban traffic without having to enlarge its station platforms, the new cars carried 148 passengers—about 50 percent more than conventional cars of the time.

Since July 12, 1856, when the first documented commuter train ran on the Illinois Central Railroad between downtown Chicago and the then-distant community of Hyde Park, the development of Chicago's outlying neighborhoods and suburbs has been tied to the railroads. The term *commute* originated with the practice of giving discounted, or *commuted*, fares to regular riders. Suburban commuting began to develop in a big way after the Chicago Fire, when many residents moved to the country to get away from city congestion. Early commuting was an adventure: Trains often got stuck in snowdrifts or were halted by prairie fires that destroyed wooden bridges. The earliest coaches were hand-me-down rolling stock, cold in winter and roasting in summer. Opening the windows just let in sparks and soot from the steam engine.

In the 1850s it took about three hours to travel the thirty-eight miles from Aurora to Chicago via two connecting railroads. By 1883, faster locomotives and better track cut the time in half, and modern rush-hour express trains make the run in less than an hour. In 1996, suburban rail service in the Chicago area carried 140,000 commuters daily, some of whom rode in car number 700, the original bi-level car delivered in 1950.

—*David Young*

◀ *For 140,000 people in the Chicago area, workdays begin and end with a train ride. In this 1967 photo, commuters settle into their routines on a Burlington bi-level train, which can carry 50 percent more passengers than a single-level.*

Playboy Magazine

Hugh Hefner launches America's sexual revolution with $10,600 and the idea that Puritanism is unhealthy.

DECEMBER 1, 1953

For a magazine that spawned dozens of imitators as it both chronicled and set a standard for sexual change in America, *Playboy* got off to a jittery start. Hugh Hefner had so little confidence in his magazine that he did not print the month of the inaugural issue—December—on the first cover. He was not sure how long it would take to sell. Neither Hefner nor anyone else can recall the exact date when the first copies went on sale, but it was sometime around December 1, 1953. Much to Hefner's surprise, the entire run of seventy-two thousand copies quickly sold out, and his monthly was born.

That first issue did contain something special: the much-celebrated nude calendar photo of Marilyn Monroe. It cost Hefner $200, a hefty bite from the $600 he had put up to go with the $10,000 he had raised selling stock to friends. "*Playboy* came at the right time, when the United States was experiencing a sexual revolution," Hefner would explain years later. "My naked girls became a symbol of disobedience, a triumph of sexuality, an end of Puritanism."

Hefner, a University of Illinois alum (class of 1949) and graduate of Chicago's Steinmetz High School, catered to the country's growing public libido with the magazine's heavy dose of photo layouts of nude women plus news and advice about all things sexual. Mixed in were interviews with public figures, articles by highly regarded writers (early contributors included James Baldwin, Ray Bradbury, and P. G. Wodehouse), and well-drawn cartoons. By 1960, circulation had hit one million copies, generating magazine-only annual profits of more than $3 million. The clubs, clothing, private Boeing jet, television shows, and movies—all displaying the famed bunny logo—were just around the corner.

▲ *Hefner and* Playboy *turned a modest America on its ear with photographs of beautiful nude women mixed with provocative writing.*

◀ *Hugh Hefner's round bed in the Chicago* Playboy *mansion often doubled as a desk. In or out of bed, pajamas were his preferred attire.*

Hefner's empire peaked in the 1970s; the magazine hit a circulation high of 7.2 million copies in 1972. After that, competition from publications that titillated readers even more ate into circulation, and Hefner came under constant attack from religious, feminist, and political groups. A series of divestitures in the 1980s refocused *Playboy*'s attention on the magazine alone.

The Playboy mansion, backdrop for many of the magazine's photo shoots as well as Hefner's living, working, and entertaining quarters, moved from its forty-eight-room North State Parkway address to Beverly Hills in the 1980s. The company headquarters shifted from the old Palmolive Building on Michigan Avenue, renamed the Playboy Building when Hefner purchased it in 1965, to nine floors of offices at 666 North Lake Shore Drive. Christie Hefner, his daughter, took charge of daily operations. But Hugh Hefner, who turned seventy in 1996, remained editor in chief of the magazine.

— *Mike Conklin*

▲ *Branching out from the magazine business in the 1960s, Hefner opened a string of Playboy clubs. Here, flanked by Playboy bunnies in 1968, he pours Chicago water into the swimming pool of his newest club, in Lake Geneva, Wisconsin.*

◀ *Whether Hefner was working or hosting a party or both, the lights usually burned late into the night at the Playboy mansion, at 1340 North State Parkway, on Chicago's Gold Coast.*

The Blues

Willie Dixon joins Muddy Waters, initiating a new era in the blues—and in popular music.

JANUARY 7, 1954

After this day Chicago blues, and by extension the popular music of the last half of the twentieth century, would never be the same. McKinley Morganfield, a.k.a. Muddy Waters, was already famous as the singer and guitarist most responsible for bringing the acoustic Delta Blues of his native Mississippi into the modern electrified era, after arriving in Chicago in 1943. And with artists such as Waters leading the way, Chicago had already become the city most closely identified with the electric blues in the postwar era, a reign that would continue through the 1950s and 1960s with such giants as Howlin' Wolf, Otis Rush, Junior Wells, and Magic Sam.

But on January 7, the music of Waters and Chicago ascended to a new level when the singer welcomed into his inner circle Willie Dixon, the bass player, arranger, and songwriter who was emerging as the secret weapon of Chess Records, the famed blues label of 2120 South Michigan Avenue. Dixon's songs would become indelibly associated with Waters, with their mixture of menace and mirth, swaggering sexuality, and ribald playfulness. More than any single factor, Dixon's words shaped Waters's stage persona for decades to come.

Dixon showed up at Chess to play string bass in Waters's soon-to-be legendary band, which included pianist Otis Spann, guitarist Jimmy Rogers, and harmonica player Little Walter. Together they would record "Hoochie Coochie Man," which would become Waters's biggest hit

▲ *After arriving in Chicago in 1943, McKinley Morganfield, a.k.a. Muddy Waters, took the acoustic Delta Blues of his native Mississippi into the modern electrified era.*

In the early 1970s, robust blues belter Koko Taylor brought new life to the local scene. ▶

◄ Willie Dixon's words would shape Waters's stage persona for decades.

▼ By the 1990s, Buddy Guy (shown here at a benefit concert, with Dr. John on keyboards) was winning Grammy awards and running his Legends nightclub on the South Side, a mecca for rock artists such as Eric Clapton.

to date, and the first of a succession of influential singles written by Dixon and sung by Waters: "I'm Ready," "I Just Want to Make Love to You," "You Shook Me."

None of those songs defined Waters like "Hoochie Coochie Man." With its immortal lines "I got a black cat bone/I got a mojo too/I got the John the Conqueroo/I'm gonna mess with you," Waters fused the ancient hoodoo mythology of the South with the electricity, both figurative and literal, of the North. "Hoochie Coochie Man" was a siren call to countless aspiring musicians from the Rolling Stones to the Allman Brothers, who would one day translate it into their own version of the blues.

In the early 1970s, grassroots labels such as Bruce Iglauer's Alligator Records, which provided a platform for the robust blues belter Koko Taylor, brought new life to the local scene. By the 1990s, Chess alumnus Buddy Guy was winning Grammy awards and running his Legends nightclub on the South Side, where rock artists such as Eric Clapton made pilgrimages. Guy said he owed his late-blooming success to the endorsement of rockers such as Clapton and Stevie Ray Vaughan. But like most of Waters's disciples, Guy also knew that if the blues had a baby named rock 'n' roll, it is likely that the Hoochie Coochie Man was the daddy.

—Greg Kot

Lyric Opera of Chicago

The internationally renowned Lyric thrives in a city where many opera companies have failed.

FEBRUARY 5, 1954

To many, it seemed nothing more than a hugely impractical scheme, like something cooked up by Mickey Rooney and friends in one of those old Andy Hardy movies: "You bring the costumes, I'll get the barn." Cassandras predicted the curtain would never go up. But it did. On this Friday evening, the Lyric Theater of Chicago presented its calling card, a performance of Mozart's *Don Giovanni* at the Civic Opera House. The company that would later reap international acclaim as Lyric Opera of Chicago was born.

In the cheers of a capacity crowd greeting Lyric's inaugural production, the company's three young founders were vindicated. They made an interesting trio: Carol Fox, a student singer; Lawrence V. Kelly, an insurance broker; and Nicola Rescigno, an Italian conductor. A love of opera, and the desire to bring resident opera back to the city after seven years, brought them together.

Between 1910 and 1946, seven opera companies—several merely different names for the same reorganized company—presented seasons at the Auditorium and Civic Opera House. All fizzled in a sea of debt. Fox, Kelly, and Rescigno knew they could do better. With donations from friends of Fox and Kelly, they scraped together $30,000 for two performances of *Don Giovanni*, engaging a dream cast that included Nicola Rossi-Lemeni, Eleanor Steber, and Bidu Sayao. Claudia Cassidy, the *Tribune's* influential critic, lauded the company's maiden effort, writing that the production was of a quality worthy of "an established troupe of long standing."

The success of the first two performances made possible a three-week autumn season consisting of sixteen performances of eight operas; twelve of those performances sold out. Starpower

▲ *For Lyric cofounder Carol Fox, running a successful opera company meant attending to matters great and small. Here she assists a member of the children's chorus with her make-up.*

▲ *Other opera companies had occupied the stunning Civic Opera House and failed, but Lyric would use a combination of starpower and skillful management to keep the theater's thirty-six hundred seats filled season after season.*

helped. That November, the fledgling company presented the American debut of soprano Maria Callas as Bellini's *Norma*. The fiery American-born diva chose to introduce herself to the United States via Lyric because it paid higher fees than New York's Metropolitan Opera. Italian singers and productions predominated in those early years. By 1956, when Fox took sole command of a rechristened Lyric Opera of Chicago, the company was being called "La Scala West."

In the mid-1990s, the Lyric cast still spoke fluent Italian but also French, German, English, Russian, and Czech. Ardis Krainik, who succeeded Fox in 1981, earned a reputation for herself as a tough businesswoman and for Lyric as a theater that took twentieth-century opera as seriously as the classics. Lyric's first integral production of Richard Wagner's *Ring* cycle, in March 1996, was its most ambitious and, at $6.5 million, most expensive artistic endeavor to date. More than four decades after presenting that calling card, *Don Giovanni*, Lyric was still taking risks.

—*John von Rhein*

▲ *In its early years, Lyric Opera's many productions of Italian operas, such as this 1959* Aida, *earned it the nickname "La Scala West."*

◄ *Nicola Rossi-Lemeni appeared as Don Giovanni in Lyric's first production. A single performance was planned (advertisement, above), but tickets sold so quickly that a second was added.*

Richard J. Daley Elected

After the Boss takes office, no one questions who runs Chicago.

APRIL 5, 1955

When Cook County Democratic leaders met in December 1954 to pick a candidate for the 1955 mayoral race, they gave Mayor Martin Kennelly three minutes and fifty-eight seconds to make his case for reendorsement. Elected in 1947 to bring an air of respectability back to the mayor's office after the long, scandal-plagued rule of Mayor Ed Kelly, Kennelly had earned the respect of the business community and the newspapers but not of the Democratic Party. After his time was up, party leaders promptly endorsed their own chairman, Richard J. Daley.

Daley, who had been Cook County clerk since 1950, defeated Republican Robert Merriam on this date to become the new mayor of Chicago at age fifty-two. Daley had promised that if elected, he would resign as Democratic Party chairman.

It was a promise he never kept. For the next twenty-one years, Daley combined the power of the mayor's office with the political clout of the Democratic organization to become perhaps the biggest—and ultimately, the last—of the big-city bosses.

During Daley's long reign, the face of Chicago changed profoundly. His friendship with Presidents John F. Kennedy and Lyndon B. Johnson brought millions of federal dollars to the city to pay for ambitious capital-works projects and to fund the jobs that Daley used to hold his political apparatus together. He presided over the construction of the city's expressway system, sprawling public-housing complexes, a greatly expanded O'Hare International Airport, the vast lakefront filtration plant for the city's water system, and the West Side campus of the University of Illinois at Chicago, a bitterly controversial project that involved the demolition of an Italian neighborhood.

Daley's national reputation was cemented in the presidential election of 1960, when legend has it that late-counted Democratic votes were responsible for Kennedy's paper-thin victory over Richard Nixon. Daley was later criticized for his

▲ *Mayor Richard J. Daley (left), Judge Abraham Lincoln Marovitz, and former Mayor Martin Kennelly shake hands shortly after Marovitz administered the oath of office to Daley in April 1955.*

▶

A high point of the year for the mayor was the annual St. Patrick's Day Parade. Daley, shown leading the 1963 march down State Street, lived his entire life in the traditionally Irish neighborhood of Bridgeport.

heavy-handed methods in dealing with the late-1960s riots, and in 1972 he and his machine allies were prevented from taking their seats at the Democratic convention because of a challenge to their credentials.

The setbacks only seemed to make him stronger with voters in Chicago, as did his lifelong struggle with the English language (for instance, calling the airport "O'Hara . . . the crosswords of the nation"). He was elected by huge margins six times, and voters followed his directives to the point that nearly every elected county officeholder and every alderman on the fifty-member City Council was a Democrat. Throughout his years as mayor, Daley maintained his image as a devout and devoted family man, living in a modest bungalow in the Bridgeport community where he was born and raised. But he saw close associates and top aides, such as Alderman Thomas Keane, press secretary Earl Bush, and Circuit Court Clerk Matt Danaher, brought down by federal investigators.

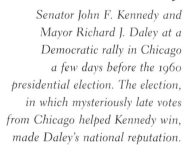

▶ Senator John F. Kennedy and Mayor Richard J. Daley at a Democratic rally in Chicago a few days before the 1960 presidential election. The election, in which mysteriously late votes from Chicago helped Kennedy win, made Daley's national reputation.

▲ Alderman Thomas Keane (left), Daley's leader in the City Council, confers with the mayor during a council session in 1969. Keane, like other key Daley associates and aides, eventually was convicted and sent to jail by federal prosecutors.

▲ *The mayor and his city: probably the most powerful of America's big-city bosses and the mayor who presided over the building of many large public-works projects in the city, Daley left an indelible stamp on Chicago. This photo, taken in 1966, was one of his favorites.*

Paradoxically, it was Daley who severely wounded the party in the early 1970s when he reluctantly signed the Shakman decree, which outlawed the firing of public workers for political reasons. But since it was issued by a federal judge, Daley had little choice. In his later years, he held the party together through the force of his personality. He remained the Boss of the "City That Works." For a generation of Chicagoans, the word "mayor" came before only one name: Daley.

—*Robert Davis*

The First McDonald's

A traveling salesman launches the fast-food revolution with that first hamburger.

▼ *The first McDonald's franchise restaurant, in the Chicago suburb of Des Plaines, featured the chain's famous golden arches and sold 15-cent hamburgers that always tasted the same. A replica of the restaurant was later built on the site and became a museum.*

APRIL 15, 1955

The journey to billions and billions began with a single humble hamburger. History does not note the name of the customer, but that first request for service on this date at the new franchise restaurant on Lee Street in Des Plaines became the order heard 'round the world. The owner of the restaurant, Ray Kroc, lived in the Chicago suburb of Arlington Heights. He chose nearby Des Plaines because he hoped to lure recreational travelers driving between Chicago and the lakes of northern Illinois and southern Wisconsin. His particular genius, however, was not so much site selection or restaurant design as it was concept recognition: a year earlier, working as a traveling salesman of malted-milk-mixing machines, he had come across a thriving hamburger joint in San Bernardino, California, run by Mac and Dick McDonald. He sensed the possibilities.

The McDonald brothers were uninterested in expanding, so Kroc entered into a franchising agreement with them, bringing first to Des Plaines and later, after he bought out the brothers in 1961, to the rest of the world a chain of drive-in restaurants defined at first by what they were not. The restaurants were not slow—food was served quickly since it was prepared assembly-line style and was ready at the moment of order. They were not expensive—the 15-cent burger (just under 90 cents in 1996 dollars) was a mainstay. They were not hangouts—Kroc kept out pay phones and jukeboxes. And they were not risky—the premises were clean and well lighted, and the food always tasted the same.

That first order began not only the spread of the McDonald's empire—swollen by the mid-1990s to around fifteen thousand locations in about seventy countries—but also the franchised-fast-food revolution in American dining. That revolution has conquered highways, airports, malls, and school lunchrooms as well as our very culture, where its fast-food slogan ("You deserve a break today") and mascot (the Ronald McDonald promotional clown) have become as common and recognizable as any quotation or icon from fiction. Kroc died in 1984, the same year his flagship Des Plaines restaurant, which had been remodeled several times, was torn down. The company then built a nearly exact replica of the original on the site and turned it into the McDonald's Museum.

—*Eric Zorn*

▲ *Ray A. Kroc, pictured in 1957, was selling malted-milk machines on the road when he came upon the McDonald brothers' hamburger joint in San Bernardino, California.*

O'Hare International Airport

The Jet Age arrives at an airfield that soon becomes the world's busiest airport.

▼ *Jet exhaust makes waiting planes look like a mirage, but they are real: with more than nine hundred thousand flights a year at O'Hare, the airport's runways are rarely empty.*

OCTOBER 29, 1955

Mayor Richard J. Daley's words were prophetic at a ceremony marking the start of scheduled passenger service at fledgling O'Hare International Airport. "I consider O'Hare's beginning as a long and firm step into the jet airline age, now upon us," Daley declared at the festivities on this date. "We have the space for expansion for vast future developments that may now be entirely unguessed."

Officials at the time believed O'Hare could serve eight million passengers annually within a few years. But who could have predicted that the airport would be handling nearly seventy million people a year four decades later? Along the way, O'Hare would secure Chicago's place as the world's premier aviation crossroads and, at the same time, become a mighty money machine for the city and surrounding suburbs. In the mid-1990s, the airport generated an estimated $12 billion a year in economic benefits and created more than three hundred thousand jobs.

For such an economic and aviation heavyweight, O'Hare had a modest beginning. Orchard Place Airport, nestled against northwest suburban Park Ridge, was just one of the many sleepy little airfields spread across the Chicago area when World War II broke out. It took on added significance, however, when the federal government turned it over to the Douglas Aircraft Company, which assembled C-54 transport planes on the site. Meanwhile, the city's busy commercial field—small and landlocked Municipal Airport (renamed Midway after the war)—was becoming increasingly congested. Several locations came under scrutiny as a site for another passenger air terminal, including a landfill in the lake off 39th Street, but in late 1945 Orchard Place won the City Council's nod.

◄ *Domestic flights use one complex of terminals (foreground), while a separate terminal (background), which opened in 1993, handles international flights. A "people mover" rail line connects the two complexes.*

The first scheduled service began with a freight carrier in 1948, but regular passenger service could begin only in 1955, when a new passenger terminal was finished. After that, O'Hare's growth was strong and steady as airlines switched over from propeller-driven planes to big jets that could not use small airports like Midway. In 1961, the number of flights at O'Hare surpassed the total at Midway, which relinquished its title as the world's busiest airport.

Hundreds of millions of dollars in subsequent investment brought new services and facilities to the airport, including two architectural gems: the United Airlines terminal, designed by Helmut Jahn, which opened in 1987; and Ralph Johnson's International Terminal, which began serving passengers in 1993. But as the suburbs grew up around O'Hare, aircraft noise produced political opposition strong enough to stifle construction of additional runways. Some leaders contended that growing aviation demand had produced a new need—for yet another Chicago-area airport.

—*Gary Washburn*

▼ *By 1962, O'Hare was already the world's busiest airport— and at times, it seemed, the most crowded.*

The Congress Expressway Opens

A new highway makes it easier to enter the city. It also makes it easier to leave.

DECEMBER 15, 1955

One dignitary who spoke on this day at the ribbon-cutting for the new highway that stretched west from the Loop noted that the project had been discussed for three decades. "That's enough talk," Cook County Board President Daniel Ryan summed up. "Let's drive it."

With that, a ceremonial ribbon was scissored and a four-and-a-half-mile stretch of what was christened the Congress Street Expressway was opened to traffic. Ryan's name later would be given to another Chicago "superhighway," part of a network of expressways and tollways that would radiate out from the central city and stretch across far-flung suburban regions that were then little more than cropland.

Although other parts of the new, divided-lane highway system were already open in outlying areas, this newest segment was the first portion close to downtown, and it was the first significant step toward the realization of Daniel Burnham's proposal for a major thoroughfare along the path of Congress Street, which had been part of his 1909 plan for Chicago. To build the $183 million expressway, hundreds of buildings had to be razed, three thousand graves in two cemeteries had to be relocated, and a tunnel had to be knocked through the base of the main post office, near Canal Street. Fortunately, the massive building had been designed to accommodate the right-of-way.

The expressway system relieved congestion, at least temporarily, on neighboring streets, and it greatly shortened travel times for cross-city trips. But it also opened vast tracts of outlying farmland to commercial and residential development. Established city neighborhoods fractured as former city residents filled up the suburban developments that sprawled across the landscape. Some critics have maintained that the expressway system also divided the city in places by separating black and white neighborhoods.

In 1955, such concerns lay in the future. Chief Michael Ahern of the police traffic division had more immediate problems in mind. "It's an expressway, but not a speedway," he declared. A forty-five-mile-an-hour speed limit would be "strictly enforced." Within a few weeks, a seventeen-year-old motorist was pinched for doing ninety miles an hour.

The final segment of the expressway opened in late 1960. Chicago being a political town, many of the area's expressways are named for local or national politicians: Ryan, President John F. Kennedy, Illinois governor and presidential candidate Adlai Stevenson. In January 1964, the Congress was renamed for Dwight D. Eisenhower, the president who had created the interstate highway system of which it was a part.

— *Gary Washburn*

▲ *The Congress Street Expressway under construction in 1953. The view is looking west from the main post office.*

◄ *Expressways made travel faster—at least some of the time. Temper-shredding traffic jams, such as this 1985 snarl on the Kennedy Expressway, quickly became all-too-regular features of expressway driving.*

The Last Streetcar

For almost 100 years, the city's streetcars provided the background music of neighborhood life.

JUNE 21, 1958

At 6:16 A.M. on this date, Al Carter hopped aboard a Vincennes Avenue trolley car a block from the end of the line, dropped a token in the fare box, and asked the conductor to sign his transfer. A South Sider with a penchant for seeking immortality in history's footnotes, Carter had been the last visitor through the turnstiles at the "Century of Progress" exhibition twenty-four years earlier. He knew that the autographed transfer ensured him a small place in Windy City lore as the last straphanger to ride a Chicago streetcar.

The green-and-cream streamlined trolley rolled into a car barn shortly afterward and closed an era that had opened on April 25, 1859, when Chicago's first streetcar began running along a single railroad track laid in the middle of State Street between Madison and 12th Streets. Horses pulled the first streetcars, but soon San Francisco pioneered a new system, with cars hooked to a moving cable underneath the street. Chicago's lines were steadily rebuilt in the 1880s until the city had the world's largest cable-car system. In the meantime, eastern cities were experimenting with electric streetcars that drew their power from a wire strung over the tracks, a method imitated in Chicago beginning in the 1890s.

By World War I, the city's trolleys held all the records: the street railroads had more miles of track, operated over more routes, and kept more electric cars running than any other city. In 1929, when the fare was 7 cents, Chicago's streetcars carried nearly nine hundred million passengers. Across much of the city, commuters were never more than a quarter of a mile from a streetcar line. The clang of the trolley bell and the click-clack sound of wheels bumping over rail joints were the background music of neighborhood life.

The streetcar's drawback was that it could only follow the tracks, making it difficult to detour around accidents and fires. A rival form of mass transit, the rubber-tired, gasoline-powered buses that first appeared on Chicago's streets in 1927, suffered no such disadvantage. After World War II, buses were rapidly introduced on former streetcar routes, even as the burgeoning of suburbia and the opening of Chicago's superhighway system was causing ridership to decline. "It's time I quit anyway, even if they continued the street cars," said William Armstrong, who had been a motorman since 1916. "Traffic is getting too heavy and too fast."

—*Ron Grossman*

▲ *Car 7213 rolls into the history books as the last Chicago streetcar. At one time, the city had the largest street railroad system in the world.*

Our Lady of the Angels Fire

With poor alarms and no sprinklers, the school was almost defenseless when a fire broke out.

DECEMBER 1, 1958

At 2:40 P.M. on this chilly Monday, the time of day when fidgeting youngsters count the minutes to the final bell, a billowing and blinding mass of flames, smoke, and gas burst out on the second floor of Our Lady of the Angels school. Within seconds, twelve hundred students at the parochial school were scrambling for their lives, many leaping from windows to escape the inferno.

The fire had begun in a paper-filled waste barrel at the bottom of a stairwell of the West Side school. After smoldering for several minutes, the blaze shot up like a cannonball into a crawl space above the second floor and then burned its way through to the classrooms beneath. The two-and-a-half-story brick-and-wood building was almost defenseless against the flames. There was no sprinkler system, and only the first floor had a fire door. Because the school's fire alarm was not connected to the fire department, it took at least two minutes from the first sight of flames before the firefighters got word of the blaze. Another three minutes—almost an eternity in such catastrophes—elapsed before emergency equipment arrived on the scene.

By then, panicked children had already begun to jump from the upper floor, landing in heaps on top of each other. From an upper window, a nun screamed, "We are trapped!" A passing milkman saw the smoke, ran inside, and dragged ten pupils to safety, including one girl frozen in terror on a stairwell, blocking the escape of others. In the horrified crowd that gathered outside was a woman with tears streaming down her face. Apparently unable to speak English, she waved a grimy, wrinkled scrap of paper in front of firemen and others in the crowd. It read: "Mary . . . Room 209."

Three nuns and eighty-seven children perished that day. During the following months, five more children died from their wounds. In the fire's wake, the city ordered sprinklers installed in all schools and linked school alarms to fire-department alarm systems. In 1961, a former Our Lady student, a fifth-grader when the fire erupted, confessed to starting the fire, but he recanted at court hearings. A judge held him responsible for other arson blazes but refused to pin him with blame for the school fire. The cause was never officially determined.

—Bob Secter

◀ *Firemen rescue an injured girl from the school's second floor, where the fire did the most damage.*

The 1959 White Sox

The team's pennant win results in a celebration that scares thousands.

SEPTEMBER 22, 1959

They were known as the "Go-Go Sox," hustlers who scraped together a 94–60 record less with bat-popping might than with clutch pitching, flawless defense, and jackrabbit speed on the basepaths. There was Luis "Little Looie" Aparicio, the Venezuelan shortstop and base-stealing whiz, and his double-play partner at second base, plucky Nellie Fox, with the ever-present chaw of tobacco in his cheek.

The biggest bopper was first baseman Ted "Big Klu" Kluszewski, and the surest arm was a thirty-nine-year-old workhorse with a name that sounded like a boast—Early Wynn. New owner Bill Veeck, baseball's clown prince, spiced the Comiskey Park atmosphere with snake charmers, clowns, and other eccentricities.

The American League pennant chase had been nip-and-tuck between the White Sox and Cleveland Indians since opening day. The South Siders took over for good in late July, but the Indians stayed in the hunt until a dramatic showdown on September 22 at Cleveland's Municipal Stadium. In the bottom of the ninth, with the Sox nursing a 4–2 lead, the Indians loaded the bases with one out. In came relief ace Gerry Staley, who threw one pitch—a low, outside sinker—to Cleveland's Vic Power. He slammed it to Aparicio's left. The shortstop speared the ball, raced to second, and then rifled it to Big Klu for a double play. The Sox had won the pennant.

Fire Commissioner Robert J. Quinn ordered a celebratory five-minute sounding of the city's air-raid sirens. The late-night wail, at a time when Soviet leader Nikita Khrushchev's threat to bury America was still fresh, frightened tens of thousands of area residents. Many rushed to the streets. Others herded hysterical children to shelter. "We had seven children under nine and woke them all up when the sirens screamed," said Mrs. Earl Gough of the South Side. "We said Hail Marys together in the basement." Quinn apologized but also argued that the inci-

◀ *A symbol of franchise futility in the 1959 World Series came when left fielder Al Smith backed up to the wall at Comiskey Park to try to catch a home run ball, only to be drenched by a beer dropped by a fan.*

◀ Shortstop Luis Aparicio (number 11), a future Hall of Famer, symbolized the "Go-Go Sox" with his base-stealing speed.

dent provided "a very good test" of the area's readiness, which he had found wanting. Mayor Richard J. Daley claimed that Quinn had acted in accordance with a city council proclamation that "there shall be whistles and sirens blowing and there shall be great happiness when the White Sox win the pennant."

In the World Series, the Sox fell to the Los Angeles Dodgers four games to two. Since then, Chicago baseball teams have given the city little reason to set off any sirens. The Sox made it to the American League championship series in 1983 but lost to the Baltimore Orioles. The Cubs glimpsed a National League pennant twice, only to falter in the championship series, falling to the San Diego Padres in 1984 and to the San Francisco Giants in 1989.

—*Bob Secter*

▶

The sirens may have scared many Chicagoans, but they did not dampen the enthusiasm of this Loop restaurant owner for his favorite team.

OUR SOX MUST BE BOMBERS!

DIDN'T THEY SET OFF THE AIR-RAID SIRENS AND THEN SCARE THE "H-LL" OUT OF THE YANKS?

The Second City's First Show

The cabaret's founders had little idea where those first laughs would lead.

DECEMBER 16, 1959

They were still tacking down the hall carpet when the doors opened on this evening for the first performance at The Second City. It all seemed so new and so tentative, even when the audience started applauding the fresh, smart comedy of the cabaret. As Bernard Sahlins, a cofounder, recalled years later, "We felt we were just opening a coffee shop, and maybe a little show, too." What they were doing, however, was opening a new era in Chicago theater and releasing an amazing flow of talent that soon came to dominate American comedy.

The roots of Second City extended back to 1953, when the Playwrights Theater Club, an outgrowth of young talent with University of Chicago connections,

▲ *Joan Rivers, shown in 1961 with Del Close, was an early cast member who went on to a bigger career in television.*

began performing. In 1955, the Compass Players, incorporating many of the same actors, started presenting their sketches in a bar close to the university's campus in Hyde Park. For various reasons, neither Playwrights nor Compass lasted long. What endured, however, were the techniques of improvisation and theater games that had been taught

▲ *The Second City's roots in improvisation and theater games led to such sketches as Paul Sand's 1960 portrayal of a slice of frying bacon starting to cook, then sizzling in the heat, and ending up well done.*

by Viola Spolin to such performers as Barbara Harris, Mike Nichols, Elaine May, Severn Darden, and Shelley Berman. In 1959, Spolin's son, Paul Sills, who had worked as house manager at a Chicago nightclub, proposed a new cabaret with the same kind of improvisational theater that Compass had embraced. Sills became the founding director of The Second City.

The new company, which took its name from the title of a famous series of articles on Chicago by A. J. Liebling in *The New Yorker*, moved into a former Chinese laundry on North Wells Street and began rehearsals. Specializing in bright, sharp sketches of political and social satire and incorporating audience suggestions into some of the pieces, the cast improvised on the spot. The cabaret steadily expanded its enthusiastic audiences in Chicago and established a Canadian branch in Toronto.

The Second City, which soon moved into a permanent home at 1616 North Wells Street, was already known by the 1960s as a star-making platform for actor-comedians, with Darden, Harris, Paul Sand, Joan Rivers, and Alan Arkin having gone on to bigger movie and television careers. The big breakthrough,

however, came in the mid-1970s with the advent of television's *Saturday Night Live*. In the show's early years, the cast included Second City veterans Dan Aykroyd, John Belushi, Bill Murray, and Gilda Radner. The astounding success of Belushi on the show and in films cemented the cabaret's reputation as a breeding ground for superstars of comedy. A few years later, the syndicated *Second City TV* (*SCTV*) television series, featuring such alumni as Harold Ramis, John Candy, and Andrea Martin, added to the troupe's fame and influence. Second City had gone from local phenomenon to international juggernaut.

—*Richard Christiansen*

▲ *In 1974, Second City's Toronto troupe included many future stars. Shown outside the cabaret's home in Chicago's Old Town neighborhood are (from left) Eugene Levy, Gilda Radner, Dan Aykroyd, Catherine O'Hara, and John Candy.*

◀ *The astounding success of John Belushi, performing here with Eugenie Ross at Second City in 1972, cemented the cabaret's reputation as a breeding ground for comedic talent.*

The Kennedy-Nixon Debate

Presidential politics enters the television age.

SEPTEMBER 26, 1960

It was clear from the outset that it was not to be Richard Nixon's night. The vice president had whacked his right knee earlier in the campaign, and an infection had set in. He was feeling drained as he got out of his limousine at the studios of WBBM-TV. Inside, he bonked his head against an overhead microphone while rising to greet Massachusetts Senator John F. Kennedy.

But clumsiness was the least of Nixon's problems. He and Kennedy had come to Chicago on this date to square off in a great experiment, the first nationally televised debate between presidential contenders. In the space of an hour, the camera-unfriendly Nixon would learn an unsettling truth about the power of television, a truth that has shaped political strategy ever since.

At the time of the debate, the Republican Nixon enjoyed the edge in the campaign. After eight years in the Eisenhower Administration, he was better known than his Democratic rival and was considered more worldly. Rhetorically, neither scored a knockout in the debate, which was moderated by broadcaster Howard K. Smith and dealt with domestic issues. But one of the lasting lessons of the event was that television is not about rhetoric; above all, it is about pictures. On that level, Kennedy was the clear winner. He seemed self-assured, youthful, vibrant. By contrast, Nixon appeared defensive, and the bright studio lighting exaggerated his jowls and sunken eyes. As the hour wore on, the pancake makeup he used to hide a five-o'clock shadow became streaked with perspiration.

The night seemed to jump-start Kennedy's campaign. The one-time longshot candidate eked out a razor-thin edge in the popular vote, besting Nixon by only 112,881 votes out of more than sixty-eight million cast. GOP leaders alleged vote fraud in several states, including Illinois, where they charged that the Chicago Democratic machine had stolen the state for Kennedy by manufacturing one hundred thousand votes in the city. However, rather than call for a recount, Nixon accepted the tally.

—*Bob Secter*

McCormick Place

A controversial lakefront exhibition hall ensures Chicago's status as the nation's convention center.

NOVEMBER 18, 1960

McCormick Place, Chicago's grand bid to establish itself as America's convention capital, first opened its doors on this date to VIPs from around the world and to plant lovers who came for the Home and Flower Show. Given its central location and transportation network, the city had long been a meeting place. But before McCormick Place was built, trade shows were accommodated at the International Amphitheatre on the South Side, the Chicago Coliseum south of the Loop, and the Chicago Stadium on the West Side. All had drawbacks; supremacy in the convention business would require a large, permanent exhibition hall.

As early as 1927, *Tribune* publisher Robert R. McCormick foresaw that speedy travel and the nationalization of markets would spur demand for huge business meetings. After World War II, McCormick told managing editor W. Don Maxwell to see what could be done about building a convention center on the lakefront. Maxwell, in turn, put veteran political editor George Tagge on the case. Many interests opposed the idea, but, given Tagge's connections and the newspaper's influence, the Illinois legislature was persuaded to pass bills in the early 1950s to create and fund a city–state exposition authority. After protracted legal objections by those who wanted the Burnham Park site preserved for recreational use, ground was broken in 1958—three years after McCormick's death—on a $35 million hall that *Tribune* reporter Chesly Manly described as "larger than Circus Maximus of ancient Rome and more durable than the Colosseum."

▲ Tribune *political editor George Tagge, shown in 1970, had the connections in state government to get legislation passed that made McCormick Place possible.*

▼ *The first McCormick Place, named for* Tribune *publisher Robert R. McCormick, was built on the lakefront at 23rd Street on a portion of the "Century of Progress" fairgrounds. It was destroyed in a 1967 fire.*

Large it was, covering the equivalent of three city blocks. Durable it was not, for in the frigid, predawn hours of January 16, 1967, fire raced through the cavernous main hall, collapsing the roof and making a complete rebuilding necessary. Architect C. F. Murphy's dramatic black-steel design opened in 1971. Over the years, McCormick Place has made Chicago the unquestioned leader of a convention industry that annually generates an average of $9 billion in economic activity for Illinois. A second hall, west of Lake Shore Drive, was added in 1986; and with a third, $1.2 billion hall, opened in December 1996, the complex totaled 2.2 million square feet. But the dedication of the first McCormick Place marked the end of an era. It was the last time the *Tribune* threw its full weight so forcefully behind a single, highly controversial civic undertaking.

—*John McCarron*

The 1961 Stanley Cup

When the Blackhawks won their first championship in twenty-three years, the possibilities seemed endless.

APRIL 16, 1961

It was not even the biggest news story in their own city. A late spring snowstorm, with drifts of up to ten feet, dominated the news. In the middle of the front page in the next day's *Tribune* was a three-line headline: HAWKS BRING STANLEY CUP TO CHICAGO. A 5–1 victory over the Detroit Red Wings on this date in Detroit gave the Chicago Blackhawks their first Cup in twenty-three years. For the city, it was the first championship in any major sport since 1947, when the old Chicago Cardinals won the National Football League title.

The Blackhawks, who played their first season in 1926–27, raised Lord Stanley's chalice for the first time in 1934 and again in 1938. After a long sentence in hockey Siberia, the Blackhawks emerged in the 1960–61 season as an almost perfect blend of youth and experience, backstopped by peerless goalie Glenn Hall, the "quiet, calm, nerveless knight of the nets," as the *Tribune* described him.

Stan Mikita and Bobby Hull, the "Golden Jet," had yet to reach their prime but were already forces in the old six-team National Hockey League. Pierre Pilote, Ken Wharram, and Eric Nesterenko were entering their glory years. Still, trailing 1–0 during the first intermission of this sixth game of the Cup final, coach Rudy Pilous had to give his players a pep talk. "I just told them," he said later, "tonight's game was worth $1,000 to the winner, and the loser gets nothing." For the rest of the game, the Hawks set about burying the Wings; the third period became an exhibition in championship hockey, with three Hawks tallying. (It turned out each Blackhawk received an extra $1,750 for winning. The Red Wings received $750 per man.)

It seemed to many that this would be the first in a series of Cup titles for the Blackhawks. Soon a prolific young scorer, Phil Esposito, would be added. But in 1967, the Hawks finished a glorious regular season, first overall, only to fall in the semifinals. Esposito was traded. Hull left for Winnipeg. The Hawks were foiled twice—in 1971 and 1973—by Montreal in the final round. The team returned to the league finals in 1992, but four games later, the Pittsburgh Penguins raised the Cup. On a mid-April night in 1961, however, the future appeared to offer endless possibilities. But there was no celebrating with the fans on that Sunday night. The Hawks' flight from Detroit was canceled because of the snowstorm.

—Bob Foltman

▲ *A happy Rudy Pilous, coach of the Blackhawks, with the Stanley Cup after the Hawks beat the Detroit Red Wings in Game Six of the Cup final. With him are players Elmer Vasko (left) and Ed Litzenberger.*

◄ *Bobby Hull, the "Golden Jet," was one of the stars of the 1961 Blackhawks. Hull, shown here during the 1959 playoffs, played with the Hawks until 1972, when he left for Winnipeg.*

Bozo's Circus

The golden age of Chicago television was brief, but the flap-shoed clown endures.

SEPTEMBER 11, 1961

The television debut of *Bozo's Circus* on WGN in Chicago on this date signaled the beginning of an enduring city-clown alliance. Bozo is not the only clown to come out of Chicago, but he is surely the most popular. Technically speaking, however, he is not a native. At least one version of Bozo the Clown was born as a record-album character in 1946, and Bozo would be launched on television in other places before he took root in Chicago (longtime weatherman Willard Scott of NBC's *Today* show played him in Washington, D.C., in 1959).

Still, the red-haired, flap-shoed, hyperkinetic master of kiddie-show ceremonies—played by Bob Bell for the first twenty-three years and Joey D'Auria after that—became more popular in Chicago than in any of the other 182 television markets where, at his late-1960s peak, a version of him appeared. Because it is broadcast on cable-television superstation WGN, the *Bozo Show* (as it was later renamed) has a national presence, but it has never aimed for television greatness; its only goal is to please children.

Year after year, the cast has accomplished this admirably single-minded goal by rehashing old vaudeville bits that have been simplified for young audiences. Over time, this stubborn reliance on formula has come to be seen as a strength, a built-in nostalgia trip for the Chicagoans whose second visit to the show's set has occurred with children of their own in tow.

But Bozo's strong identification with the city has obscured Chicago's early television history. In TV's infancy, before New York and Hollywood became the twin—and only—peaks of the programming world, Chicago enjoyed a brief burst of sunshine with such shows as *Kukla, Fran and Ollie*, the deceptively simple sock-puppet theater of Fran Allison and Burr Tillstrom; *Studs' Place*, set in Studs Terkel's mythical corner pub; and, especially, *Garroway at Large*, a prototypical talk show with inventive, studio-roaming host Dave Garroway.

▲ Bozo's *original cast: Bob Bell as Bozo and, from left to right, Don Sandburg as Sandy, Ray Rayner as Oliver O'Oliver, Bob Trendler as Mr. Bob, and Ned Locke as Ringmaster Ned*

Unable to find a sponsor, *Garroway at Large* was dead by 1951. Garroway moved on to New York and greater fame as inaugural host of NBC's *Today*. Other talent followed similar paths, and by 1954 television production was virtually kaput in Chicago. There have been few gasps of air since those days. Movie critics Gene Siskel and Roger Ebert and talk-show hosts Phil Donahue and Oprah Winfrey gained national fame from a Chicago production platform. But only Winfrey's show has stuck around after celebrity was assured. Only Winfrey, that is, and—of course—Bozo.

—*Steve Johnson*

Robert Taylor Homes

Built with high hopes, America's largest public-housing project evolves into an emblem of failure.

MARCH 5, 1962

As a sort of welcome-wagon gift for the first family to move into the Robert Taylor Homes on this date, Mayor Richard J. Daley presented James Weston with flowers. Handing the bouquet to Weston, a glass inspector and married father of two children, Daley declared: "This is a great thing for the city. It provides decent housing for fine families." Thus was inaugurated the nation's largest public housing project, with more than forty-four hundred units. Within five years, the mayor said, the city hoped to eliminate most of the worst apartment buildings in Chicago and replace them with new housing.

Half of his dream was realized. Large chunks of black neighborhoods were covered with towering monoliths run by the Chicago Housing Authority (CHA): Cabrini-Green on the Near North Side; Henry Horner Homes on the West Side; and a four-mile swath of high-rises on the South Side, including the Taylor projects. CHA row houses, such as those built in the decade after the authority's 1937 founding, were overshadowed in the late 1950s and early 1960s by huge high-rise projects that planners hoped would house many more poor families relatively cheaply. But instead of supplanting shoddy housing, the complexes became hot zones for an array of social problems.

Even as the mayor welcomed the Weston family, the idea that places like Robert Taylor Homes would be humane replacements for slums was starting to crack. Many of the high-rise complexes were poorly constructed; two thousand workers slapped together Taylor's twenty-eight buildings at a rate of twenty-one floors a week, with elevator shafts exposed to the city's extreme weather. In CHA developments unemployment ran as high as 90 percent, and residents were at least twice as likely to be the victims of serious crime as other Chicagoans. The concentration of the poorest of the poor transformed Chicago's public housing into a national emblem of the failures of government-run shelter.

◀ *Housing projects were supposed to be way stations on the road to a better life, but they quickly became dead ends for most residents. Poorly constructed and inadequately maintained, the projects and their surroundings deteriorated rapidly. By 1995, some high-rises had been demolished, and more were slated for razing.*

While many of the CHA's high-rises were built at a time when the civil rights movement seemed to be making progress toward racial and economic equality, Chicago and many other cities were sowing the seeds of a mostly black underclass consigned to live their lives in vertical ghettos. James Weston and his family moved out of the Taylor project after five years, but that was a rare example of public housing as a stopping place on the way to a better life.

Admitting the failure of densely packed high-rises, the CHA began demolishing buildings at Cabrini-Green and Horner in 1995 and has planned to raze many more, including the one the Westons moved into that late winter day in 1962.

— *Flynn McRoberts*

▲ *The twenty-eight buildings at the Robert Taylor Homes contain more than forty-four hundred dwelling units. Although meant to be an improvement over the slums they replaced, the buildings turned into hot zones for a host of social problems, as did many high-rise projects across America.*

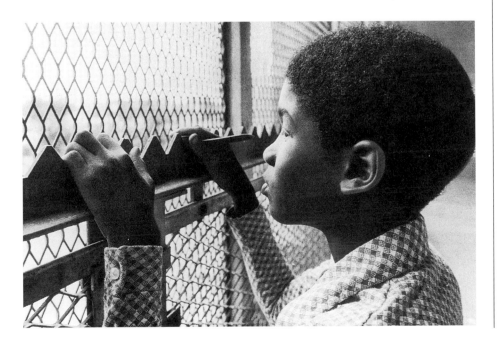

◄ *With drab exteriors and chain-link fences on the balconies, high-rise projects like the Robert Taylor Homes came to be seen by many residents and by outsiders as prisons for the poor.*

Sandburg Village

A risky urban renewal project convinces middle-class residents to stay in the city.

APRIL 19, 1963

It required Chicagoans of fearless spirit to become pioneer tenants at Sandburg Village. So it was fitting that Anthony Yasillo, a lion keeper at Lincoln Park Zoo, was among the first ten occupants to move in on this date. The giant project, which ultimately totaled twenty-six hundred units in nine high-rises and adjacent town houses, was built amid a Near North Side area of blight, brothels, and banditry, all pressing in on Chicago's exclusive Gold Coast.

Other large urban-renewal projects preceded it, notably in Hyde Park near the University of Chicago and on the Near South Side; but Sandburg, so close to downtown and the Gold Coast, was a crucial test of the ability of the city to repair itself.

Security concerns were high at the development, whose sixteen acres were bounded by North Avenue and LaSalle, Clark, and Division Streets. A block away was Wells Street, lined with raucous bars. The violence and squalor of the Cabrini-Green public housing complex loomed farther west. The new construction was a $40-million-plus gamble to save the Near North Side and, in turn, stave off the blight threatening Chicago's business core to the south and the Lincoln Park neighborhood to the north. "The whole area would have gone down the drain," declared Arthur Rubloff, Sandburg Village's chief promoter, a flamboyant, indefatigable real-estate baron who was known neither for understatement nor small plans.

He had a point. Sandburg Village was a model at a time when middle-class flight was devastating Chicago and older cities across the nation. Sandburg Village attracted eight thousand residents, who formed a nucleus that slowly transformed the entire area. Encouraged by the presence of a prosperous anchor, venturesome

▲ *These buildings along North Clark Street were torn down to make way for Sandburg Village. With changing tastes, they might have been preserved in later years for their vintage charm.*

▼ *With its core of middle-class residents, Sandburg Village was able to support such events as an annual art fair, shown here in 1973.*

◄ *Covering sixteen acres on Chicago's Near North Side, Sandburg Village's nine high-rises and adjacent town houses provided housing for eight thousand people. Those residents formed a nucleus that slowly transformed the entire area.*

urbanites began to fix up homes in nearby Old Town, south Lincoln Park, and the western blocks of the Gold Coast. By the late 1970s, prices in those areas had sky-rocketed, real-estate money had begun to move to working-class sections of the North and Northwest Sides, and the word "gentrification" had entered the city's vocabulary. In the 1990s, high-priced homes even began to encircle Cabrini-Green. And, with changing tastes, housing of the sort razed to make way for Sandburg was being preserved for its vintage charm.

Other cities have attempted similar redevelopments around their central areas, but few have been as effective in sparking private investment as Sandburg, which was converted to condominiums in 1979. Moreover, Sandburg Village encouraged two other publicly supported developments that have provided an arc of middle-class residential buffers for the Loop on the west and south: Presidential Towers and Dearborn Park. The three projects were contrived to provide critical masses of people to preserve the blight-threatened edges of downtown. All spawned the hoped-for revitalization, and many thousands of new middle-class residents have made downtown Chicago one of America's most vibrant central areas.

—*J. Linn Allen*

▼ *The renovation of old buildings and the construction of new houses for middle-class buyers in formerly working-class areas added the word "gentrification" to the city's vocabulary. The influence of Sandburg Village can be seen in this development in Wicker Park.*

Kennedy's Assassination

A president dies in Dallas. So does a kind of innocence.

NOVEMBER 22, 1963

On this day, a Friday, President John F. Kennedy was assassinated while riding in a motorcade through Dallas. Chicago froze in horror, the moment sealed in memories people would carry for the rest of their lives. Office workers on their lunch hours when the news broke stood on the street, some too shocked to speak, some openly weeping. Crowds gathered around loudspeakers strung up in the Loop, listened to radios in hotel lobbies, and watched television sets in restaurants and bars.

A middle-aged woman who heard the news in front of a Michigan Avenue hotel grabbed her husband by the arm but could not say anything, according to a story in the *Tribune*. Neither could her husband: "He put his hand over his mouth. Finally, the silence was broken by the woman, who said, 'Oh, my God!' That was all she was able to say. Then the two shocked, suddenly grief-stricken people looked at each other and there were tears streaming down both of their faces."

Mayor Richard J. Daley, a close ally whose delivery of Illinois during the 1960 election was crucial to Kennedy's victory, burst into tears during a lunch meeting of the Cook County Democratic Central Committee. He dictated a statement and then left for his home. "I cannot express my deep grief and sorrow over the tragic death of President John F. Kennedy," the statement read in part. "His vital spirit, sincerity, and warm personality have given us all a memory that we will cherish and never forget." Black mourning drapes were placed around the LaSalle Street entrance to City Hall.

On Monday, the official day of mourning, the city essentially shut down. Virtually all public offices were closed, as were most businesses. Chicago public schools closed after a morning memorial service. Catholic schools and suburban schools closed, and most colleges and universities suspended classes. When funeral services began in Washington, Chicago Transit Authority trains and buses halted for a minute of silence. The city's sidewalks were nearly empty. Highway traffic slowed to a trickle. Lake Shore Drive was deserted. The cars, buses, trains, and people slowly returned; but for many, in Chicago and across the nation, a kind of innocence never did.

—*Barbara Brotman*

The 1963 NFL Championship

On a freezing winter day, the Bears win the Bears' way—with defense.

▼ *Bears linebacker Larry Morris brings down Y. A. Tittle, hitting the Giants quarterback in the knee with his helmet. Tittle was much less effective for the rest of the game.*

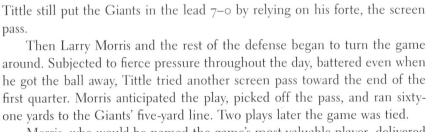

▲ *The heart of the 1963 Bears' league-leading defense—and of the entire team—was its corps of linebackers: (from left) Larry Morris, Bill George, and Joe Fortunato.*

December 29, 1963

Grit, savvy, and sheer brutality—those are classic Chicago traits, no matter what the endeavor, and they brought the National Football League championship to Chicago on this date, when the Bears defeated the New York Giants 14–10. The Bears had not been a dominant team since the early 1940s, and there were doubts that such success would ever come their way again, given owner-founder George Halas's tight-fisted ways ("He throws nickels around like manhole covers," said tight end Mike Ditka) and his supposed resistance to new offensive strategies. The Bears would be smash-mouth or not be at all—that was the team image, and this game epitomized it.

▲ *Owner-coach George Halas embraces linebacker Larry Morris after the Bears' 14–10 victory, the last championship that Halas would live to see. Morris was named the game's most valuable player.*

Led by linebackers Bill George, Joe Fortunato, and Larry Morris, and defensive ends Doug Atkins and Ed O'Bradovich, the 1963 Bears held their opponents to a then-league-record-low 144 points and finished 11–1–2 to win the Western Conference, twice beating Vince Lombardi's defending champion Green Bay Packers. By contrast, the Giants' strength was their offense—in particular, the passing of veteran quarterback Y. A. Tittle. Stopping Tittle was the Bears' game plan. Some of their work was done for them—at kickoff the temperature was nine degrees at Wrigley Field, not conducive to a wide-open offense—but Tittle still put the Giants in the lead 7–0 by relying on his forte, the screen pass.

Then Larry Morris and the rest of the defense began to turn the game around. Subjected to fierce pressure throughout the day, battered even when he got the ball away, Tittle tried another screen pass toward the end of the first quarter. Morris anticipated the play, picked off the pass, and ran sixty-one yards to the Giants' five-yard line. Two plays later the game was tied.

Morris, who would be named the game's most valuable player, delivered a second, and literal, blow to the Giants a few minutes later when he broke in on Tittle and hit him in the knee with his helmet just as the quarterback threw. From that point, the gutty but limping Tittle was much less effective, the coup de grâce being delivered in the third quarter when O'Bradovich, working in concert with Fortunato, picked off another screen pass deep in Giants territory. That led to the Bears' second touchdown and gave them the lead for the first time. There was no way this team was going to relinquish it.

—Larry Kart

The Beatles at the Amphitheatre

The Fab Four finds delirious fans and jelly beans on their first visit to Chicago.

SEPTEMBER 5, 1964

The Beatles' Chicago debut must have been a blur for John Lennon, Paul McCartney, George Harrison, and Ringo Starr: on their first major North American tour the quartet traveled twenty-two thousand miles in twenty-nine grueling days. But for their fans in that first summer of Beatlemania in America, it was a thrill they would never forget. A few hours after their 4:30 P.M. landing on this date at Midway Airport—where a crowd of five thousand greeted them—the Beatles performed a concert at the International Amphitheatre typical of their whirlwind visit.

For $30,000, they played thirty-four minutes to a screaming audience that made the effortless melodies and lovelorn lyrics of the eleven songs—from "I Want to Hold Your Hand" to "Can't Buy Me Love"—virtually an afterthought. The thirteen thousand mostly teenage, mostly female concertgoers showered their heroes with jelly beans, in response to an innocent remark by Harrison earlier in the year about his favorite snack food. Critics around town reacted bemusedly, with a condescending pat on the head to the youngsters for not starting a riot. "No, we wouldn't have missed it," declared *Tribune* columnist David Condon, who covered the concert in a departure from his normal sports duties. "Not because the Beatle noise beats anything that can't be stirred up around the piano bar at the Singapore, but because the Saturday show gave us a chance to be proud of the juveniles, who are pretty much maligned in this turbulent age."

Another *Tribune* account quoted a pair of mothers after the show. "I feel sorry for them," one said. "Who do you mean, the Beatles or the girls?" the second responded. "The Beatles," replied the first. "What will happen to them when all this adulation has passed them by?" More than thirty years later, there was still no answer to that question. Rock took off in many directions after that first concert tour by the lads from Liverpool, changed forever by them and the other groups of the "British Invasion," such as the Rolling Stones and the Who. But some of the simple joy of that time lived on. When McCartney returned to Soldier Field in 1990 to perform many of his old band's hits, the screams were just as loud, as though Chicago still had not gotten over its first bout of Beatlemania.

—Greg Kot

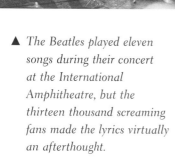

▲ *The Beatles played eleven songs during their concert at the International Amphitheatre, but the thirteen thousand screaming fans made the lyrics virtually an afterthought.*

▶

Some five thousand Beatlemaniacs were on hand to greet the band at Midway Airport.

The Richard Speck Case

Eight young women die at the hands of a drifter during a night of senseless horror.

JULY 13, 1966

The hiring hall for merchant seamen on Chicago's Southeast Side was just down the street from a town house where nine student nurses lived. On the night of July 13, a drifter who had been looking for work on a Great Lakes freighter broke into their townhouse. His name was Richard Franklin Speck.

Armed with a knife and a revolver, he woke and hog-tied the women and then methodically strangled and stabbed eight of them, spending at least a half-hour on each victim and washing his hands before going to the next. The ninth woman was Filipino exchange student Corazon Amurao, who escaped death by scooting under a bed and hiding until Speck left.

After dawn on July 14, Amurao made her way to a ledge outside a second-floor window. "They are all dead," she screamed. "My friends are all dead. Oh God, I'm the only one alive." Her description of the killer and fingerprints at the scene fueled a massive manhunt for the man responsible for the slaughter.

A twenty-four-year-old high school dropout and drifter, Speck was born in Monmouth, Illinois, but spent much of his youth in Texas, where he floated in and out of trouble. By the spring of 1966, he was wanted for questioning in connection with an attempted rape and murder in Monmouth, to which he had returned. He seemed destined to play the part of the fiendish loser, right down to his tattoos: "Born to Raise Hell" on his left forearm, "Love" and "Hate" on his knuckles.

As police scoured the nation, Speck spent the next three days hiding in Chicago flophouses and then tried to slit his wrists. He was taken to Cook County Hospital, where a doctor spotted the tattoos and called authorities.

Speck never denied committing the murders, but he claimed he blacked out after a binge of drinking and taking drugs and had no idea what he had done that night. In 1967, he was condemned to death, but the U.S. Supreme Court overturned the sentence. Speck spent the rest of his life in Stateville Correctional Center, near Joliet. In a bizarre videotape made years later by fellow prisoners, he was asked why he had killed the young nurses. "It just wasn't their night," he said and then laughed. Speck died in December 1991 after a heart attack.

—*Bob Secter*

▲ *Born to raise hell: Richard Speck in 1967 with public defender Gerald Getty.*

Martin Luther King Jr. in Chicago

During his stay in the city, the civil-rights leader faced a "hateful" crowd.

AUGUST 5, 1966

On this muggy Friday afternoon, Martin Luther King Jr. stepped out of the car that had ferried him to Marquette Park, on Chicago's Southwest Side, to lead a march of about seven hundred people. The civil-rights leader and his supporters were in the white ethnic enclave to protest housing segregation. Thousands of jeering, taunting whites had gathered. The mood was ominous. One placard read: "King would look good with a knife in his back."

As King walked past the police who separated the marchers from the hostile crowd, someone hurled a stone. It struck King on the head. Stunned, he fell to one knee. He stayed on the ground for several seconds, shaking off the blow. As he rose, aides and bodyguards surrounded him, holding placards to protect him from the rocks, bottles, and firecrackers that rained down on the demonstrators. King was one of thirty people who were injured; the disturbance resulted in forty arrests. He later explained why he put himself at risk: "I have to do this—to expose myself—to bring this hate into the open." He had done that before, but Chicago was different. "I have seen many demonstrations in the South, but I have never seen anything so hostile and so hateful as I've seen here today," he said.

King brought his protest movement north in 1966 to take on black urban problems, especially segregation. Chicago seemed like the perfect arena. Many in its large black community hailed from the South, the city had numerous activists, and white real-estate agents generally did not sell property in white neighborhoods to blacks or other minorities. To show his commitment to the northern campaign, King rented a $90-a-month, four-room apartment in January at 1550 South Hamlin Avenue, on the West Side.

◀ King, with his wife, Coretta, waves to a crowd after moving into an apartment on the city's West Side in January 1966, at the start of his Chicago campaign against segregated housing. With him is Andrew Young (far left), who later became mayor of Atlanta.

▲ King's stay in Chicago resulted in an agreement by local real-estate agents to abide by the city's fair-housing ordinance in exchange for an end to protest marches. King is shown in November 1966, reviewing a copy of the ordinance with a West Side real-estate agent.

The Marquette Park march was one of many staged by King's movement that summer in Chicago. The protests were designed to pressure the city's white leaders into making solid commitments to open housing. But King's battle was not only against racism. He also faced Mayor Richard J. Daley, whose love for his city was so profound that he disdained those, particularly outsiders, who pointed out its faults. King got little sympathy from Daley. "Maybe he doesn't have all the facts on the local situation," the mayor said. "After all, he is a resident of another city."

The marches and the threat of marches that had the potential to be more violent than at Marquette Park led to an accord that year between the protesters and the Chicago Real Estate Board. The board agreed to end its opposition to open-housing laws and ask its members to abide by Chicago's fair-housing ordinance in exchange for an end to the demonstrations. Many blacks viewed the settlement as a sellout. Before he left town, a weary King acknowledged the modest gains. It was "a first step in a thousand-mile journey," he said.

—*Frank James*

▲ *Supporters shield Martin Luther King Jr. after the civil-rights leader was hit on the head by a stone during an open-housing march in Marquette Park.*

▶

At another march two days after the Marquette Park incident, white youths demonstrate the intensity of racial feeling in the city that summer.

The Blizzard of 1967

Winter in Chicago has never been easy, but this one was a record-setter.

JANUARY 26, 1967

At 5:02 A.M. on this date, it began to snow. Nothing remarkable about that. It was January in Chicago, and four inches of snow had been predicted. But it kept on snowing, all through this miserable Thursday and into early Friday morning, until it finally stopped at 10:10 A.M. By then, twenty-three inches covered Chicago and the suburbs, the largest single snowfall in the city's history.

Thousands were stranded in offices, schools, and buses. About fifty thousand abandoned cars and eight hundred Chicago Transit Authority buses littered the streets and expressways. Most people simply wanted to get home. One woman who worked downtown on Wacker Drive and lived on the city's North Side—normally a thirty-five-minute trip—spent four hours en-route. In south suburban Markham, 650 students at four schools camped out in libraries and gymnasiums because school buses could not get through. "They are all enjoying themselves," Superintendent J. Lewis Weingarner told the *Tribune.* "This is a night that will go down in many memory books."

Some memories were not as cheerful. Looting was rampant. Long lines formed at grocery stores, and shelves were emptied in moments. As a result of the record snow, twenty-six people died, including a minister who was run over by a snowplow and a ten-year-old girl who was accidentally caught in the crossfire between police and looters. Several others died of heart attacks from shoveling snow.

The Blizzard of '67 proved the wisdom behind the Chicago saying, "If you don't like the weather, just wait a minute." Only two

◀ *Abandoned vehicles made even major streets and highways impassable.*

days before, the temperature had reached an unseasonable *sixty-five degrees*. Generally, winter is the time that tries the soul of even the most devoted Chicagoan. Temperatures frequently fall below zero in January and February, and futile battles with big snows are a regular—but thankfully not an annual—occurrence. In the month of January 1918, forty-two inches of the white stuff descended on the city. The 20.3 inches of snow that fell in mid-January 1979 piled up on top of snow already on the ground, producing a record accumulation of 29 inches.

The paralyzing strength of the '67 storm suspended normal routines for days. The latticework of stranded cars, trucks, and buses plugged up roads. Thousands of air travelers and workers were stranded at Chicago's three airports, which were closed for unprecedented long stretches. Drifts ten feet high covered Midway Airport's runways. Though Mayor Richard J. Daley had workers clearing streets around the clock, he appealed to owners of snow-removal equipment to donate their services. Still, it was great to be a child during the Blizzard of '67. There were mountains of snow to play in, and plenty of time to play in them: schools were closed for several days.

—*Allan Johnson*

▲ *The heavy snowfall of the 1967 blizzard turned the landscape white and forced many motorists to leave their cars behind, as happened here on the Oakwood Drive entry to Lake Shore Drive.*

▶

After the snowing stopped, the cleanup began. Fierce winds whipped the snow into drifts as high as twelve feet.

◀ *At least some enjoyed the snow. Children frolic among buried cars in the Edgewater neighborhood, on Chicago's North Side.*

Chicago's Picasso

The unveiling of the puzzling sculpture changes the public art landscape.

▼ *The Picasso, which celebrated art rather than civic achievement, paved the way for other works of modern public art, such as Claes Oldenburg's 1977* Batcolumn, *at Madison and Jefferson Streets.*

► *Alexander Calder's* Flamingo, *another legacy of the Picasso, stands in Federal Plaza. It was erected in 1974.*

AUGUST 15, 1967

Just after noon on this date, Mayor Richard J. Daley pulled a cord attached to twelve hundred square feet of blue-green fabric, unwrapping a gift "to the people of Chicago" from an artist who had never visited—and had shown no previous interest in—the city. The artist was Pablo Picasso, who at age eighty-five had dominated Western art for more than half a century. He had been approached by William E. Hartmann, senior partner of Skidmore, Owings and Merrill, one of the architectural firms collaborating on Chicago's new Civic Center. Hartmann had wanted a sculpture for the plaza bordered by Washington, Randolph, Dearborn, and Clark Streets.

The architect visited Picasso at his home in southern France, presenting several gifts (including a Sioux war bonnet and a White Sox blazer) plus a check for $100,000 from the Chicago Public Building Commission. Picasso responded not with an original design but one from the early 1960s that he modified, combining motifs from as far back as the beginning of the century. The result was a forty-two-inch maquette, or model, for a sculpture made of Cor-Ten steel, the same material used on the Civic Center building. The American Bridge division of U.S. Steel, in

Gary, Indiana, translated the maquette into a piece that weighed 162 tons and rose to a height of fifty feet. It was the first monumental outdoor Picasso in North America.

At the unveiling, Daley said, "We dedicate this celebrated work this morning with the belief that what is strange to us today will be familiar tomorrow." The process of familiarization brought trouble. Picasso's untitled sculpture proclaimed metamorphosis the chief business of an artist by crossing images of an Afghan dog and a woman. However, the effort at first did not count for much, in part because Chicago's earlier monuments—statues of past leaders—commemorated a different idea: civic achievement. Colonel Jack Reilly, the mayor's director of special events, immediately urged removal of the sculpture. Alderman John J. Hoellen went further, recommending that the City Council "deport" the piece and construct in its place a statue of "Mr. Cub . . . Ernie Banks."

In 1970, a federal judge ruled that since the full-size sculpture was technically a copy of the maquette, it could not be copyrighted by anyone. This opened the way to countless reproductions that bred familiarity, the first step toward love. The name-brand quality of the sculpture inspired other commissions—from Alexander Calder, Marc Chagall, Joan Miró, Claes Oldenburg, Henry Moore—that found easier acceptance among Chicagoans, though not the same awestruck affection. As much as the Water Tower, the Picasso became a symbol of the city.

—Alan G. Artner

▲ *Mayor Richard J. Daley (closest to the sculpture) unveils the Picasso "with the belief that what is strange to us today will be familiar tomorrow."*

The Closing of Riverview

To generations of Chicagoans, it was a place to "laugh your troubles away."

▼ *With heart-pounding drops like this one, the Bobs was justifiably considered Riverview's scariest roller coaster.*

OCTOBER 3, 1967

Children would beg their parents to drive by slowly—especially at night—so they could savor the lights, watch one of the Pair-O-Chutes float to the ground from an Erector-Set tower, and listen to the squeals of terrified riders on the roller coasters. It was Riverview, a place where, in the words of well-named entertainer and television pitchman Dick "Two-Ton" Baker, you could "laugh your troubles away."

Opened in 1904 on what was the German Sharpshooters club at Western and Belmont Avenues, on Chicago's North Side, Riverview began with three rides on seventy-four acres and the promise of "an avalanche of novelties, a whirlwind of surprises." Over the years the novelties and surprises grew, and the park became a second home to generations of youngsters. Toward the end there were 120 rides, including six roller coasters, plus a midway complete with freaks and barkers and Kewpie dolls.

More than 1.7 million people visited the park in 1967, nearly as many as watched the Cubs and White Sox at home that year combined. But it was not enough to save the park. On this date—a month after the park's annual Labor Day "Mardi Gras" had ended its season—came the announcement that Riverview had been sold to developers for more than $6 million. Aladdin's Castle and the Pair-O-Chutes and the Tunnel of Love and the Flying Turns and the Water Bug and the Rotor and the Ghost Train and—was this really happening?—even the revered Bobs would be flattened, gone, history.

In truth, Riverview, though still profitable, had in its final years lost some of its sparkle. By the mid-1960s, some troubles could not just be laughed away. "'Midst all the dripping nostalgia over the demise of Riverview," wrote the *Tribune's* Herb Lyon in his Tower Ticker column, "one sorry fact stands out. It was sold to industrial interests primarily because of the unprecedented leap in juvenile delin-punksy this past season. In fact, it was a tinder-box nightly, with violence lurking behind the rollercoaster fun—and is one more casualty of the way things are."

—*Alan Solomon*

▲ *World War II–era couples put the Tunnel of Love to good use.*

▲ *Riverview as it appeared on the day of the announcement that the sixty-three-year-old amusement park had been sold to developers. In the foreground is the Belmont Avenue bridge over the North Branch of the Chicago River. In the upper-left corner is Lane Technical High School, at the corner of Addison Street and Western Avenue.*

The King Riots

The city erupts in violence following the killing of Martin Luther King Jr.

APRIL 5, 1968

Before darkness fell on this day, a Friday, the plumes of smoke from the West Side already were visible to Loop office workers. In Chicago and across the nation, rioting was breaking out in response to the news that Martin Luther King Jr. had been gunned down in Memphis the day before. On Friday evening, at the beginning of what would become a hellish weekend, commuters jammed Lake Shore Drive in an effort to avoid the chaos along the Eisenhower Expressway, which ran through the worst of the riot area.

Many American cities—including Detroit, Newark, and Los Angeles—were convulsed by riots in the mid-1960s. Chicago had not escaped unscathed; riots in the Humboldt Park neighborhood in 1966 had seemed major when they happened. Yet the city had been spared the kind of devastation left in the wake of Los Angeles's Watts riots of 1965. With the assassination of King, the city's luck ran out.

Throughout the weekend, police in the Lawndale and Austin neighborhoods on the West Side and in the Woodlawn neighborhood on the South Side rushed from emergency call to emergency call as mobs of men, women, and children moved from store to store, breaking plate-glass windows and taking what they found. Television sets, clothing, food, and liquor were carted away from largely white-owned businesses that lined Madison Street and Homan and Kedzie Avenues. Fires blazed out of control across the West Side.

Not long after sunset Friday, army units and the first of three thousand Illinois National Guard troops arrived to back up police, who had no training for such a civic catastrophe. Military units and fire department crews were greeted by sniper fire, but no soldiers, police, or firefighters were killed or seriously hurt. By Saturday afternoon, soldiers in Jeeps bristling with machine guns had secured the overpasses along the Eisenhower Expressway from downtown almost to the city's western edge. The fires, shootings, and looting continued through Sunday night, but by Monday morning relative quiet had returned.

◀ *Widespread looting devastated blocks of West Side shops during the riots. Looting also broke out in the Woodlawn neighborhood, on the South Side.*

Mayor Richard J. Daley later told reporters that he had ordered police "to shoot to kill any arsonist or anyone with a Molotov cocktail in his hand . . . and . . . to shoot to maim or cripple anyone looting any stores in our city." In the first two days of rioting, police reported numerous civilian deaths but were unable to determine whether they were caused by the riots or other crimes. No official death toll was given for the tragedy, although published accounts say nine to eleven people died during the rioting. Three hundred fifty people were arrested for looting, and 162 buildings were destroyed by arson. Bulldozers moved in to clean up after the rioters, leaving behind vacant lots that remained empty three decades later.

—*James Coates*

▲ *On the first day of rioting, smoke from fires on Madison Street fills the sky above the West Side.*

▼ *Chicago police, rifles at the ready, crouch behind a patrol car to take cover from a sniper.*

The 1968 Democratic Convention

At the height of a stormy year, Chicago streets become nightly battle zones.

AUGUST 26, 1968

Across the country and in Chicago, tensions were already at near-hysterical levels by the time delegates to the Democratic National Convention arrived for the convention's opening session on this date. The flames and destruction of the King riots on the West and South Sides in April were still vivid memories. In June, Senator Robert F. Kennedy's final words had included the phrase "On to Chicago" when his presidential candidacy was cut short by an assassin's bullet in California.

And during the summer, colorful, publicity-seeking young activists such as Abbie Hoffman and Jerry Rubin had vowed to lead thousands of Vietnam War protesters to Chicago to disrupt the convention. Chicago police fueled the paranoia by publicizing reports that demonstrators were planning

▲ *Antiwar demonstrators march down Michigan Avenue in one of the peaceful events of the convention week, which attracted thousands of young protesters to the city.*

▶

By the time the 1968 Democratic convention began, tensions were already high. Security at the International Amphitheatre was so heavy that the Tribune called the convention site "a veritable stockade."

to spike the city's water supply with LSD. Daley, a major influence in the Democratic Party, made it clear he would brook no attempts to disrupt the convention or sully the city's name. The Illinois National Guard was called up, and roads to the International Amphitheatre were surrounded with such heavy security that the *Tribune* called the convention site "a veritable stockade."

As delegates jammed into Chicago's downtown hotels, thousands of young demonstrators, and some sightseers, moved into Lincoln Park. Demonstration leaders' attempts to get city permits to spend nights in the park had failed. So each night police moved in, sometimes using tear gas and physical force to clear them out. At first, the news media focused on events at the Amphitheatre, where, in spite of the inevitable conclusion that Hubert Humphrey would secure the presidential nomi-

▲ *Each night, Chicago police cleared Lincoln Park, where the demonstrators gathered during the day. Sometimes the police used tear gas, as here. Sometimes, they used physical force.*

◀ *Protesters as well as police braced for trouble. Here, anti-Vietnam War demonstrators gather in Lincoln Park for self-defense lessons.*

► *As the week wore on, confrontations between protesters and police became more violent, reaching a peak on the night of Wednesday, August 28, when police charged and beat demonstrators with their clubs.*

▼ *The confrontation in the streets led to commotion at the International Amphitheatre, where Senator Abraham Ribicoff denounced the "gestapo tactics" of Chicago police. An outraged Mayor Richard J. Daley (hand to mouth) shouts at the senator, joined by his sons Richard M. (the future mayor, also with hand to mouth), John (left of mayor, shouting), and Bill (behind Richard M.).*

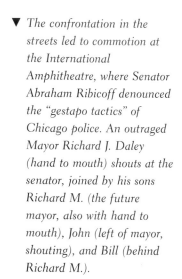

nation, tempers flared during debate on the Vietnam War. CBS reporters Mike Wallace and Dan Rather were roughed up on camera by security guards, causing anchor Walter Cronkite to intone to a national audience, "I think we've got a bunch of thugs here, if I may be permitted to say so."

The nightly clashes between demonstrators and increasingly angry Chicago police reached their pinnacle on the night of Wednesday, August 28. Television cameramen in the Conrad Hilton Hotel (the former Stevens Hotel), at Michigan Avenue and Balbo Drive, turned their cameras down on the crowd, which chanted "The whole world's watching." Someone threw a beer can. Police charged and dragged off protesters, beating them with their clubs and fists. "Many convention visitors and others watched the battle from upper windows of the hotel," the *Tribune* wrote the next day. "Many were appalled at what they considered unnatural enthusiasm of police for the job of arresting demonstrators." It would later be called a "police riot." The street battle led to another confrontation that night at the Amphitheatre. In his speech nominating George McGovern, Connecticut Senator Abraham Ribicoff criticized the "gestapo tactics on the streets of Chicago." Television cameras zoomed in on an enraged Mayor Daley, shouting back at the rostrum.

The convention chaos was cited as a major factor in the election later that year of Republican Richard M. Nixon. Daley launched a campaign to restore the city's tarnished image, but Chicago, which had hosted more political conventions than any other city by far, was shunned by both parties for the next twenty-eight years. Not until August 1996, with a different Mayor Richard Daley running Chicago, did the Democrats return. That convention, at which President Bill Clinton was nominated for a second term, was a calm, carefully managed affair. But the whole world was not watching.

—*Robert Davis*

◀ Demonstrators swarm over the statue of General John Logan in Grant Park across from the Conrad Hilton Hotel. Many delegates and Vice President Hubert Humphrey, the Democratic presidential nominee, stayed at the hotel, later renamed the Chicago Hilton.

▶

Antiwar demonstrators seek relief from tear gas at Buckingham Fountain, in Grant Park.

The Chicago Seven Trial

High drama and high jinks fill the courtroom as the counterculture confronts a straitlaced judge.

SEPTEMBER 24, 1969

Everybody knew it would be interesting, the trial of eight people charged with conspiring to incite the riots that erupted during the 1968 Democratic National Convention in Chicago. How could it not be, with a cast of characters that included hippie leaders Abbie Hoffman and Jerry Rubin, Black Panther Party leader Bobby Seale, activist ideologues Tom Hayden and Rennie Davis, old-time liberal David Dellinger, and strict and conservative Federal District Judge Julius J. Hoffman? But nobody knew as the trial began on this morning that it would drag out over four and a half months and disintegrate into a chaotic shambles that came to symbolize the widening gap between generations cleaved by the war in Vietnam.

Beginning as the Chicago Eight trial, it quickly became the Chicago Seven when Seale, after loudly disrupting the trial when he could not have the lawyer of his choice, was at first bound and gagged in the courtroom and then severed from the case for a later trial, which never occurred. Judge Hoffman, a stickler for courtroom decorum, was challenged daily by the defendants, especially Abbie Hoffman, who called the judge "Julie" and once entered the courtroom wearing judicial robes, which he threw to the floor and trod upon. The trial became a three-sided war between the defendants and their lawyers, William Kunstler and Leonard Weinglass; the prosecutors, Thomas Foran and Richard Schultz; and the judge.

That war extended to the streets as well, with almost daily demonstrations in Chicago's South Loop. On October 11, a Saturday Loop rally turned violent in the

▼ *Defendants Hoffman (left) and Rubin sport judicial robes to mock the proceedings. Later, Hoffman wore his robes into the courtroom and then threw them on the floor and trod upon them.*

▼ *The Days of Rage riots erupted on October 11, 1969, to protest the trial. Richard Elrod (left), an assistant city corporation counsel at the time who later became Cook County sheriff, was partially paralyzed during a scuffle later in the day.*

▲ *The Chicago Seven at one of their many news conferences: (from left) Lee Weiner, Rennie Davis, David Dellinger (holding his granddaughter), Abbie Hoffman, Jerry Rubin, Tom Hayden, and John Froines*

▼ *Federal Judge Julius Hoffman, a stickler for courtroom decorum, was challenged at every turn.*

notorious Days of Rage riots, when members of the Weatherman faction and other antiwar groups ran amok in the city streets, breaking windows, fighting police, and leaving an assistant city corporation counsel, Richard Elrod, partially paralyzed when he tried to seize a demonstrator.

The defense presented a parade of witnesses that included singers Judy Collins, Pete Seeger, and Arlo Guthrie; cultural icons Allen Ginsburg and Timothy Leary; writers Norman Mailer, Paul Krassner, and William Styron; and Mayor Richard J. Daley.

The trial ended on February 18, 1970, with the jury deciding that five of the defendants—Rubin, Hoffman, Hayden, Davis, and Dellinger—had incited riots but had not conspired to do so. Defendants Lee Weiner and John Froines were acquitted of all charges. But Judge Hoffman sentenced all seven defendants and two defense lawyers to contempt-of-court jail sentences. Eventually, all of the contempt sentences and the riot charges were either dismissed by higher courts or dropped by the government. At the time, it was the Trial of the Century, untelevised but reported extensively. In the end, though, the Chicago Seven trial seemed to amount to nothing at all.

—*Robert Davis*

The 1969 Cubs

The North Siders flirt with pennant glory but fade as summer wears on.

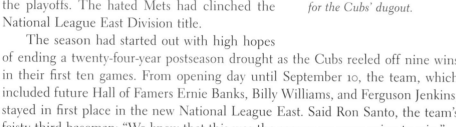

SEPTEMBER 24, 1969

*For of all sad words of tongue or pen,
the saddest are these: 'It might have been!'*
—John Greenleaf Whittier (1856)

Those words were lamentably appropriate for the Chicago Cubs on this painful day, when the team's legendary futility reached a record low. Barely three weeks after holding a four-game lead over the New York Mets, the Cubs found themselves mathematically eliminated from the playoffs. The hated Mets had clinched the National League East Division title.

The season had started out with high hopes of ending a twenty-four-year postseason drought as the Cubs reeled off nine wins in their first ten games. From opening day until September 10, the team, which included future Hall of Famers Ernie Banks, Billy Williams, and Ferguson Jenkins, stayed in first place in the new National League East. Said Ron Santo, the team's feisty third baseman: "We knew that this was the season we were going to win."

Ken Holtzman pitched a no-hitter August 19 against the Atlanta Braves, but by then the teasing baseball gods were warming up. A nine-and-a-half-game lead over the New York Mets started to disappear—oh, so slowly. By the end of the month, the Mets had chipped the Cubs' lead to four games. Salt in the wound was an eight-game losing streak from September 3 to the eleventh that coincided with a Mets' seven-game winning streak. "If I'd known we were going to lose eight straight," Manager Leo Durocher said later, "I would have just played nine pitchers every day and let everyone else go home and rest."

▲ *A black cat wanders onto the field during a Cubs–Mets game in New York in September. It heads, naturally, for the Cubs' dugout.*

Explanations for the Cubs' collapse abounded, from the team becoming too wrapped up in off-the-field endeavors to the remote possibility that the Mets, who would go on to win the World Series, simply had a better team. Wrote *Tribune* sports columnist Robert Markus: "My theory is that the Cubs simply had to shoulder their burden too long. It is impossible to endure the kind of pressure the Cubs were under for six months." Whatever the reason, it was the Mets who celebrated the night of September 24. "The Mets served champagne, shaving cream and bath towels tonight to one and all, including themselves," wrote the *Tribune's* Edward Prell from New York that evening. It might have been the Cubs.

—*Steve Nidetz*

▼ *Dejected Cubs players leave Wrigley Field following another loss during their infamous September swoon.*

The Black Panther Raid

Controversy rages after seven minutes of gunfire silence two members of the revolutionary group.

DECEMBER 4, 1969

With sunrise more than an hour away, eight policemen from the Cook County state's attorney's office crept to the front of a tattered two-flat on Chicago's West Side on this date. Another six officers were at the back door. Inside, nine people slept in the first-floor apartment, where nineteen guns and more than one thousand rounds of ammunition were stored. This apartment, at 2337 West Monroe Street, was a stronghold of the Illinois Black Panther Party, a branch of a national group known for revolutionary politics and for killing cops.

About 4:45 A.M., Sergeant Daniel Groth knocked on the front door. When there was no answer, he knocked with his gun. The next seven minutes of gunfire became one of the most hotly disputed incidents of the turbulent 1960s. After the shooting stopped, Illinois Black Panther leader Fred Hampton, twenty-one, and a party leader from Peoria, Mark Clark, twenty-two, were dead.

Racial tensions, police suspicion, and the Panthers' radical politics had already proved a volatile combination. Founded in 1966, the party quickly became a menacing, yet romanticized, force. In the two years before the raid, police and Panthers had engaged in eight gun battles nationally, in which three police officers and five Panthers died. Four of the shootouts, including one in which two police officers were killed, occurred in Chicago.

In the angry controversy after the raid, police maintained they were justified in opening fire, but the Panthers saw the raid as a pretext for killing Hampton. The *Tribune* became part of the uproar when it published a photograph showing holes in a doorjamb that it identified as coming from bullets fired from inside the apartment. They proved to be nail heads. Months later, a federal investigation concluded that only one shot was fired by the Panthers, although that number remained in dispute. Police fired eighty-two to ninety-nine shots.

The raid ended the promising political career of Cook County State's Attorney Edward V. Hanrahan, who was indicted but cleared with thirteen other law-enforcement agents of charges of obstructing justice. Bernard Carey, a Republican, defeated him in the next election, in part because of the support of outraged black voters. Some have seen the Black Panther raid as a factor in the emergence of a separate black voting bloc that would no longer automatically back the Cook County Democratic machine.

—*Ted Gregory*

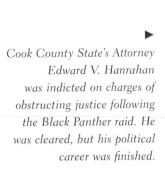

▲ *Illinois Black Panther leader Fred Hampton in October 1969. Two months later, he was dead.*

▶

Cook County State's Attorney Edward V. Hanrahan was indicted on charges of obstructing justice following the Black Panther raid. He was cleared, but his political career was finished.

Sears Tower

The world's largest retailer constructs the world's tallest building.

MAY 3, 1973

Several thousand employees of Sears, Roebuck & Company gathered outside the soaring Sears Tower on this blustery day for a topping-out ceremony that would see a twenty-five-hundred-pound steel girder bearing twelve thousand signatures hoisted more than a quarter-mile into the sky. It was now officially the tallest building in the world.

The ceremony had been anticipated since the company's decision in 1970 to move its headquarters from Homan Avenue, on the West Side, to a new building. To the city's relief, the new location would not be in the suburbs but at Wacker Drive and Jackson Boulevard, on the western edge of downtown Chicago. "I want to thank them [Sears] for staying in Chicago when so many are leaving," Mayor Richard J. Daley said. Retired Sears chairman Gordon Metcalf, who had decided to build the tower when he headed the retailing company, finally explained what many had assumed. "Being the largest retailer in the world, we thought we should have the largest headquarters in the world," he told the shivering crowd.

Three months later, Sears would begin moving its employees into what became known as a "vertical city"—fifteen thousand people working, shopping, and dining inside one building. Architect Bruce Graham and engineer Fazlur Khan designed the 110-story tower as a bundle of nine square tubes, seven of which end at either the fiftieth, sixty-sixth, or ninetieth floors, mainly to reduce the wind load on the upper stories. Only two of the nine squares reach the full 1,454-foot height of the building.

For twenty-three years, the tower remained the world's tallest building, but its reign ended in 1996 with the completion of the Petronas twin towers, in Kuala Lumpur, Malaysia, which surpassed it by twenty-nine feet. Still, with Sears Tower and two other giant skyscrapers built at about the same time—the Amoco Building (1,136 feet) and the John Hancock Center (1,127 feet)—Chicago is home to three of the six tallest buildings in the world.

Before the Sears Tower ceded its lofty title, its stature had slipped in a different way. After using the building for only nineteen years to house its headquarters staff, Sears—no longer the world's largest retailer—began moving to a new location in 1992. That site was in Hoffman Estates, a suburb northwest of the city.

—*John Schmeltzer*

◀ *Seemingly oblivious to the height or the view, a welder works near the top of Sears Tower in 1973.*

▲ At 1,454 feet, the 110-story Sears Tower was the tallest building in the world until 1996, when a twin-tower project in Kuala Lumpur, Malaysia, surpassed it. In the background are two other behemoths of the Chicago skyline, the John Hancock Center, with its tapered sides and twin antennas, and, at the far right, the Amoco Building.

Richard Nixon Resigns

After the release of transcripts of the Watergate tapes, support for the president drops away.

AUGUST 9, 1974

The botched 1972 burglary of the headquarters of the Democratic National Committee in Washington's Watergate complex led two years later to an unprecedented event in American history: the resignation, on this date, of a president. Republican Richard Nixon's tearful farewell to the nation had the earmarks of Greek tragedy. Having won his second term by the biggest landslide in history, Nixon was hounded from office by public outrage and the threat of impeachment.

Chicago and the Midwest had been strongholds of Nixon support as the drama of political shenanigans, intrigue, cover-up, and betrayal unfolded. That support dropped away after April 30, 1974. That was the day Nixon, forced by mounting congressional pressure, released a 1,308-page transcript of edited Watergate-related conversations between him and his key aides. Nixon had taped the conversations in his White House office for his own use.

The transcript led the *Tribune* to publish one of the most extraordinary editions in newspaper history. The *Tribune* was the only newspaper in the country that decided to print the entire, 246,000-word transcript the next day. It was a herculean undertaking, marshaling the efforts of hundreds of *Tribune* secretaries, office clerks, reporters, editors, and printers to copy and typeset the text in a few hours in an era before the widespread use of computers. The forty-four-page special section was added to the eighty-page Wednesday paper. It was a technical and entrepreneurial coup acclaimed as a "miracle" by leading journalists nationwide.

Tribune Editor Clayton Kirkpatrick, who spearheaded the effort, had long admired Nixon's political leadership. However, the contents of the transcript changed Kirkpatrick's mind. He was a principal author of a devastating editorial on May 9 titled "Listen, Mr. Nixon . . .," which began: "We saw the public man in his first administration, and we were impressed. Now in about 300,000 words we have seen the private man, and we are appalled." The editorial called for Nixon to be impeached or to resign, citing the transcript's revelations of White House treachery and amorality. The loss of the staunchly Republican newspaper's support was particularly disheartening to Nixon. It was a clear signal that middle America had abandoned him, helping to clear the path to his resignation.

—William Mullen

American Buffalo Premieres

David Mamet's play brings the raw intensity of Chicago theater to national attention.

OCTOBER 23, 1975

David Mamet had already established himself as a promising Chicago writer when, in early 1975, he submitted the script of his *American Buffalo* to the Goodman Theatre, guaranteeing the management that, if produced, it would win the Pulitzer Prize for drama. Mamet, then twenty-seven, had to wait nine years for the Pulitzer, when his *Glengarry Glen Ross* took the 1984 prize. But *Buffalo*, which the Goodman premiered on this date as part of its experimental Stage 2 series, securely established him as a major American playwright and firmly anchored Chicago as an important center of theater activity.

Before *American Buffalo*, there had been a lively, youthful off-Loop theater scene in the city. The musical *Grease*, which originated in a small Lincoln Avenue house, had gone on to become a 1972 Broadway smash, and director Bob Sickinger's pioneering Hull House Theater, established in 1963, had produced a series of cutting-edge dramas. But the power of *American Buffalo*—its dynamic use of language and its vision of the underbelly of American life—boosted the city's theatrical stock beyond anything that had gone before.

▶

The original production of American Buffalo *in 1975 starred (from left) J. J. Johnston, William H. Macy, and Bernard Erhard.*

Immediate reaction to the gritty drama of three petty thieves in a bungled burglary attempt was mixed. The *Tribune* dismissed the play as "almost two hours of bleep-rated dialogue," while the *Daily News* called it "a triumph for Chicago theater—and a treasure for Chicago audiences." But by the time a Broadway production of *American Buffalo* won the New York Drama Critics Circle Award as best American play of the 1976–77 season, Chicago was viewed as a breeding ground for hot new talent in all fields of theater.

Dozens of small theaters, encouraged and challenged by Mamet's leap to fame, planted their flags and established an energetic, hard-driving "Chicago style" of home-grown, home-made theater. In 1975, for example, the year of *American Buffalo*, a cocky young group of actors banded

▲ *Playwright David Mamet (right) and director Gregory Mosher, whose long association with Mamet began with* American Buffalo

▶

The home-grown, home-made style of Chicago theater is reflected in the simple stage set for this 1974 Apollo Theater production of Mamet's Sexual Perversity in Chicago. *The actor is Cosmo White.*

together in a church basement in the northern suburb of Highland Park and launched themselves as the Steppenwolf Theatre Company. Within ten years, many of these actors—John Malkovich, Gary Sinise, Joan Allen, John Mahoney, and Laurie Metcalf among them—had become stars of international reputation on stage, film, and television.

As the years passed, the young artists who were just out of college in the 1970s grew to become the leaders of a strong, confident theater tradition. For example, Robert Falls, who made his Chicago directorial debut in 1976, was by the 1990s the artistic director of Goodman Theatre, the city's largest and oldest resident not-for-profit theater. It was a remarkable period of growth for Chicago theater artists, made possible in large part by the achievement of *American Buffalo*.

—*Richard Christiansen*

▲ *Laurie Metcalf, shown in 1980, was one of the original members of the Steppenwolf Theater Company, which began in a suburban church basement.*

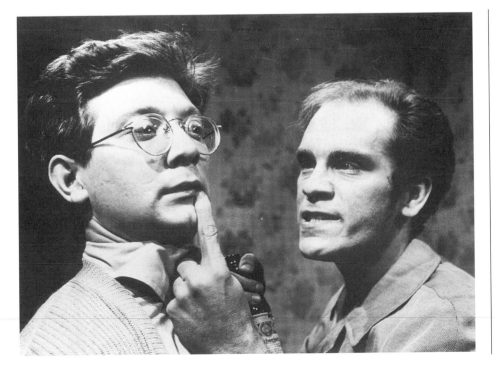

◀ *Jeff Perry (left) and John Malkovich in a tense scene from the 1982 Steppenwolf production of Sam Shepard's* True West

The Death of Mayor Daley

An era comes to an end with the exit of the last big-city boss.

▼ *A few days after Mayor Daley died, the Chicago City Council held a memorial session at which he was eulogized at length. Purple-and-black velvet bunting covered the chair he had occupied for twenty-one years, longer than any other Chicago mayor.*

DECEMBER 20, 1976

A jovial, confident, seemingly healthy Mayor Richard J. Daley started his day on this frigid Monday by attending a pre-Christmas breakfast with his loyal department heads. By most accounts, the twenty-first year of Daley's record-breaking reign as mayor was one of his happiest. Two years before, he had suffered a potentially debilitating stroke but had recovered fully and won an unprecedented sixth term in 1975.

After breakfast, he looked at some ice sculptures on display at the Civic Center Plaza (soon to be named after him) and then took a long ride in his limousine to the farthest southern reaches of his city to attend a Chicago Park District event, where, on a basketball court, he even made a basket on his first try.

On the way back to City Hall, Daley told his security detail that he had chest pains, and they drove him to his doctor's office on North Michigan Avenue. After a quick examination, his doctor said Daley would have to go to nearby Northwestern Memorial Hospital and left the mayor alone while he made the necessary arrangements. When he returned, the mayor had collapsed. He was rushed to the hospital, but it was obvious that Richard J. Daley, at the age of seventy-four, was dead.

In the days that followed, an estimated one hundred thousand people came to the Nativity of Our Lord Catholic Church in Daley's native Bridgeport community to pass by his casket. The mourners at his funeral included Vice President Nelson Rockefeller, President-elect Jimmy Carter, and Senators Edward Kennedy and George McGovern, and mayors from throughout the nation.

Michael Bilandic, the Bridgeport alderman, was chosen to succeed Daley, but he was not the politician Daley was. Nor was the Democratic machine what it once was. Already crippled by a federal court decree that restricted patronage, it could no longer guarantee elections without Daley. "Many will say it was an era that should have ended, perhaps long ago," said the *Tribune*, which had endorsed him in four of six mayoral campaigns. But "before cheering the end of the Daley machine, it is worth pausing to ask to what extent it has been the city that worked, and to what extent it was the Daley machine that worked." Despite the mayor's flaws, most agreed he did what he thought was best for the city he loved.

—*Robert Davis*

▲ *At the funeral mass for Mayor Richard J. Daley, Cardinal John Cody consoles the mayor's widow, Eleanor Daley. The funeral was attended by dignitaries from across the nation.*

The Final *Chicago Daily News*

The "Front Page" town's last afternoon paper puts a period on a proud tradition.

MARCH 4, 1978

Chicago's last afternoon newspaper, the brilliant and brawny *Chicago Daily News*, refused to go quietly. Its final edition on this date was breezily headlined SO LONG, CHICAGO. It died at the age of 102, the last of a long line of newspapers that tried to survive by reporting and writing from the heart and failed. In the process, though, they gave Chicago its reputation as the city of the "Front Page."

In the newspaper cemetery, the *Daily News* had plenty of company. Less than four years earlier, Tribune Company's afternoon paper, *Chicago Today*, had closed. The *Inter-Ocean*, the *Journal*, the *Post*, the *Herald and Examiner*—all these and others had already gone to their graves. The city was down to two papers: the *Tribune* and the *Sun-Times*.

The death of the *Daily News* was one more sorrowful testament to changing times. People did not read newspapers—especially afternoon newspapers—as they once did. With jobs and people moving to the suburbs, there were fewer straphangers commuting home on public transportation. Instead, people were in their cars, homebound on expressways. Traffic made it harder for delivery trucks to get the paper to the readers who remained. And for many people television's evening news was enough. Circulation had skidded from about 614,000 in the 1950s to 327,000. *Daily News* publisher Marshall Field V, who inherited the legendary paper from his father, decided to shut it down.

The *Daily News* had always been a writer's newspaper. It hired Carl Sandburg and Mike Royko and scores of lesser-known door kickers and Balzacs. The *Daily News* invented the daily newspaper columnist. The first was Eugene Field, whose children's poems "Wynken, Blynken, and Nod" and "Little Boy Blue" were originally published in the *Daily News*. The last was the Pulitzer Prize–winning Royko, voice of Chicago for more than thirty years. Ben Hecht, coauthor of the play *The Front Page*, was a reporter for the *Daily News*. Groundbreaking reporter Lois Wille won a Pulitzer Prize for the paper and went on to win another after joining the *Tribune*. In all, the *Daily News* won fifteen Pulitzers, five of them by members of its renowned foreign service. "It was a reportorial staff half daft with literary dreams," said Hecht. In the end, that was not enough to save it.

—*Ellen Warren*

◀ *The writing talent at the* Chicago Daily News *was impressive throughout its history: Carl Sandburg (top) toiled there before gaining fame as a poet, Ben Hecht was coauthor of* The Front Page, *and Mike Royko and Lois Wille earned two of the paper's fifteen Pulitzer Prizes.*

The John Wayne Gacy Murders

A crawl space becomes the graveyard for victims of the country's worst serial killer.

▼ *Numbered stakes indicate where the bodies of John Wayne Gacy's victims were found in the crawl space beneath his suburban home.*

DECEMBER 22, 1978

During the chilly nighttime hours on this date, police began one of the grisliest excavation projects in the history of American crime. For weeks to come, Chicago and the nation watched in horror as the crawl space under the home of thirty-six-year-old John Wayne Gacy, a onetime children's clown, revealed itself as a ghastly, makeshift tomb. Twenty-nine bodies, all young males, were recovered from the Gacy home in suburban Norwood Park. Four others were found in Illinois rivers. The first died in 1972, the last in 1978—only ten days before Gacy's arrest. Eight of the victims were never identified.

Formerly a businessman in Iowa, where he had served a sentence for sodomy, Gacy was a successful contractor in Chicago's northwest suburbs in the 1970s. First killing homeless male prostitutes and later suburban teenagers, Gacy usually lured his victims into his car, knocked them out with chloroform, and sometimes tortured them at his house for hours before stabbing or strangling them to death. His final victim was a Des Plaines high school student named Robert Piest. Before disappearing, the fifteen-year-old youth told his mother he was going to meet a man about a construction job. Des Plaines police quickly learned that Gacy was that man.

After police found the first three bodies in Gacy's home, Cook County medical examiner Robert Stein was called in. "I opened the door and, my God, there was the odor of death," Stein told a *Tribune* reporter. In a search for bodies and other evidence that went on for months, Gacy's home was reduced to rubble. A bulldozer was brought in, and investigators tore up his garage, driveway, barbecue pit, and yard. Barricades were set up to ward off souvenir hunters.

Gacy claimed he killed to rid society of bad elements. His defense attorneys said he was insane. He was found guilty in 1980 of thirty-three counts of murder, making him the country's worst convicted serial killer. In prison, Gacy gained notoriety for his paintings, many depicting clowns. He claimed innocence near the end, though he said at the time of the verdict, "All the jury did was . . . the same thing I have been trying to do for the last ten years: destroy myself." He was executed at the Stateville Correctional Center, in Joliet, in 1994. One attorney remarked: "John Gacy is the poster child for the death penalty."

—*Sid Smith*

▲ *Gacy, a onetime children's clown, was a successful contractor at the time of his arrest.*

Jane Byrne Elected

Chicago's first female mayor slays the machine and then brings it back to life.

FEBRUARY 27, 1979

Paralyzing blizzards set up Mayor Michael Bilandic for defeat, but it was bright, warm sunshine on this date that did him in. The fair weather on the day of the mayoral primary election brought out the voters, and the memory of the city's inept handling of record January storms drove them to overturn the nearly half-century rule of the Democratic machine. Maverick candidate Jane Byrne won the Democratic nomination.

Byrne's campaign, launched after she was fired from a City Hall job by Bilandic, was dismissed at first as a bid for retribution. But events buried Bilandic. Two huge snowstorms dumped more than thirty-five inches of snow on Chicago in little more than two weeks, and the city's response to the blizzards was a disaster. Streets were not plowed, garbage was not collected, and mass transit was staggered by the snow. Chicago was the city that could not get to work, and revelations that the city's "snow emergency plan" was a sham written by a political crony disgusted city residents even more. By Election Day, many voters who had been faithful to the machine were ready to dump Bilandic. "The people of Chicago freed themselves tonight," crowed Byrne, who easily defeated a Republican opponent in the April general election. "I'm going to run it straight, and I'm going to run it clean."

Almost immediately, she spurned the independent activists who had helped her and cut a deal with Democratic insiders to run the city. It was only the first about-face in her tempestuous four-year reign. In just the first year, she battled strikes by transit workers, schoolteachers, and firefighters. Byrne is probably best remembered for moving in to the Cabrini-Green housing project in an attempt to quell violence there, but she was also praised for steering the schools through a financial crisis and for appointing a majority of blacks and Hispanics to the school board. She was criticized, however, for another reversal when she replaced two black board members with whites who opposed school busing. Top administrators were hired and fired, seemingly at whim. In the end, Byrne's chaotic governing style overwhelmed the achievements of her administration, but her election showed that the days of automatic victories by the Democratic organization were over.

—R. Bruce Dold

▲ *Coffee and the morning paper: Jane Byrne savors her victory in the Democratic primary.*

▼ *During the winter of 1978–79, a record 89.7 inches of snow blanketed the city and buried Mayor Michael Bilandic. Chaotic scenes such as this were commonplace.*

The Crash of Flight 191

The worst air disaster in American history claims 273 lives.

MAY 25, 1979

As an American Airlines DC-10 jet roared into the sky over O'Hare International Airport on this Friday afternoon, its left engine fell off. Flight 191, bound for Los Angeles at the beginning of the Memorial Day weekend, rolled over in the air and plunged to the earth less than a mile from the runway. The plane "burst into a pillar of flame and smoke that could be seen up to eight miles away," the *Tribune* reported. Nearby resident Abe Marmel, who was working in his vegetable garden, heard the explosion: "By the time I looked up, there was a rain of fire falling down on me."

All 271 people on board and two people on the ground were killed. As of the mid-1990s, it remained America's worst aviation disaster. The plane just missed hitting a trailer park north of the airport. A priest at a Catholic church in the suburb of Elk Grove Village reached the scene within minutes. "It was too hot to really do anything but administer the last rites," he told the *Tribune*. "I just walked around trying to touch a body here or there, but I could not. It was too hot to touch anybody, and I really could not tell if they were men or women. Bodies were scattered all over the field." An assistant state's attorney said he saw "kiddie books and briefcases and business papers strewn all over the place. And a child's book entitled *The Beginning of Life*."

As the nation's center of commercial aviation, Chicago had been the scene of more than its share of airplane tragedies. In 1940, a United Airlines DC-3 laden with ice crashed while trying to land at Municipal (later Midway) Airport, killing ten people. One disaster had a rather bizarre twist: Among the forty-five people killed in the 1972 crash of a United 737 was Dorothy Hunt, wife of E. Howard Hunt, one of the conspirators in the Watergate break-in. After it was discovered that she had been carrying a briefcase containing $10,000 in cash (later linked to the scandal), some convoluted sabotage theories surfaced. But the accident was blamed on pilot error at a critical stage of the plane's descent to Midway, causing it to stall and crash into a Southwest Side neighborhood.

◀ *The explosion of the DC-10, which was loaded with fuel for a long flight, left few large pieces of the jet intact. This aerial photograph shows how close the plane came to hitting a trailer park.*

In the investigation following the Flight 191 disaster, the National Transportation Safety Board found that two months before the crash American Airlines mechanics in Tulsa, Oklahoma, had taken a shortcut in removing the engines from the plane's wing pylons for maintenance. This mistake had cracked an aluminum component in the pylon. Normal wear and tear widened the crack until the piece broke, and as the engine tore loose, it damaged electrical and hydraulic systems, a combination that left the plane unable to fly. When the DC-10 was certified for service eleven years earlier, engineers calculated the odds of such a simultaneous failure at ten billion to one.

—David Young

▲ *American Airlines Flight 191 (above left) goes into a roll after losing its left engine following takeoff from O'Hare International Airport. Moments later (above right), a cloud of black smoke billows from the site of the crash. These photos were obtained by the* Tribune *from a student pilot on a layover at O'Hare.*

◄ *A firefighter walks amid the wreckage of Flight 191. Triage flags and stakes mark the spots where bodies were found.*

Disco Demolition

Who knew that so many people hated disco this much?

JULY 12, 1979

Comiskey Park had seen more than its share of oddball promotions, what with White Sox owner Bill Veeck's penchant for the colorful (a scoreboard that lit up and exploded with fireworks) and the offbeat (having his players wear shorts). But nothing compared to Disco Demolition Night, staged at Comiskey on this summer Thursday evening. Anyone bringing a disco album to the game—a twi-night doubleheader between the White Sox and Detroit Tigers—would be admitted for just 98 cents. Between games, radio personality Steve Dahl—then the morning man for rock music station WLUP-FM—would blow up those disco albums with fireworks.

Dahl, who had been fired from WDAI-FM the year before when that station switched to an all-disco format, had garnered national recognition for his crusade against what he called "Disco Dystrophy." Dahl and his "Insane Coho Lips Antidisco Army" had staged two previous antidisco rallies—both well attended but nothing compared to this night. Comiskey Park was filled to capacity; the official attendance was more than fifty-nine thousand. An estimated fifteen thousand fans milled outside the park, unable to get in.

After the first game, which the Sox lost 4–1, Dahl ceremoniously blew up a crate filled with disco records. All was orderly up to that point. But as Dahl finished, thousands of fans stormed onto the field, tearing up clumps of sod, burning signs, knocking over a batting cage, and flinging records like so many Frisbees. Police arrested thirty-seven people; by the time order was restored, the grounds were little more than a grassy moonscape. The second game was canceled and later awarded to the Tigers by forfeit.

Later, some blamed Dahl; some blamed Veeck. Howard Cosell even blamed White Sox announcer Harry Caray, saying Caray contributed to a "carnival" atmosphere. In reality, a handful of rowdies had taken advantage of a situation for which stadium security was woefully unprepared. "In my wildest dreams, I never thought that I, a stupid disc jockey, could draw seventy thousand people to a disco demolition," Dahl said in a *Tribune* interview. "Unfortunately, some of our followers got a little carried away." That was the last antidisco rally for WLUP. But it brought Dahl national attention and established him as a radio superstar in Chicago.

—*Phil Vettel*

Thousands of disco-despising spectators (below) ignore the message on the White Sox scoreboard on Disco Demolition Night. By the time order was restored, the field was so churned up that the second game of the doubleheader had to be canceled. The promotional stunt was the brainchild of radio personality Steve Dahl (right).

Pope John Paul II in Chicago

For forty hours, the visitor from Rome unites the city in spirit.

▼ *The highlight of Pope John Paul II's visit to Chicago was a three-hour Mass in Grant Park, attended by an estimated two hundred thousand people.*

OCTOBER 5, 1979

The man previously known as Karol Cardinal Wojtyla had been in Chicago before, most recently in 1976, when he visited a Northwest Side church as a little-known Polish cardinal. But by the fall of 1979, he had become John Paul II, the first Polish pope in history, the 264th successor to the apostle Peter, and head of the world's seven hundred million Roman Catholics. His visit this time would make him only the second pope to visit the United States and the first ever to come to Chicago.

The city held a double attraction as a stop on his first American tour, made less than a year after he became pope. With 2.4 million Catholics, the Chicago archdiocese was the largest in the country at the time. And, with some five hundred thousand residents of Polish ancestry, after Warsaw it was home to the second largest Polish community in the world. His stay in Chicago would last all of forty hours, but it became one of those unique events that brought the city together, regardless of race, ethnicity, or belief. Large, joyful crowds greeted him wherever he went, from his arrival at O'Hare International Airport on the evening of October 4 to his departure on the morning of the sixth.

His crowded schedule on this date included an address to 350 American bishops at Quigley Preparatory Seminary South. Delivering a message early in his papacy that he would repeat often over the years, he said that the Catholic Church under his leadership would continue to oppose abortion, extramarital sex, homosexuality, and divorce. Then he traveled to Grant Park for the largest Mass ever celebrated in Chicago. "The skyscrapers of Chicago's Loop resembled cathedral spires as they soared over the crowd," reported the *Tribune*, which described the gathering of an estimated two hundred thousand people as "festive yet solemn, happy but devout." Many wore ethnic clothes, and worshippers of all ages, races, and even religions came to see the pontiff. In his homily, John Paul II said, "Looking at you, I see people who have thrown their destinies together and now write a common history. . . . This is the way America was conceived; this is what she was called to be. . . . But there is another reality that I see when I look at you . . . your unity as members of the People of God."

—Robert Davis

The Closing of Wisconsin Steel

One Southeast Side plant seemed to symbolize the decline of industrial Chicago in the 1980s.

▼ *The closing of Wisconsin Steel was a major blow to the city's Southeast Side, once a leading center of American steel production.*

MARCH 28, 1980

It was a decision as cold and hard as the steel bars that rolled out of the mills at Wisconsin Steel. Envirodyne Inc., the last owner of the plant, did not offer the employees any buyouts. It did not notify them of its intentions. When the last shift ended on this date, the corporation locked the gates and put more than three thousand people out of work.

To some, Wisconsin Steel was a symbol of America's shift from making things out of natural resources and human sweat to providing services dependent solely on ingenuity and brainpower. It seemed to be another painful example of the collapse of industrial Chicago, where one heavy industry after another had laid off workers or shut down plants. The pattern was widespread around the Great Lakes manufacturing states, an area that came to be known as the Midwestern Rust Belt.

To others, the darkened blast furnaces and empty lockers were the inevitable result of inept management and strong competition. International Harvester had owned Wisconsin Steel for seventy-five years, using it as a captive supplier of steel for its farm equipment. But Harvester did not invest in Wisconsin Steel, sustained years of losses, and finally sold it in 1977 to Envirodyne, a California company with no steelmaking experience. Envirodyne had planned to spend $50 million to update the facility, but it never did. The company had purchased Wisconsin Steel just as old-line companies in the industry began to be buffeted by foreign competition and low-cost domestic minimills. The plant lost money for three more years until a strike at Harvester, still its best customer, forced it to close.

Wisconsin Steel's demise was a major blow to Chicago's Southeast Side, once a leading center of steel production in the United States. More layoffs and plant closings followed. By the mid-1980s, Chicago's steel industry had been decimated. But even as the large steelmakers were closing inefficient plants, others were investing in mills in Gary, Indiana, and elsewhere. By the early 1990s, plants in northwest Indiana were making steel efficiently, and the region was being

▲ *Laid-off workers in an office at U.S. Steel's South Works in Chicago: closings of industrial plants in the Chicago area shattered the lives and dreams of many working-class families.*

◀ *Suddenly out of work, angry steelworkers questioned Wisconsin Steel and union officials at a meeting shortly after the plant was shut down. Although many workers protested the closing for years, the jobs were gone forever.*

referred to as the steel capital of the world. Other Midwest manufacturers also invested heavily to improve productivity. In the mid-1990s, one Chicago bank economist called the Midwest the nation's "Growth Belt." The region had become a global center of professional services and high-tech manufacturing, with one urban planner forecasting steady growth in jobs and population for many years.

On Chicago's Southeast Side, however, Wisconsin Steel and U.S. Steel's South Works were gone and so were the jobs they had provided. Where many steelworkers' homes once stood, there were vacant lots. The closings shattered the lives and dreams of many working-class families.

—*Terry Brown*

▼ *By 1995, a scale house was one of the few remaining buildings at the site of the South Works, which had opened in 1880 and at one time employed more than twenty thousand workers.*

The Election of Harold Washington

A bitter, divisive campaign results in the election of Chicago's first black mayor.

APRIL 12, 1983

Other black politicians had run for the office of Chicago mayor before. In fact, even Harold Washington had. Most of those past campaigns had been quixotic, symbolic, and, in the end, futile. But things were different in 1983. Black community leaders and politicians sensed that the combination of dissatisfaction with Mayor Jane Byrne and unusually high numbers of newly registered black voters had made the time right for a major campaign for the mayor's office in a city that was about evenly divided between black and white residents.

Washington, a United States congressman who had once done prison time for failing to file federal income tax returns, was a reluctant candidate. He demanded financial backing, and he got it. He demanded even more new voter registrants, and he got them. Finally, he agreed to challenge Byrne and join the field, which included Cook County State's Attorney Richard M. Daley, son of the late Mayor Daley. As a Daley Democrat, Washington had been elected to six terms in the Illinois House, but he had broken with the Democratic machine in 1977, when he first ran for mayor. Because of that, he had support in white liberal wards along the lakefront, where he was seen as the reform candidate. Because Byrne and Daley split the remaining white vote and Washington got nearly all of the black vote, the mathematics were simple. Washington won.

Although winning the Democratic nomination historically was tantamount to election, racial tensions were so high in Chicago that Republican candidate Bernard Epton, a liberal former state legislator, became the favored son in blue-collar and white ethnic neighborhoods. A poorly conceived and quickly withdrawn Epton campaign slogan, "Before it's too late," fueled racial strife; Washington was subjected to some nasty and well-publicized verbal assaults during visits to white neighborhoods. But Chicago was still a Democratic city, and on this date, Harold Washington, bigger than life, was elected the first black mayor of the city of Chicago.

◀ *A young supporter congratulates Washington the day after his victory in the Democratic mayoral primary in February 1983.*

In his inaugural address at Navy Pier, Washington was not conciliatory. "Business as usual will not be accepted by the people of this city," he said. "Business as usual will not be accepted by this chief executive of this great city." The battle was joined. Alderman Edward Vrdolyak quickly solidified a majority bloc of twenty-nine anti-Washington aldermen, and the so-called Council Wars had begun. The "Vrdolyak Twenty-Nine" blocked much of the Washington agenda. His appointments were held up for months, even years. His annual budget proposals were attacked. Every issue was hard fought, with stalemate often the result. But in April 1986, court-ordered special elections resulted in a Washington majority in the City Council for the first time. The Washington administration was ready to begin its work.

—*Robert Davis*

▲ *Harold Washington takes the oath of office as mayor of Chicago in April 1983. Looking on are Cardinal Joseph Bernardin, outgoing Mayor Jane Byrne, and her husband, Jay McMullen.*

During the first three years of Washington's first term, much of his agenda was blocked because of "Council Wars." Two of the principal combatants on the City Council floor were aldermen Tim Evans (left) and Edward Burke. ▶

Operation Greylord

A federal probe of court corruption sets the standard for future investigations.

▼ *In the halls of the Criminal Court Building, attorney Terrence Hake burrowed into the dark side of justice as the mole in the Greylord investigation.*

AUGUST 5, 1983

It was a Friday, and a group of lawyers—some prosecutors, some defense attorneys—had gathered in a Loop hotel on this day for a bachelor party. But the celebrating stopped when the television news broke this stunning story: for three years, the Federal Bureau of Investigation had been running an undercover operation aimed at Cook County's court system. It featured at least one undercover operative and a listening device in a judge's chambers.

"DO YOU SWEAR YOU'RE NOT AN FBI AGENT, NEVER HAVE BEEN AN FBI AGENT, AND NEVER WILL BE AN FBI AGENT, SO HELP YOU GOD?"

One lawyer in the room—Terrence Hake—was not surprised by the news. Disgusted with the corruption that permeated the Cook County court system, he had become the FBI's mole in its unprecedented investigation of judicial corruption. First as a prosecutor and later as a defense lawyer, Hake had burrowed into the dark side of justice, handing out bribes to fix cases concocted by the FBI.

Four months after the Greylord investigation was revealed, the first indictments were announced, naming two judges, a former judge, three attorneys, two court clerks, and a police officer. "I believe this will be viewed as one of the most comprehensive, intricate, and difficult undercover projects ever undertaken by a law-enforcement agency," U.S. Attorney Dan Webb said in announcing those charges.

The allegations ranged from fixing drunk-driving cases to more serious felony charges. One lawyer was caught on tape bragging that "even a murder case can be fixed if the judge is given something to hang his hat on." By the end of the decade, nearly one hundred people had been indicted, and all but a handful were convicted. Of the seventeen judges indicted, fifteen were convicted. The tally of convictions included fifty lawyers as well as court clerks, police officers, and sheriff's deputies.

Greylord was not the first federal investigation of public corruption in Chicago, but it was a watershed in its use of eavesdropping devices and a mole to obtain evidence instead of relying on wrongdoers to become government informants. Over the next fifteen years, federal authorities launched similar investigations targeted at corruption in Chicago's City Hall (including Operations Incubator and Silver Shovel), other governmental bodies (Operation Lantern), and organized crime (Operation Gambat and Safebet). Scores of public officials, including aldermen, judges, and legislators, were convicted.

—*Maurice Possley*

►

Judge Richard F. LeFevour was sentenced to twelve years in prison for his role in the Greylord scandal. He was convicted of taking thousands of dollars in bribes to fix traffic cases.

Chicago Goes Cellular

A new era in telecommunications arrives first in Chicago, reviving the consumer-electronics industry.

In a car, in a shopping mall, or on the street, cellular phones quickly became a popular means of communication.

OCTOBER 13, 1983

A new age in communications technology began on this date with one of those silly stunts concocted by publicists: a bunch of grown men ran a race to determine who would be the country's first commercial mobile cellular telephone customer. The event at Soldier Field, with play-by-play commentary by Cubs announcer Jack Brickhouse, was in keeping with the technology's image: another marginally useful gadget for the very rich.

Radio-spectrum limitations meant that throughout the Chicago area the old car-phone system could handle fewer than two thousand calls an hour. Engineers at AT&T's Bell Laboratories thought they could boost capacity by fifty times or more by reducing signal power and dividing a region into smaller units called *cells*. Computerized switches would transfer calls from one cell to the next as drivers passed through their territories.

The first large-scale experimental cell-phone system was built in the Chicago area in the late 1970s after successful tests of prototypes in New Jersey. One advantage of the location was the large Bell Labs office in west suburban Naperville, where engineers could monitor the system and iron out start-up problems. In 1983, Ameritech Corporation, the local successor to Bell, won government permission to convert the experimental system into a commercial one. Other areas of the country soon followed.

It was far from obvious that the new phones would have mass appeal. They cost around $3,000 at first, and monthly bills could average up to $200. Cell phones looked like a nice niche market to Motorola, which, along with other companies such as Zenith and Admiral, had once made Chicago a center of radio and television manufacturing. Like others, Motorola had abandoned the manufacture of television sets to the Japanese. Instead, it focused on two-way radio systems for police departments, cab dispatchers, and others.

But as prices for cell phones fell, demand shot up. By the 1990s, they had become a fixture in American life, and Motorola found itself back in the consumer-electronics market as the leading maker of cell phones. The popularity of the phones and other new technologies, such as paging services and computer modems, created a new industrial base for the region.

—*Jon Van*

▲ *With the advent of cellular phones, signal towers were constructed throughout the Chicago area. Computerized switches transfer calls from one cell to the next as drivers pass through their territories.*

The State of Illinois Center

Upon landing in the Loop, a dazzling building looks like nothing else in Chicago.

▼ *The man behind the building, architect Helmut Jahn, in the Center's sixteen-story atrium*

MAY 6, 1985

I n a cityscape long associated with the flat, black facades of architect Ludwig Mies van der Rohe, the arrival of Helmut Jahn's State of Illinois Center was akin to Carmen Miranda crashing a black-tie ball. From the outside, where it boldly looks out on the classically styled City Hall–County Building and the monolithic Daley Civic Center, the State of Illinois Center is a scalloped structure of blue glass gridded by beams of salmon-red steel. The inside opens up into a dramatic, sun-lit, sixteen-story-high atrium with balconied, curved floors and more of that delectable salmon-and-blue color scheme.

▲ *Even the building's floor, with its kaleidoscopic pattern, is dazzling.*

"Helmut Jahn's State of Illinois Center is the most cerebral, the most abstract, yet easily the most spectacular building ever constructed in the Loop," began *Tribune* architecture critic Paul Gapp's initial critique of the building. "In a city where architects so long worshiped the ninety-degree angle and black curtain walls, the center's asymmetry and multicolored skin appear as almost impudent nose-thumbing at the past." He was dazzled by the interior but turned off by the exterior, "a chunky wedge of little grace or elegance."

It stands as one of the city's prime monuments to postmodernism, a style that broke away from the rigid geometry of modernism and freely employed decoration and forms from the past. The decade also produced such celebrated postmodern structures as Kohn Pedersen Fox's 333 Wacker Drive (1983) and Bloomingdale's Building (900 North Michigan Avenue, 1989) and Skidmore, Owings, and Merrill's AT&T Corporate Center (1988) and NBC Tower (1989).

The audacity of the state center would have been unusual in any city structure, but this was a government building constructed with public funds: $172 million in the final tally, up from the originally budgeted $85 million. Indoor temperatures during the first two summers spiked to 110 degrees as a faulty air-conditioning system proved no match for the sun blazing through the glass. The state spent additional millions to fix the problem. The General Assembly voted in 1992 to give credit—or blame—where it was due, renaming the structure the James R. Thompson Center after the four-term governor who chose Jahn's flamboyant design over seven more conservative ones.

The Bavarian-born Jahn, who previously won acclaim for his curved, modernist-inspired Xerox Centre (1980) and his art deco revival addition to the Chicago Board of Trade (1982), continued to put his mark on the city with his widely praised glass-and-exposed-steel United Airlines terminal at O'Hare International Airport (1987). The Thompson Center also may claim as its legacy—though it may not want to—a new generation of glassy, color-happy, vertical shopping malls on North Michigan Avenue.

—Mark Caro

▲ *Like a visitor from another planet, the State of Illinois Center, dubbed by some "Starship Chicago," sits amid the skyscrapers of the Loop. In 1992, it was renamed the James R. Thompson Center.*

▶

French artist Jean Dubuffet's Monument with Standing Beast *joined the collection of modern sculptures on display in front of Chicago civic structures.*

Deep Tunnel Opens

An ambitious project aims to "bottle a rainstorm" in a vast system of tunnels.

▼ *Deep Tunnel and other pollution-control efforts have prompted planners and developers to take advantage of the river's dramatic setting. One example is this walkway with a fountain and water cannon.*

MAY 24, 1985

Superlatives filled the air at the dedication on this date of thirty-one miles of tunnels that had been constructed deep underground, the first section of a vast project to control water pollution and flooding in the Chicago area. Deep Tunnel "is the largest undertaking of its kind ever attempted by mankind," declared Raymond Rimkus, general superintendent of the Metropolitan Sanitary District of Greater Chicago, the agency that planned the project. For once, many of the superlatives were deserved. Deep Tunnel, or the Tunnel and Reservoir Plan, is the largest public-works project in Chicago's history and one of the biggest in the United States. The tunnel system, which was still under construction in the mid-1990s, will be 130 miles long when finished, each inch bored out of rock 150 to 350 feet below the surface. Its estimated cost is $3.6 billion.

With the reversal of the Chicago River in 1900, the city's sewage was directed away from Lake Michigan, its source of drinking water. But during severe storms, sewage-tainted stormwater still backed up into the lake. In addition, one of the consequences of the continued development of the flat metropolitan region was that storms frequently flooded basements—or worse. In 1954 and 1957, the Chicago River overflowed and flooded downtown Chicago.

Deep Tunnel is intended to "bottle a rainstorm" by channeling stormwater that overflows from sewers into the system's tunnels, which are up to thirty-three feet in diameter. The tunnels will connect with massive reservoirs, which are to be finished in the early twenty-first century. When complete, the system will have a capacity of forty-one billion gallons and will serve Chicago and fifty-one suburbs in Cook County. In the meantime, as they are completed, the tunnels are put to use to hold water that is pumped to a sewage treatment plant after a storm.

▲ *A worker stands in a newly finished section of Deep Tunnel, which is designed to hold sewage-tainted stormwater that would otherwise end up in streams and basements. The tunnels have diameters of up to thirty-three feet.*

Deep Tunnel is the biggest and most ambitious project to attack the problem of pollution in area streams and Lake Michigan. Other efforts include federal and local laws to restrict discharges of industrial pollution into waterways, and improved sewage treatment facilities. Often these measures came about only after lengthy and bitter public controversies. The *Tribune* chronicled and sometimes spurred those battles, most notably with its "Save Our Lake" campaign, launched in 1967, which focused on pollution of the Great Lakes and particularly Lake Michigan. Those articles "prompted thousands of readers to resolve that Lake Michigan shall not be destroyed," the *Tribune* reported. By the 1990s, periodic testing by the sanitary district—by then renamed the Metropolitan Water Reclamation District—showed marked declines in many water pollutants.

—*Casey Bukro*

▶

To bore through solid rock, the Deep Tunnel project uses large tunnel-boring machines. Here, the machine breaks through the last remaining rock to join two sections of tunnel.

The 1986 Super Bowl

The super talented, super colorful Bears end a rollicking season with an overwhelming win.

▼ *Quarterback Jim McMahon signals a touchdown as William "Refrigerator" Perry smashes into the end zone. Perry, a defensive lineman, became a national celebrity after Ditka played him at fullback in several games during the 1985 season.*

JANUARY 26, 1986

The Chicago Bears devastated the New England Patriots on this date in Super Bowl XX by an appropriate score, 46–10, stamping their ravaging "46" defense on National Football League history. The victory in the New Orleans Superdome, the first major championship for a Chicago team since the 1963 NFL title, was a near-perfect ending to a near-perfect season.

Coach Mike Ditka had shocked the team in 1982 when he predicted that the Bears would win the Super Bowl in three years. Ditka, who had played tight end for the Bears, had just been named head coach by owner George Halas. The team was numbed by a tradition of losing, despite outstanding performances by such stars as running back Gayle Sayers and linebacker Dick Butkus. To change that tradition, Ditka brought in younger players and instilled in them his fierce determination. Ditka broke his hand when he slammed it into a locker following a loss in 1983, the same year Halas died. Soon Ditka's rugged personality came to symbolize the Bears.

A loss to San Francisco denied the team a trip to the 1985 Super Bowl, but the next season would be different. At quarterback was Jim McMahon, the "Punky QB," who, despite an injury, threw three touchdown passes to win an early game against the Minnesota Vikings. Future Hall of Fame running back Walter Payton rushed for 1,551 yards. The defense, featuring such forces of nature as Mike Singletary, Richard Dent, Dan Hampton, and Gary Fencik, terrorized opponents with their unconventional "46" blitzes under the aggressive coaching of defensive coordinator Buddy Ryan. And William "Refrigerator" Perry, a 310-pound-plus defensive lineman, became a national celebrity when Ditka started to play him occasionally at fullback. Perry even scored three touchdowns.

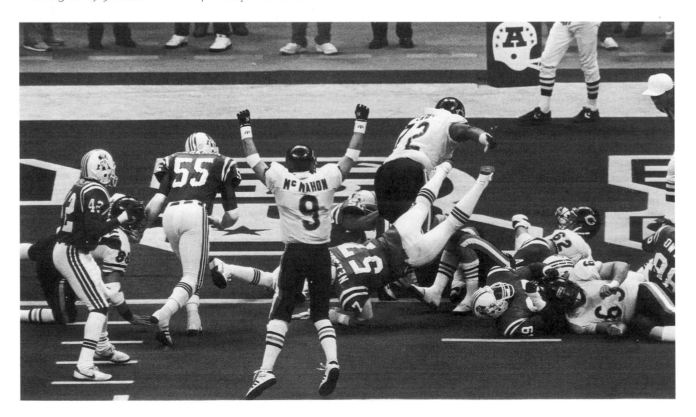

▲ *Capping an almost perfect season, the Bears carry defensive coordinator Buddy Ryan (left) and head coach Mike Ditka off the field after the team's 46–10 victory over the New England Patriots in Super Bowl XX. Ryan, with whom Ditka feuded bitterly, left the following season.*

Chicago became obsessed with the Bears. The Picasso wore a headband. The Art Institute's lions donned helmets. The Chicago Symphony Orchestra performed the team song, "Bear Down, Chicago Bears." Before the Super Bowl, many players made a music video called "The Super Bowl Shuffle," a gloating, highly premature celebration of a rollicking season that had been spoiled only by a loss to the Miami Dolphins. The game itself became lopsided so early that the only suspense concerned McMahon's ever changing headbands, which advertised various charities. However, the cries of "Payton! Payton!" went unanswered. The league's all-time leading rusher failed to score.

Ditka talked about the Bears becoming the team of the 1980s, but Ryan, who feuded openly with Ditka, left the following season. Distractions, such as commercial endorsements, and player attrition took their toll. The team won only two more playoff games under Ditka. In 1993, Halas's grandson, Bears president Mike McCaskey, replaced Ditka with Dave Wannstedt, and in 1996, Wannstedt fired placekicker Kevin Butler, the last remaining player from the super season of 1985.

—Don Pierson

▶

The only suspense in the Super Bowl occurred whenever McMahon unveiled a new headband with an advertisement for a charity. The league's all-time leading rusher, running back Walter Payton, got into the headband act, too, but failed to score in the game.

Vietnam Veterans Parade

An enthusiastic, emotional "welcome home" honors those who served in America's most controversial war.

JUNE 13, 1986

The city was expecting a maximum of 125,000 marchers in the Welcome Home parade for Vietnam veterans. An estimated 200,000 showed up on this day, cheered by nearly 500,000 spectators, who may have seen the march as a chance to heal a long-standing wound in the nation's soul; the parade came eleven years after the war ended. The official route ran for less than three miles, starting in Olive Park, named for a Vietnam War hero, and ending in Grant Park, where Vietnam War protests had once raged. But the parade lasted for nearly five hours; it was perhaps the largest parade for Vietnam vets held in the United States.

About 250,000 young men and women from the Chicago area fought in the protracted, divisive struggle in Southeast Asia. The names of 964 Chicagoans are part of the list of those killed in action that is engraved on the wall of the Vietnam Veterans Memorial in Washington, D.C. Those who came back alive returned to an America that would not look them in the eye. Vietnam was not only a war that did not have the wholehearted support of the country; it was the first war America had lost. For the war's opponents and supporters alike, the veterans were at first uncomfortable reminders of the futility and the humiliation of the American war effort. But with the passage of time, the emotions of the era cooled, and increasingly people began to realize that, regardless of the outcome of the war, the men and women who had fought in Vietnam had suffered and sacrificed for their country.

▲ *Banners and a blizzard of confetti express the feelings of spectators along LaSalle Street.*

"During the Vietnam War, you didn't come home with your buddies," said Tom Stack, chairman of the Chicago Vietnam Veterans Parade Committee. "Nobody got a parade. You got off the plane, trashed your uniform, and went home through the back alley. They are coming to this parade to reunite with the rest of America. And we are all ready for it." The march gave them a voice for their emotions. "If I was asked to write a love poem today," said Vietnam veteran poet Steve Mason, "I don't know what I'd say, but I'd mail it to Chicago."

Loral Valley, thirty-five, of Chicago, stood with a group of children and adults who held a long red-and-white banner inscribed "Thank you, Vets" in blue letters. "I was with the 'Hell, no, we won't go' group during the war," Valley said. "I participated in a lot of marches. Today, it's like a catharsis. It's a way to say I'm sorry I didn't support them then."

Sitting in a chair in Grant Park, Steve Benson, thirty-seven, of Freeport, Illinois, watched with his son, Mike, as the parade came to an end. "I wanted to show my son the closeness and friendships between the veterans," Benson said, "and I wanted him to meet guys that I fought with and know what we went through. He didn't have to come, but he said, 'Dad, I just want to be with you.' I think after today, I'll be able to talk about it a little more openly with him than in the past. I feel like I have had a ton of bricks taken off me. I've cried and I wasn't alone."

—*Ted Gregory*

▲ *Spontaneous embraces (above and opposite page) were the order of the day during the Welcome Home parade, perhaps the largest in the country for Vietnam veterans.*

The Death of Mayor Washington

His legacy was "not what he did, but what he was on the verge of doing."

NOVEMBER 25, 1987

By the final months of 1987, Mayor Harold Washington was finally having things his own way. Elected to a second term earlier in the year in a campaign devoid of much of the racial heat that marked the 1983 contest, Washington had a majority of the city's fifty aldermen working with him. He was a Democratic political power, helping forge election tickets and exerting influence over careers. A racially divided city seemed to be accepting the reality of a black mayor.

▲ *On the day of Washington's funeral, in early December 1987, high school students salute the late mayor as the hearse carrying his casket passes by.*

Sitting in his fifth-floor office in City Hall on this morning, talking to a press aide, he suddenly slumped over, his face resting on the desktop. He had suffered a heart attack. Although he was rushed to a hospital emergency room, it was clear to all that Washington was dead. In the days that followed, the city came together as it never really had when he was alive. Thousands lined the frigid sidewalks outside City Hall, waiting to file through the rotunda where his body lay in state. The lines contained blacks, whites, Hispanics, friends, foes—the entire spectrum of Chicago's population.

With time, even Chicagoans who disagreed with him had found themselves charmed by his easy wit, his sometimes obscure vocabulary, his self-deprecating humor, and his sarcastic digs at his political opponents. The *Tribune* said in an editorial: "It may be his laugh that will stay with us longest: a sound of merriment not loud but deep, a kind of total chuckle. Harold Washington's grin gave off a personal glow that was his own, as individual as a radio wavelength. Chicago will seem colder without it."

During his time as mayor, he had chipped away at the remnants of the Democratic machine's patronage system by appointing professionals, minorities, and women to city positions. He had worked for economic development in city neighborhoods rather than just downtown. But the bulk of his time had been spent fighting his opponents in the City Council. "In many ways, Washington's legacy is not what he did, but what he was on the verge of doing," said the *Tribune*.

The days following Washington's death were as raucous as the days of "Council Wars," culminating in a marathon City Council session to name a new mayor. Finally, in the early-morning hours, the white aldermanic bloc chose Eugene Sawyer, a black alderman from the South Side, to take over as mayor until a special election could be held in 1989.

—*Robert Davis*

◀ *In the days following his death, thousands filed through City Hall to pay their last respects to Mayor Harold Washington. The city came together as it never had when he was alive.*

Lights at Wrigley Field

The last stronghold of daytime baseball finally glows in the dark.

AUGUST 8, 1988

At 6:05 P.M. on this date, ninety-one-year-old Cubs fan Harry Grossman began the countdown. "Three . . . two . . . one . . . let there be lights!" Grossman pressed a button, and to the cheers of thousands of fans, six light towers flickered to life. Night baseball had come to Wrigley Field.

It had taken six years of arguing, cajoling, and bluffing to bring lights to Wrigley, which for years had been the only major league baseball park where night games could not be played. When then–general manager Dallas Green first proposed installing lights in 1982, many neighborhood residents took up the cause of keeping the field dark. Largely because of their efforts, the Illinois General Assembly and the Chicago City Council passed legislation that effectively banned night games (a grandfather clause excluded Comiskey Park, which had had lights since 1939).

The Cubs, owned by the Tribune Company, persisted. Management hinted darkly that the team might abandon Wrigley for the suburbs. Major league baseball decreed that should the Cubs ever make it to the World Series, their home games would have to be played at an alternate, lighted site. Eventually a city ordinance was passed that allowed the Cubs a maximum of eighteen night games per season.

The first game with lights drew far more attention than normally accorded a Monday matchup between fourth- and fifth-place teams. Among the dignitaries in the sellout crowd were Mayor Eugene Sawyer, Governor James R. Thompson, baseball commissioner Peter Ueberroth, and National League president A. Bartlett Giamatti.

Starting pitcher Rick Sutcliffe was nearly blinded by the thousands of flashbulbs that went off as he delivered the first pitch. Perhaps that was why Philadelphia Phillies outfielder Phil Bradley deposited Sutcliffe's fourth pitch into the bleachers. Then, with the Cubs leading 3–1 in the fourth inning, the rains came—not a light drizzle but a downpour. After a two-hour rain delay, the game was called, obliterating it from the record books. "This proves that the Cubs are cursed," said one fan as she ran from the ballpark. The following morning, the *Tribune* editorialized, "Someone Up There seems to take day baseball seriously."

The first *complete* night game at Wrigley Field took place the following evening. The Cubs beat the Mets, 6–4.

—Phil Vettel

Richard M. Daley Elected

Chicago votes for another Daley—a son eager to create his own legacy.

APRIL 4, 1989

As Richard M. Daley claimed victory on this date in a special mayoral election that put him on a path to follow his famous father, he declared an end to a tumultuous decade in Chicago political history. "We ran a campaign that will be remembered not for its angry words but for the hand of friendship we extended," Daley said after easily vanquishing two rivals to become the city's forty-fifth mayor. Indeed, he had waged a low-key campaign, promising a conciliatory administration guided by common sense and fairness. It was a welcome prescription for mending political divisions that dated back to Jane Byrne's election in 1979. The rancor of Chicago politics had once led the *Wall Street Journal* to call the city "Beirut by the Lake."

Daley's winning coalition included Democratic Party loyalists from the predominantly white Bungalow Belt on the Southwest and Northwest Sides, lakefront independents, and Latinos. A three-term Cook County prosecutor and onetime state lawmaker, Daley had been thwarted in his first mayoral bid six years earlier. This time, he took advantage of a political rift in the black community caused by battles between interim mayor Eugene Sawyer and Alderman Timothy Evans.

In his quest to fill the remaining two years of the late Harold Washington's second term, Daley ousted Sawyer in the February primary and, in the general election five weeks later, crushed Evans, a third-party candidate, and Republican nominee Edward Vrdolyak. It was the second time in Chicago's history a son had followed his father into the office; Mayors Carter Harrison and Carter Harrison II served a combined twenty-two years between 1879 and 1915.

▲ *Daley, age thirteen, with his father, the first Mayor Richard Daley, in 1955. Shown with them are the managers of Chicago's baseball teams, the White Sox' Marty Marion (left) and the Cubs' Stan Hack.*

▼ *The duties of a big-city mayor run the gamut, from presenting plans for the future (left) to mingling with Chicago youths in a park (second from left), greeting important visitors such as the Dalai Lama (left, next page), and presiding over—and occasionally suffering through—long City Council meetings.*

Daley the son, who turned forty-seven on the day of his April 24 inauguration, assumed the mantle without the political patronage and federal largesse available to his father. He inherited a budget deficit and impending crises in public education, housing, and transportation. But backed by a City Council majority, Daley imposed managerial reforms and privatized many city jobs. He dispatched experienced aides to the park and transit systems as troubleshooters and obtained the power to reform the four-hundred-thousand-student public school system, one of the nation's worst. Daley also renovated Navy Pier into a year-round lakefront attraction and expanded Chicago's convention facilities.

By winning reelection in 1991 and 1995, he ensured that a Daley would serve as mayor in every decade of the second half of the twentieth century. The son broke with part of his heritage by moving from Bridgeport, cradle of Chicago mayors, to a new development in the South Loop. But he was widely seen as a chip off the old block, from his frequently fractured syntax to his love for Chicago. "You don't hand down policies from generation to generation," he said at his first inauguration, "but you do hand down values."

—*Thomas Hardy*

▲ *Confetti showers down on Richard M. Daley on the night of his election in 1989. "We ran a campaign that will be remembered not for its angry words but for the hand of friendship we extended," he said, declaring an end to a tumultuous decade in Chicago politics.*

Transplanting Healy Road Prairie

The movement to preserve the Prairie State's native grasslands comes of age.

JULY 14, 1990

To save a pristine remnant of the grasslands that once covered the Prairie State, conservationists on this date attacked it with bulldozers. The Healy Road prairie, in far northwestern Cook County, was especially valuable because it was on an Ice Age gravel hill, which produced a rare combination of prairie plants with such evocative names as flowering spurge, shooting star, and Scribner's panic grass. But the landowner, a gravel company, was determined to mine the site. As a last resort, some two hundred volunteers dug up the prairie and trucked the clumps of sod to a nature preserve six miles away.

The effort marked a milestone for the young prairie preservation movement, in which the Chicago area took a leading role. No one had ever moved a prairie. In short order, organizers had to convince several governmental agencies that the experiment could succeed and marshal the equipment and people to pull it off. Rounding up volunteers was the easy part. Specialists had long been aware that these unique grasslands were fast disappearing, and that concern had spread in the 1980s to many ordinary citizens. "The only way these poor plants are going to have a chance is if we come here and help," one volunteer told the *Tribune*. "This is more important than anything else I could be doing today."

Prairies, which became the natural ecosystem of North America's midsection after Ice Age glaciers retreated ten millennia ago, were nearly eradicated by intensive farming and urban development; by the 1990s, far less than 1 percent of the original prairie acreage survived. Odd patches held on in pioneer cemeteries, along railroads, and in a few other niches. Preserving the remaining prairies is labor-intensive. Cutting down non-native trees, periodically burning prairies to remove dead plants, and other chores require many people willing to work for free. In a testament to the power of these quietly beautiful landscapes, more than five thousand Chicago-area residents volunteered annually for prairie work in the mid-1990s.

After the Healy Road move, the acreage being preserved or restored steadily increased. In 1996, thirty-four government, nonprofit, and cultural entities announced plans to restore two hundred thousand acres in the metropolitan region to natural conditions. And, at its new home, the Healy Road prairie had settled in, with lower densities of some rare plants than naturalists had hoped for, but with the likelihood that it would continue to thrive.

—*Stevenson Swanson*

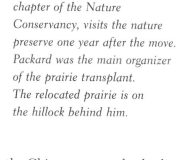

▲ *Steve Packard, of the Illinois chapter of the Nature Conservancy, visits the nature preserve one year after the move. Packard was the main organizer of the prairie transplant. The relocated prairie is on the hillock behind him.*

▼ *Volunteers transplant clumps of sod taken from the Healy Road prairie. The grassland's new home is a man-made hill in a nature preserve near northwest suburban Elgin. Thousands of Chicago-area residents annually volunteer for prairie restoration or preservation projects.*

The Last Game at Old Comiskey Park

The oldest ballpark in the major leagues dies with a win at age eighty.

SEPTEMBER 30, 1990

On this final day, a crowd of 42,849 fans turned out on a glorious, sunny, autumn afternoon to say farewell to what had been proclaimed the "Baseball Palace of the World" when it opened July 1, 1910. Many fans were teary-eyed, realizing that the place where they had spent so many happy times would soon be turned into a parking lot for the new Comiskey Park, which was rising just to the south at 35th Street and Shields Avenue.

"Years from now," the Chicago White Sox ads had said all season, "you'll say you were there." On this day, one of the many banners hanging from the upper-deck railings read, "Years from now, you'll park here." Several more read, "Good-bye, Old Friend." That is exactly what Comiskey Park had been. Besides being the home of Chicago's American League team, the venerable ballpark with the exploding scoreboard had been the site of several heavyweight title fights, the home field for the Chicago Cardinals in the National Football League, the stadium where the Negro League All-Star Games were played, and the place where the Beatles had performed two concerts.

Former Sox vice president Charles Comiskey, grandson of the man for whom the park was named, was on hand for the final game, against the Seattle Mariners. Mayor Richard M. Daley, who practically grew up at the ballpark, threw out the first ball. Former Sox great Minnie Minoso brought the lineup card out to the umpires. And then it began. Jack McDowell's first pitch to Harold Reynolds was a strike. The crowd—which included Hollywood types such as Ron Howard, Kurt Russell, and Goldie Hawn—roared as if it were the World Series. By the sixth inning, the Mariners were leading 1–0, but a triple by Lance Johnson, a single by Frank Thomas, and a triple by Dan Pasqua put the Sox ahead 2–1. And that is how it stayed.

When it was over, after the crowd had joined organist Nancy Faust for a final rendition of "Na-Na Hey-Hey Good-bye"—the unofficial victory song of the Sox—veteran catcher Carlton Fisk looked out across the green grass and summed up the feelings of many others in the park. "I don't know if I want to see it as it's being torn down," he said. "I think I'd rather see it now, when it's all up, and then not see it. That way, I've got it in my mind what it was and what it continues to be. I have a lot of things from this ballpark, right between my ears, and I'll keep them right there."

—*Bob Vanderberg*

◀ *The original Comiskey Park (left) would soon be razed, the land it occupied since 1910 turned into a parking lot. Across 35th Street, the new Comiskey Park was almost ready for action.*

The Harold Washington Library

Chicago's library had some odd homes before settling into its new address on State Street.

OCTOBER 7, 1991

After being a vagabond in its own city for more than a decade, the Chicago Public Library on this date settled into a permanent home, a ten-story, classically styled building that cost $144 million. It was heralded, in true Chicago fashion, as the largest public library in the world. The library's central collection had been shifted among several warehouses while a protracted civic debate considered the question of where a new library should be built. At one point, the city even considered renovating an empty State Street department store for the library's collections.

Not that a department store would have been the oddest location the library had ever occupied. After the fire of 1871, the people of Great Britain sent eight thousand books to the city to help in what they assumed would be the restoration of the city's incinerated public library. In fact, in the course of growing into the commercial center of the mid-continent, Chicago had never gotten around to starting a library. With nowhere else to put it, the British benefaction was deposited in an empty water tank.

In 1897, the library moved into a grand edifice at Michigan Avenue between Randolph and Washington Streets. This stately structure, designed by Shepley, Rutan, and Coolidge, was richly ornamented with mosaic tile and a Tiffany dome, but it was a schizophrenic building. Part of it was set aside for the Grand Army of

The Harold Washington Library Center, named for a mayor who loved to read, opened in 1991 at the northwest corner of State Street and Congress Parkway. Two years later, flamboyant foliate designs and ornamental owls were added (left) to the top of the building.

the Republic, an organization of Civil War veterans, which had been promised a Civil War museum on the site. The building quickly became too small for the library's rapidly expanding collections. After the library moved out in 1975, the Michigan Avenue building was renovated and rededicated as the city's cultural center.

When the department store proposal was finally rejected in the mid-1980s, an architectural competition was held, with five teams of architects displaying their designs at the Cultural Center to crowds of curious Chicagoans. The winning design, by Thomas Beeby of Hammond, Beeby, and Babka, did not meet with universal approval. *Tribune* architecture critic Paul Gapp called the building a "heavy, lackluster statement." But the fact that the city at last had a permanent home for the library's six million books, periodicals, photographs, and other items was cause enough for celebration. "Chicago finally has a public library worthy of a world-class city," the *Tribune* said in an editorial.

In 1996, Bill Gates, chairman of the computer software firm Microsoft Corporation, gave the library system $1 million to install fiber-optic links to the Internet at all of the library's eighty-two branches. That seemed to guarantee the library a role in the electronic future. As for its printed past, more than seventy-six hundred books of the original eight thousand donated by the British have disappeared over the years—lost, stolen, or, at the very least, long overdue.

—Stevenson Swanson

▶

After the library moved out of its old quarters on Michigan Avenue in 1975, the building was renovated into the Chicago Cultural Center, a setting for concerts and exhibitions.

▲ *The light-filled winter garden on the ninth floor of the library provides a tranquil spot for reading or reflecting.*

◀ *After receiving a donation of eight thousand books from the British people, the city set up its first library in an empty water tank at LaSalle and Adams Streets that had survived the 1871 fire.*

The Great Chicago Flood

An odd calamity turns the Loop into a "soggy ghost town."

APRIL 13, 1992

Tens of thousands of office workers and store clerks streamed into the Loop as usual on this morning, only to be sent home for an unscheduled holiday. For many, that holiday lasted a week; for some, it went on for over a month. The reason was one of the oddest calamities in American history: the Great Chicago Flood.

Earlier that morning, some 124 million gallons of murky Chicago River water poured through a crack in a little-used, all-but-forgotten forty-seven-mile network of freight tunnels under the central business district. After filling the tunnels, the river water rose into the basements of many downtown buildings, knocking out electric power and natural-gas service.

It was a flood that no one at street level could see, a flood in which no one was injured. No one, except those trying to stop the water's spread, got wet. But, as the *Tribune* reported, the invisible disaster turned the Loop into a "soggy ghost town" and caused damage and business losses of at least $1 billion. Trials at the Daley Center were postponed. The Chicago Board of Trade and the Chicago Mercantile Exchange closed. Rapid transit trains were rerouted for weeks while water was pumped out of subway tunnels. City Hall was evacuated.

▼ *For most people, the Great Chicago Flood was an invisible disaster, evident only in the many hoses that snaked over sidewalks and streets as water was pumped out of Loop basements.*

One of the biggest shocks of the first day of the calamity was that city officials had known about the potential problem—for three months, it turned out—but had moved too slowly to approve the $10,000 contract to fix it. In September 1991, a private contractor had driven new wooden pilings into the riverbed next to the Kinzie Street drawbridge to protect the bridge from passing barges and other traffic on the north branch of the Chicago River. The pilings had been placed in the wrong spot and punctured the ceiling of the freight tunnel below. A slow leak was discovered in January by cable television company workers who were inspecting the cables that ran through the tunnel. City officials were notified, but, because of bureaucratic hemming and hawing, nothing was done. "This was no minor oversight," said Mayor Richard M. Daley, "and the costs to the city will be enormous."

Daley demanded and received the resignation of a city official who was in charge of the department that was responsible for inspecting the tunnels. Pumping the water out of buildings and the tunnel system took weeks; but even three years later, city government was feeling the invisible disaster's financial effects. On August 11, 1995, city lawyers agreed to pay up to $36 million in damages to settle lawsuits brought by Marshall Field and Company and insurers for about a dozen buildings damaged by the flood waters.

—*Patrick T. Reardon*

◀ *The streets stayed dry during the flood, but it was a different story underground.*

▲ *Sandbags, dirt, stones, even mattresses were dumped in the river to try to plug the hole that flooded Loop buildings. The flooding resulted from pilings, shown in the photograph, being placed in the wrong spot and puncturing an old freight tunnel underneath the Chicago River.*

The Death of Dantrell Davis

An innocent boy becomes a random victim of a growing gun and gang culture.

OCTOBER 13, 1992

Dantrell Davis, a lively seven-year-old with an electric smile, was crossing the street to attend classes at Jenner Elementary School, just one hundred feet from his apartment building. But in the Cabrini-Green public-housing complex where Dantrell lived, every step was fraught with danger, and innocence could provide no shield against violence. Neither could the police officers who sat in a squad car near the school on this morning. Helpless, too, was the volunteer parent patrol that watched for trouble. Not even Dantrell's mother, who held his hand tightly as they crossed the street, could protect her son. A stray bullet fired by a sniper in a nearby building tore through the boy's head and killed him.

▲ *Police officers, a parent patrol, and even his mother could not shield Dantrell Davis from a gang member's stray gunshot.*

Dantrell Davis was one of sixty-one children killed in Chicago in 1992. Yet his death was the year's most symbolic. For many in Chicago and across the nation, Dantrell's slaying epitomized one of the worst problems in American society: crime had run amok in urban America and no one—not even the smallest child—was safe. Much of the bloodshed was caused by the growth of gangs, which imperiled and often ruled the lives of people whose neighborhoods they claimed as their turf. Gangs transformed communities into illegal drug markets and recruited young people into their ranks. While relationships with families decayed, teenagers' ties to gangs thrived. Armed with high-powered handguns, teens created carnage that denied some of their peers the chance to live beyond puberty.

This cycle of violence spurred the *Tribune* to chronicle the death of every child under age fifteen in 1993 as part of a series entitled "Killing Our Children." The articles sought to personalize the victims and shed light on their short—and, at times, troubled—lives. Sixty-two children were killed that year. "The unceasing proliferation of handgun violence in Chicago and across the U.S. is a national disgrace," the paper said in an editorial (one in a series on children and violence that earned the *Tribune* the 1993 Pulitzer Prize for editorial writing). "The toll in deaths and shattered lives, particularly on our children, has reached staggering numbers."

▲ *Annette Freeman, mother of Dantrell Davis, weeps during a choral performance at a memorial service for her son.*

Police arrested a man named Anthony Garrett for Dantrell Davis's death. Garrett was a gang member seeking revenge, authorities said. From a tenth-story window, the Army-trained marksman fired a burst of bullets from an assault-style weapon at a group of rivals in front of Dantrell's building. Dantrell was the only person hit. Garrett was convicted of the crime and sentenced to one hundred years in prison.

But the cycle of violence became, if anything, more appalling. In 1994, Robert "Yummy" Sandifer, an eleven-year-old gang member, accidentally killed a fourteen-year-old girl on the city's South Side while trying to shoot a rival gang member. A few days later, Robert himself was dead, executed by two fellow gang members, ages fourteen and sixteen.

—*Joseph A. Kirby*

◀ *A pupil at Jenner Elementary School expressed the raw facts of urban life—a dead boy and a man with a gun—in this view of Dantrell Davis's death.*

The 1995 Heat Wave

Record temperatures and humidity result in a deadly weekend.

JULY 13, 1995

The temperature soared to 106 degrees at Midway Airport on this date, a Thursday, setting a new record for Chicago. The temperature was officially listed as 104 degrees, as measured at O'Hare International Airport, the official reporting station, but such technicalities mattered little to sweltering Chicagoans. Between Wednesday and Sunday, Chicago felt as if it were roasting under a wet wool blanket. The city had sweat through hot spells before—scorching summers in Chicago seem to go with the freezing winters—but by the time this heat wave was over, it had been blamed for an unprecedented number of deaths.

▲ *The elderly were especially susceptible to the hot weather. This 101-year-old woman was overcome by heat later in the summer when an electrical fire knocked out the power in her apartment building.*

The misery of triple-digit temperatures was made worse by especially high humidity, making it difficult to sweat and cool off, and by nights that seemed almost as hot as the days. At first people complained, made jokes, cranked up their air conditioners, and gulped ice cream and cold beer. Overheated Chicagoans opened an estimated three thousand fire hydrants, leading to record water use. The Chicago Park District curtailed recreation programs to keep children from exerting themselves in the heat. Swimming pools were packed, while some sought relief in cool basements. People attended baseball games with wet towels on their heads. Roads buckled and some drawbridges had to be hosed down to close properly.

By Saturday, dozens of deaths had been attributed to the heat. The next day, refrigerated semitrailers were set up at the Cook County medical examiner's office to accommodate the hundreds of bodies that a steady line of ambulances brought in. Only with the return of more normal summer temperatures did the deadly pace finally slacken. Ultimately, Dr. Edmund Donoghue, Cook County medical examiner, listed heat as the primary or contributing factor in more than 550 deaths in the county. In September, an epidemiological study by the Chicago Board of Health blamed 733 July deaths in the city on the heat. The varying numbers depended on how deaths were counted.

Many of the dead were elderly. Some did not want to lose their independence, even temporarily, by moving in with family members. Others had no one who would take them in. Some lived in high-crime areas and were afraid to open their windows. And some probably never thought that hot weather could kill.

—*Cindy Schreuder*

▼ *Many of the victims of the 1995 heat wave left no family or were indigent. Of the sixty-eight unclaimed bodies that county workers are shown burying here, forty-one died of heat-related causes.*

The 1995 Northwestern Wildcats

A wild season earns the Cats a trip to the Rose Bowl.

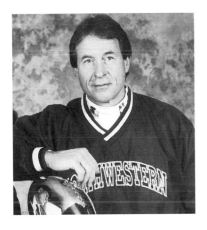

▲ *Northwestern Coach Gary Barnett with the 1995 Big Ten trophy.*

JANUARY 1, 1996

Northwestern University playing in the Rose Bowl? Even a winning season had seemed too much to hope for. But in 1995, Northwestern accomplished the impossible, even pushing Michael Jordan and the Bulls off the front page for a while. The Wildcats came out of nowhere to win the Big Ten Conference championship and earn a trip to the Rose Bowl.

Coach Gary Barnett told his players not to carry him off the field after upsetting Notre Dame; that was only the first game, just part of a larger goal. Likewise, he hated it when people called Northwestern's run a "miracle," but what word better described these facts? Before 1995: twenty-four years without a winning season, forty-seven without a bowl appearance, fifty-nine without a Big Ten title. After 1995: a 10–2 record, a Rose Bowl bouquet, a Big Ten title. Before: lots and lots of empty seats at Dyche Stadium (the team's home field), marshmallow fights in the student section, torn-down goalposts to celebrate *any* victory. After: three consecutive sellouts, a student body that finally cared as much about football scores as SAT scores, and fired-up fans who flooded the field to congratulate their heroes after a 21–10 win over Penn State on national television. Before: Rick Venturi goes 1–31–1 as head coach, lands head coaching job with a pro team. After: Gary Barnett corrals seventeen coach-of-the-year awards, rejects UCLA's offer to coach the Bruins. He stays because he *wants* to be at Northwestern.

By the end of the year, the Wildcats' success had brought a bevy of accolades: they even got a spot on the *Tonight Show* before the Rose Bowl. Despite the glitz, the team was still able to focus on the New Year's Day game. After falling behind the USC Trojans 24–7, the Cats stormed back, using two field goals by Brian Gowins and a perfectly executed onside kick. When running back Darnell Autry rambled for a two-yard score early in the fourth quarter, Northwestern had its first lead at 32–31. But an interception of a Wildcats pass late in the game and a record-setting day by USC wide receiver Keyshawn Johnson, who caught twelve passes for 216 yards, were too much. The final: 41–32 in favor of the Trojans. The result: no lost respect for what Northwestern had accomplished. The Mildcats? They became history in 1995.

—*Teddy Greenstein*

▶

Northwestern's remarkable season brought the team a bevy of accolades and unprecedented media exposure. A few days before the Rose Bowl, the Wildcats appeared on the Tonight Show *with host Jay Leno and Northwestern alum Charlton Heston.*

The 1996 Chicago Bulls

Before capturing a fourth trophy, an all-time great team wins a record seventy-two games.

JUNE 16, 1996

Michael Jordan, Phil Jackson, Scottie Pippen, Dennis Rodman, and the rest of the Chicago Bulls cared little about history on this muggy Sunday night. After they defeated the Seattle Super-Sonics 87–75 to win a fourth National Basketball Association championship in six years, the talk was not about whether the victory had cemented the Bulls' place as the greatest team in basketball history. Lighting a victory cigar or hugging a teammate was what mattered.

Of course, the Bulls had created the debate by becoming the first team in NBA history to break the seventy-victory plateau. They finished 72–10 and won each game by an average of twelve points. In the franchise's thirty-year history, no other season could compare. Players such as Jerry Sloan, Chet Walker, Bob Love, and Norm Van Lier provided plenty of thrills during the 1960s and 1970s—but no championships. Hard times followed, until the arrival of Jordan in 1984. As his legend grew, so did the Bulls' success.

When they won three straight championships, starting with the 1990–91 season, they ruled not just basketball but Chicago sports. For the fourth title, the Bulls returned to the United Center on the West Side with a tenuous three-games-to-two lead in the Finals after losing two straight in Seattle. On that Sunday night, Jordan scored twenty-two points, Rodman sparked a decisive third-quarter run—finishing with nineteen rebounds—and the Bulls returned to the pinnacle.

The Bulls' bench clears in celebratory glee (right) at the final buzzer in Game Six of the 1996 NBA Finals, at Chicago's United Center. Later in the week, with four NBA championship trophies at their feet, the Bulls (above, from left, Dennis Rodman, Scottie Pippen, 1996 Coach of the Year Phil Jackson, and Michael Jordan) savor their success at a victory celebration in Grant Park.

The city has had Death Valley–size dry spells in baseball, football, and hockey, relieved by a Super Bowl here, a Stanley Cup there, a World Series—where? To say the city was overjoyed to have not just a championship team but one of such history-making accomplishments is to say too little. Chicago wrapped the Bulls in a feverish embrace, with fans flooding into the streets the night of the win and later filling Grant Park for a victory celebration. "That is the great and curious gift of sports," wrote the *Tribune*'s Bernie Lincicome, "to provide a common memory for all, to unite neighbors and generations. Championships make the 'them' into 'us.'"

To be sure, this championship belonged to many, even oft-ridiculed General Manager Jerry Krause, the grand architect behind it all. But Jordan stood out. He had done so since his rookie season, when he burst onto the scene with a shoe named after him and a dazzling array of dunks. His talents earned him scoring titles, most valu-

able player awards—and a reputation as a brilliant individual player who could not win the big one. That changed with the three championships. Then on October 6, 1993, Jordan stunningly "retired." After an eighteen-month hiatus to try his hand at professional baseball, he returned to the Bulls near the end of the 1994–95 season. That his comeback ended in failure—Orlando knocked the Bulls out of the playoffs; in Chicago, no less—burned Jordan.

He rededicated himself to basketball, won his fourth regular-season MVP award, his eighth scoring title, and displayed his legendary competitiveness. "He's a work of art, but he's also all about the art of work," wrote the *Tribune*'s Bob Verdi on the night of the championship. "Some guys worry about how to spend it, Michael Jordan figures out how to earn it."

When he did earn it, becoming the first player in NBA history to win the Finals MVP award four times, Jordan was moved to emotions that seemed to surprise even him.

▲ *Scottie Pippen and Tony Kukoc, named the NBA's best sixth man in 1996, contributed offensive firepower of their own to the Bulls as well as double-teaming on defense to make life difficult for opponents such as the Sonics' Detlef Schrempf.*

▶

The irrepressible Dennis Rodman, shown here smiling after being fouled in Game One, added a certain attitude to the Bulls, but he was also the league's leading rebounder.

"This is the sweetest," Jordan said with tears in his eyes. "This is the most special of all." In 1993, Jordan's father James was murdered shortly after the Bulls won their third championship. June 16, 1996, was not only the day of the Bulls' fourth championship. It was also Father's Day.

—*K. C. Johnson*

▶

Gravity-defying leaps such as this one in the third game of the 1996 NBA Finals became a Michael Jordan trademark after he joined the team in 1984.

◀ *Starter Ron Harper developed into one of the best defenders in the league during the season, his second with the Bulls. Here he swipes the ball from the Sonics' Gary Payton in Game One of the Finals.*

The Museum of Contemporary Art

A new building provides a home for the art of today — and tomorrow.

▼ *James Lee Byars's* The Monument to Language *(1955), a bronze sphere almost ten feet in diameter, dominates the museum's atrium.*

JUNE 21, 1996

At 6:55 P.M. on this date, eight civic leaders cut the ribbon on a new $46 million building to house Chicago's Museum of Contemporary Art. The ceremony began a continuous twenty-four-hour preview of the largest single space in North America—151,000 square feet—devoted to contemporary art. Designed by German architect Josef Paul Kleihues on the site of the old National Guard Armory on East Chicago Avenue, the staid rectilinear building with classical references quintupled the area of the original museum, which had opened in 1967 in a former bakery on East Ontario Street.

The prime mover back then had been lawyer and collector Joseph Randall Shapiro, known equally for his holdings in surrealist art and the breadth of his civic involvement. He became the museum's first president; Jan van der Marck became its first director. The MCA was conceived as a *Kunsthalle*, or "art hall," that would organize and host only temporary exhibitions. But in fairly short order, museum trustees decided to add a permanent collection, and thenceforth, a new, larger building became inevitable. The argument to remain free from the responsibility of caring for a permanent collection was bolstered by such unorthodox exhibitions as Dan Flavin's neon sculpture (1967), Christo's first wrapping of a building (1968), and *Art by Telephone*, which had participants phone in specifications for artworks (1968).

Van der Marck's *Kunsthalle* approach was not, however, shared by a majority of trustees, and in 1970 he became the first of four directors to leave the museum under less than happy circumstances. The MCA marked its tenth anniversary with a drive to purchase a three-story town house immediately west of the Ontario Street museum. Its renovation in 1979 added four new galleries, which were used for the display of works by Chicago artists as well as pieces from the permanent collection. In the absence of purchase funds, the museum's holdings were formed entirely with gifts.

▼ *German architect Josef Paul Kleihues designed a staid, rectilinear building that quintupled the area of the original museum.*

▲ *The new home of the Museum of Contemporary Art, the largest single space in North America devoted to the art of recent times, lies between Lake Michigan and Michigan Avenue. At the right is the chimney of the old pumping station on Michigan Avenue.*

Kleihues intended nearly all the galleries on the top floor of his structure to display works from the permanent collection, which at the time of the opening included some thirty thousand pieces, half of which were artist-designed books. The sculpture garden to the east of the building also shows works from the collection, and sculpture commissions have been planned for two huge platforms flanking the museum's main entrance. After a decade of planning and fund-raising, the MCA finally had a home worthy of its holdings, and on the strength of it, officials hope to attract more gifts of art while at the same time providing a full program of temporary exhibitions, films, live performances, and expressions in media still unimagined in the mid-1990s.

—Alan G. Artner

▶

The museum's permanent collection, on display in the new building's spacious galleries, ranges across several artistic styles, mostly from the second half of the twentieth century. In the foreground is Bruce Nauman's untitled 1965 fiberglass sculpture.

Picture Credits

Chicago Tribune Photographers

Pages ii–iii (title page): Godfrey Lundberg. *Page 11t*: Michael Fryer. *Page 29b*: Russell Hamm. *Page 35*: John Bartley. *Page 42m*: John Dziekan. *Page 43t*: Charles Osgood. *Page 53t*: John Bartley. *Page 53m*: Jack Mulcahy. *Page 60b*: Charles Osgood. *Page 61t*: Walter Kale. *Page 61m and b*: John Bartley. *Page 63mb*: Charles Osgood. *Page 81b*: Guy Bona. *Page 113b*: George Wheeler. *Page 117m*: Bruzee. *Page 122*: Anne Cusack. *Page 125l*: Earl Gustie. *Page 125b*: George Quinn. *Page 127t*: Swain Scalf. *Page 127b*: Gerald West. *Page 129b*: Barlow Wolff. *Page 131b*: Josef Szalay. *Page 143t*: Chris Walker. *Page 155*: Swain Scalf and William Loewe. *Page 163t*: George Quinn. *Page 164t*: Don Casper. *Page 164b*: Bill Aldrich. *Page 166*: Ed Smith. *Page 170t*: John Austad. *Page 171t*: Michael Budrys. *Page 172t*: Val Mazzenga. *Page 172b*: Michael Fryer. *Page 173t*: Val Mazzenga. *Page 173b*: Charles Osgood. *Page 177t*: Jim O'Leary. *Page 180b*: José Moré. *Page 181b*: Val Mazzenga. *Page 182*: Paul Gero. *Page 183*: George Quinn. *Page 186*: Ray Gora. *Page 187b*: Luigi Mendicino. *Page 188t*: Ron Bailey. *Page 189t*: Jim O'Leary. *Page 191t*: Walter Neal. *Page 194*: Ovie Carter. *Page 195t and b*: Walter Kale. *Page 196b*: James Mayo. *Page 197t*: Roy Hall. *Page 197b*: Charles Osgood. *Page 199b*: Ray Gora. *Page 200b*: John Austad. *Page 202l*: Bill Vendetta. *Page 202r*: Jack Mulcahy. *Page 205r*: Otto Kleiber. *Page 206l*: Arthur Walker. *Page 206r*: Carl Hugare. *Page 209*: Luigi Mendicino. *Page 211t*: Cy Wolf. *Page 211b*: Don Casper. *Page 212t*: Bill Yates.

Page 213t: Walter Kale. *Page 213b*: Bill Kelly. *Page 215t*: James Mayo. *Page 216l*: Bill Yates. *Page 217t*: Don Casper. *Page 217b*: Bill Vendetta and Luigi Mendicino. *Page 219b*: Walter Kale. *Page 220*: Bill Yates. *Page 221*: John Bartley. *Page 225t*: Carl Gustie. *Page 226t*: Michael Budrys. *Page 226b*: Frank Hanes. *Page 227b*: William Hogan. *Page 229t*: Carl Hugare. *Page 229b*: Michael Budrys. *Page 230*: Karen Engstrom. *Page 231tl and tr*: Michael Laughlin. *Page 231b*: Jay Needleman. *Page 234l*: Ovie Carter. *Page 234r*: Quentin Dodt. *Page 235t*: Chris Walker. *Page 235b*: Jose Osorio. *Pages 236 and 237t*: Ernie Cox Jr. *Page 237b*: Anne Cusack. *Page 238l*: Val Mazzenga. *Page 238b*: Frank Hanes. *Page 239t*: Walter Neal. *Page 239ml*: John Irvine. *Page 239mr*: Gerald West. *Page 239b*: Stan Policht. *Page 240t*: Michael Fryer. *Page 240b*: Bill Hogan. *Page 241t*: Walter Kale. *Page 241b*: James Mayo. *Page 242*: Gerald West. *Page 243t and b*: José Moré. *Page 245t*: Ed Wagner. *Page 246t*: Walter Kale. *Page 246b*: Phil Greer. *Page 247*: Charles Cherney. *Page 248t*: Anne Cusack. *Page 248b*: Michael Fryer. *Page 249*: Frank Hanes. *Page 250bl*: David Klobucar. *Page 250br*: Carl Wagner. *Page 251t*: Chris Walker. *Page 251bl*: Charles Osgood. *Page 251br*: David Klobucar. *Page 252t*: John Kringas. *Page 252b*: John Dziekan. *Page 254t*: Nancy Stone. *Page 254b*: Charles Osgood. *Page 255t*: Nuccio DiNuzzo. *Page 255b*: Anne Cusack. *Page 256b*: Chris Walker. *Page 257t*: Michael Fryer. *Page 257b*: Charles Osgood. *Page 259*: Chris Walker. *Page 260l*: Walter Kale. *Page 260b*: John Smierciak. *Page 261t*: Bill Hogan. *Page 262b*: Nuccio DiNuzzo. *Page 263t*: Charles Cherney. *Page 263b*: Paula Bronstein. *Page 264t*: Charles Cherney. *Page 264b*: Nuccio DiNuzzo. *Page 265t*: Nuccio DiNuzzo. *Page 265b*: Charles Cherney. *Pages 266l and r, 267b*: Charles Osgood.

Other Sources

CHS = Chicago Historical Society

Page vii: Col. Robert R. McCormick Research Center. *Page 1*: engraving by Seth Eastman, U.S. Army, from a sketch by H. R. Schoolcraft, CHS. *Page 2*: Raoul Varin, CHS. *Pages 3, 4t and b, 5t*: CHS. *Page 5b*: Justin Herriott illustration, CHS. *Pages 6, 7, 9b*: CHS. *Page 10b*: The Chicago Public Library, Special Collections Div. *Page 11b*: Univ. of Illinois at Chicago, the Univ. Library, Dept. of Special Collections, Chicago Board of Trade Records. *Pages 12, 13b*: Illinois State Historical Library. *Page 13t*: I and M Canal Collection, Lewis University. *Page 14t*: John Carbutt photo, CHS. *Page 14b*: C & NW Railway photo, CHS. *Page 15t*: Regional History Center, Northern Illinois Univ. *Page 16t*: Northwestern Univ. Archives. *Page 16b*: 108th Observation Squadron photo, Illinois National Guard, CHS. *Page 17t*: Copelin and Son, Northwestern Univ. Archives. *Page 17b*: Evanston Photographic Studio, Northwestern Univ. Archives. *Pages 18t, 19t and b*: Col. Robert R. McCormick Research Center. *Pages 20, 21t and b*: CHS. *Page 22*: Knox College. *Page 23t*: Alexander Hesler photo, CHS. *Page 23b*: CHS. *Page 24*: Brady photo, CHS. *Pages 25bl and br*: CHS. *Page 26t*: Alexander Hesler photo, CHS. *Page 26b*: William Shaw photo, CHS. *Pages 27, 28b*: CHS. *Page 29t*: George Lawrence photo, CHS. *Page 30*: John Carbutt photo, CHS.

Page 31t: CHS. *Page 31b*: Napoleon Sarony photo courtesy National Portrait Gallery, London; the National Portrait Gallery, Smithsonian Institution. *Pages 32 and 33t*: National Park Service, Frederick Law Olmsted National Historic Site. *Page 33b*: CHS. *Page 36b*: Col. Robert R. McCormick Research Center. *Page 37t*: CHS. *Page 37b*: George N. Barnard photo, CHS. *Page 38t*: CHS. *Page 38b*: Col. Robert R. McCormick Research Center. *Page 39t and b*: CHS. *Page 40t and b*: Montgomery Ward Archives. *Page 41*: CHS. *Page 42t and b*: detail of photos © 1996, The Art Institute of Chicago. All rights reserved. *Pages 44, 45*: CHS. *Page 46t and b*: CHS. *Pages 48, 49t and b*:

Key to picture location on page:
t = top
m = middle
b = bottom
l = left
r = right

CHS. *Page 51m and b:* CHS. *Page 52:* CHS. *Page 54t:* Frank Lloyd Wright Home and Studio Research Center. *Page 54b:* Jon Miller © Hedrich Blessing, Frank Lloyd Wright Home and Studio Foundation. *Page 55t:* Frank Lloyd Wright Home and Studio Foundation. *Page 56b:* Barnes Crosby photo, CHS. *Page 57t:* Essanay Film Mfg. *Page 57b:* Univ. of Illinois at Chicago, the Univ. Library, Jane Addams Memorial Collection. *Page 58t:* Univ. of Illinois at Chicago Library, Manuscript Collection. *Page 58b:* CHS. *Page 59:* Barnes Crosby photo, CHS. *Page 60t:* Ravenswood-Lakeview Historical Society. *Page 62l:* Chicago Symphony Orchestra. *Page 62r:* Chicago Symphony Orchestra photo, CHS. *Page 63t and b:* Chicago Symphony Orchestra. *Page 64t:* Mellen photo, CHS. *Page 64b:* CHS. *Page 67t:* Chicago Aerial Survey photo, CHS. *Page 68:* C. D. Arnold photo, CHS. *Page 69t and m:* CHS. *Page 69b:* Dr. G. Hunter Bartlett photo, CHS.

Page 70t: Dept. of Special Collections, Univ. of Chicago Library. *Page 70m:* CHS. *Page 70b:* detail of photo © 1997, The Art Institute of Chicago, Ryerson and Burnham Library. All rights reserved. *Pages 71t and b, 72t:* CHS. *Page 72b:* Stephen Deutsch photo, CHS. *Page 73b:* CHS. *Page 74r:* National Air and Space Museum, Smithsonian Institution. *Page 76:* CHS. *Page 77t:* Geiger photo, collection of Metropolitan Water Reclamation District of Greater Chicago. *Pages 77b, 78b:* CHS. *Page 79t:* Univ. of Pennsylvannia Library. *Page 80t:* UPI/Corbis-Bettmann. *Page 82bl:* Chicago Newsphoto Service. *Page 83:* Burke and Koretke photo. *Page 84t and b:* Chicago Defender. *Page 85t:* United States Steel Corp. *Page 85b:* George Lawrence photo, Library of Congress, LC-USZ62-41396. *Pages 86–87, 88, 89t:* CHS. *Page 89b:* Kobal Collection. *Page 92t:* CHS. *Page 94t:* Evanston Historical Society. *Page 94b:* Daniel H. Burnham and Edward H. Bennett, partnership 1903–1912. "Plan of the Complete System of Street Circulation," plate 110 from *Plan of Chicago*, 1909, delineated by Jules Guerin (American, 1866–1946), ink and wash on paper. On permanent loan to The Art Institute from the City of Chicago, 18.148.1966. Photo © 1996 The Art Institute of Chicago. All rights reserved. *Page 95:* Plate 125, *Plan of Chicago*, by Burnham and Bennett, CHS. *Page 96t and b:* CHS. *Page 97t:* Chicago Park District. *Page 97b:* CHS. *Page 99b:* Kaufmann and Fabry photo. *Page 100t:* from *Western Architect*, Susan Dart Collection, Lake Forest College, Donnelly Library.

Pages 100–101: Lake Forest–Lake Bluff Historical Society, photo from Harold G. Mason. *Page 102t:* Col. Robert R. McCormick Research Center. *Page 103:* CHS. *Page 106:* New York News photo, Col. Robert R. McCormick Research Center. *Page 109t:* Col. Robert R. McCormick Research Center. *Pages 109m, 110t:* CHS. *Page 110b:* International News photo. *Page 112:* National Baseball Library, Cooperstown, N.Y. *Page 114b:* UPI/Corbis-Bettmann. *Page 118:* Acme photo. *Page 120:* © Field Museum of Natural History, negative #44679. *Page 121t:* © Field Museum, negative #48823. *Page 123t:* Theatre Historical Society of America. *Page 123b:* Balaban & Katz. *Page 126:* William Ransom Hogan Jazz Archive, Tulane Univ. Library. *Page 131t:* NBC photo. *Page 132t:* CHS. *Page 132b:* Chicago Aerial Survey. *Page 133t:* CHS. *Page 136:* CHS. *Page: 137r: Chicago Herald and Examiner. Page 141: Chicago Herald-American.* *Page 142:* Frank Driggs Collection. *Page 143b:* courtesy Specialty Records. *Page 144:* Kirk M. Kandle © 1990. All rights reserved. *Page 145l and r:* UPI/Corbis-Bettmann. *Page 147t:* CHS. *Page 147b:* Hedrich Blessing Collection, CHS. *Page 150t:* CHS. *Page 150b:* Chicago Architectural Photographing Co. *Page 151t:* Chicago Architectural Photographing Co. photo, Museum of Science and Industry Archives. *Page 152b:* CHS. *Page 156:* AP/Wide World. *Page 158:* CHS. *Page 159r:* Hedrich Blessing Collection, CHS. *Page 161b:* National Air and Space Museum, Smithsonian Institution. *Page 162t:* Judt photo, *Chicago Herald-American*. *Page 163b:* CHS. *Page 167t:* Park Forest Public Library.

Page 167b: Chicago Aerial Survey. *Page 168:* UPI/Corbis-Bettmann. *Page 169:* Burlington Railroad. *Page 170b:* courtesy *Playboy*. *Pages 174, 175:* Lyric Opera of Chicago. *Page 176: Chicago Herald-American.* *Page 177m:* Bob Rea photo, *Chicago's American*. *Page 179b:* McDonald's Corp. Archives. *Page 181t:* Peter Schulz photo, Chicago Department of Aviation. *Page 184:* Chicago Transit Authority. *Page 188b:* courtesy Second City Archive. *Page 189:* AP/Wide World. *Pages 190, 192t:* UPI/Corbis-Bettmann. *Page 192b:* AP/Wide World. *Page 199t and m:* UPI/Corbis-Bettmann. *Page 200t:* CHS. *Page 201: Chicago's American. Pages 203t, 210:* UPI/Corbis-Bettmann. *Page 208r: Chicago Herald-American.* *Page 212b:* UPI/Corbis-Bettmann. *Page 214t:* ACLU. *Page 214b:* AP/Wide World. *Pages 215b, 218t:* UPI/Corbis-Bettmann. *Page 219t: Chicago Today.* *Pages 223, 224t:* courtesy Goodman Theatre. *Page 224b:* Jennifer Girard. *Page 225b:* Lisa Ebright. *Page 227tl:* Univ. of Illinois. *Page 227r: Chicago Daily News.* *Page 232b:* UPI/Corbis-Bettmann. *Page 233:* AP/Wide World. *Page 238t:* courtesy Tribune Media Services. *Page 244:* Ruben Ramirez photo, UPI/Corbis-Bettmann. *Page 245b:* AP/Wide World. *Page 253:* Chicago White Sox. *Page 255m:* CHS. *Page 256:* courtesy Tribune Media Services. *Page 261b:* AP/Wide World. *Page 262t:* Beth Keiser photo, AP/Wide World. *Page 267t:* Steve Hall © Hedrich Blessing, courtesy Museum of Contemporary Art.

All other images are from *Tribune* files.

Index